JP ON JAMMU AND KASHMIR

JP ON JAMMU AND KASHMIR

Balraj Puri

GYAN

GYAN PUBLISHING HOUSE

NEW DELHI - 110002

JP on Jammu and Kashmir

Rs. 690

ISBN : 81-212-0859-9

Published in 2005 in India by
Gyan Publishing House
5, Ansari Road, Daryaganj,
New Delhi-110002
Phones: 23261060, 23282060
Fax: 91-011-23285914
Email: gyanbook@del2.vsnl.net.in
Visit our Website at http://www.gyanbooks.com

Lasertype Setting by: Tact Computer Graphics, Delhi
Printed at: Salasar Imaging Systems, Delhi

Contents

Preface

This book presents Jayaprakash Narayan's views on Jammu and Kashmir state, expressed in press statements, public speeches and articles from pre-independence era till the late years of his life, collected through all possible sources.

There were several reasons I undertook this task viz my personal association with him as also his eminence in the public life of the country and his impact on its Kashmir policy and on Kashmiri mind. Above all, he represented an alternative approach to the problem.

JP did change his stand on it from time to time depending on new developments and it is not necessary to agree with him on all aspects of his stand. But what is relevant even today is his broad approach, marked by empathy for the people of the state and emphasis on moral values tempered with pragmatic realities. His sincerity touched an emotional chord in the hearts of the people of the state, even when he had to do some blunt speaking. Likewise, he was listened to with respect by his country men and women, even when he defied traditional nationalistic sentiment on the sensitive issue of Kashmir. His exchange of views with Pakistani leaders were also most cordial, even when he did not accept their claim on Kashmir.

In the battle for winning hearts and minds of the people of the state, which might eventually prove more decisive than battle of arms in shaping its future, a study of JP's approach to the problem is likely to be rewarding for all those who are interested in it, from policy and opinion makers to every enlightened citizen, including that in the state.

Balraj Puri

Preface

Introductory

Jayaprakash Narayan once began his address to a seminar on Jammu and Kashmir state with a statement that he had spoken and written more on the state than any body else in the country. In a light hearted interruption, I claimed that quantitatively I had exceeded his record. He graciously conceded my claim amidst a hearty laugh of the audience.

However, the fact remained that out of all leading personalities of the country he paid maximum attention to the Kashmir problem and as tallest Indian, next perhaps only to Nehru, and as most authentic Gandhian, every word spoken and written by him was noticed, influenced public opinion, shook the conscience of the people or provoked angry reactions. But his voice could not be ignored. After Nehru's estrangment with Kashmir's most popular leader Sheikh Abdullah in 1953, JP remained major emotional link between the people of Kashmir and those in the rest of India; which eventually led to a reconciliation in seventies. What happened after that is another story.

Apart from commonness of our interest in and amount of attention to the affairs of J&K state, as indicated above, I owe a lot to his inspiration and moral and political support for the role I was able to play in the state, the establishment of which was often intolerant to any non-conformist voice. I have constantly interacted with him from 1946, when I and my colleagues organised public reception for him at Jammu during his first visit to the state, to almost his last days. Not that we always agreed on every point. Wherever, I disagreed with him, I expressed my views either publicly through my articles or privately in person. I had, for instance, strong disagreement with him when he appealed to Sheikh Abdullah to merge his party National Conference with the Janata Party. (See page 255). On other occasions, when I expressed my disagreement, I have mentioned in the text of the book. On the whole, I have remained convinced that his broad approach to Jammu and Kashmir — humane and democratic — is ever relevant. But I never found him lacking in an urge to understand a contrary view point, explain his own and modify it, if necessary.

Above all he was deeply human. I have personally received his affection and consideration in generous measure. I may quote just one incident to demonstrate this aspect of his multi-faceted personality. During one of his visits to Delhi, he somehow missed an appointment with me. I wrote a protest letter to his permanent address at Patna. In reply, he not only apologised for the lapse but also requested me to spare a full day with him, from breakfast to dinner during his next visit to Delhi. In between, he might have a few brief formal appointments. Accordingly on the appointed day, I reached the house of his host JJ Singh in Delhi for a breakfast with JP. After a few hours discussion, I accompanied him to the residence of the then Home Minister Gulzarilal Nanda. Our morning discussion was mainly about the situation that had developed in Kashmir following the theft of holy relic (a hair of the prophet (PBUH) enshrined in the Hazratbal Dargah) towards the end of 1963, which, according to me, had deteriorated due to bungling of the Home Ministry. JP discussed the matter with Nanda. As the latter came out to see him off, where I was waiting, he asked me "for how long have you been away from Kashmir." I replied that it might be around ten days. Nanda commented that he got reports every day and the situation was well under control. I retorted "Nanda ji, do you want to maintain that any body who stays in Kashmir ten days longer becomes a better expert of it than me". I pointed out the discrepencies in the official version of the day to day report he had mentioned. On JP's advice Nanda assured to satisfy me.

I had lunch with JP and Prabhavati. We continued to talk, with a few interruptions, till dinner time on all possible issues facing the country and of mutual interest. JJ Singh had arranged a formal dinner in honour of JP where ambassadors, cabinet ministers, political leaders and VVIPs had been invited. JP was supposed to sit at a table at the centre along with some important personalities. He declined to sit there and insisted on getting a separate table for two of us. He said, "I have to make amends for my lapse." This act of great magnanimity made me feel guilty for having made the complaint.

I owe a heavy debt of gratitude to one of the greatest men I have come across in my humble life; as a public man and as a person. This book is a token of acknowledgment of my debt to him. I have tried to collect all possible material — his statements, articles, letters and speeches — from various sources, including archives, libraries, local and national newspapers and my personal records. It took me more than a year and help from a number of friends. I had added my comments wherever needed to give the background of the event I knew of.

Jayaprakash Narayan's name, it will be seen, has been spelled in different ways by his correspondents. I have retained original spellings which might give an indication of how differently he was addressed and understood by his contemporaries.

Balraj Puri

1

Author's Assessment of Impact of JP on Kashmir

J.P.'s Role in Kashmir

(The following article written by me and published in the socialist weekly, the Janata, on 11 December 1977, summed up JP's role in Kashmir which is elaborated and supported by evience in the rest of the book. Ed.)

Jayaprakash Narayan's contribution to politics of Jammu and Kashmir has not been adequately appreciated; it was particularly not popular among many a staunch nationalist. But it would not be an exaggeration to say that he was mainly responsible for the final solution of what had come to be known as Kashmir problem. (So it seemed at that time. Ed.)

My own political and personal-which also became emotional-association with JP dates back to 1946, when he first visited the State to lend his support to the "Quit Kashmir" movement launched by the National Conference led by Sheikh Abdullah. We succeeded in organizing a public meeting addressed by him against all attempts by Hindu militants and the supporters of the Maharaja to sabotage and disturb it.

Support to "Quit Kashmir" Movement

As the movement against the Dogra Maharaja was basically motivated by sentiments of Kashmiri nationalism, confined to Kashmir valley, it could not endear itself to Dogras of Jammu among whom the traditional sentiments of loyalty to the ruler, who was one of them, prevailed among a large section of the people—both Hindus and Muslims. The Congress party, though formally committed to support the movement for responsible government in princely states, did not approve of any demand for the end of the princely system altogether.

JawaharLal Nehru, however, tried to reconcile the Congress stand and the objective of the "Quit Kashmir" movement by saying that it was not addressed to the person of the Maharaja but to the system and hence amounted to no more than the responsible government. In any case, the "Quit Kashmir" movement did not challenge the basic spirit of the Congress stand and at the most could have exceeded it, according to him.

Jayaprakash Narayan did not believe in such sophistications and rationalizations. His support to the "Quit Kashmir" movement was categoric and unreserved.

He wanted complete end of the monarchical system. He had differed with the Congress party in his attitude towards the other princes also. While the party accepted a compromise formula regarding the ratio of the respective representation of the rulers and the people in the Constituent Assembly, JP insisted that "all representatives of the states should be elected by the people of the states and none of them should be the nominee of the princes."

JP's support to the "Quit Kashmir" movement was thus consistent with his policy towards all the princely states. He had maintained his close contacts with the developments in the crucial state of the country since then, and staked his popularity by sticking to a consistent moral stand. It has been my proud privilege that throughout all vicissitudes of Kashmir politics-or the Kashmir problem as it used to be called-I have always found myself in broad agreement with him, notwithstanding my non-conformist, irreverent and critical attitude towards all heroes.

Opposition to Communal Politics

There was hardly any issue, at any phase of the political development in the state, on which I did not get his advice, support and blessing. I owe my political survival-under ruthless and unscrupulous local rulers and despite vicious campaign of character assassination by Hindu chauvinists-mainly to the inspiration and strength I have received from JP.

To revert to the role of JP in Kashmir politics, he did not want to interfere in it the initial period of the National Conference regime, after the state's accession to India in 1947, which, partly due to the Communist influence in it, did not retain close or friendly relations with JP or his socialist followers within the state. But that did not affect his objectivity in opposing the movement launched by the Jammu Praja Parishad-supported by the Bhartiya Jan Sangh-in 1952 for abrogation of Article 370 of the Constitution which guaranteed a special status for the state.

Again his opposition to the Jan Sangh did not prevent him from criticizing the Abdullah Government for its "criminal negligence" in treating a leader of the stature of Dr. Shyamaprasad Mukherjee, who died in a Kashmir jail. Sheikh Abdullah retorted angrily and described him as a Hindu leader who "has no right to interfere in the affairs of our state."

JP Condemned Sheikh's Arrest

The relations between the two leaders were thus strained in 1953. But JP was one of the few national leaders who condemned the arrest of Sheikh Abdullah in August 1953, unreservedly. For him it was basically a moral question and nothing to do with his personal relations. He criticized the Government of India for arresting him without a trial.

From 1953 up to 1975 he continued his campaign for a settlement of the Kashmir issue through negotiations between the Government of India and Sheikh Abdullah as also with Pakistan. During this period he was condemned by Indian chauvinists as a traitor and many of his public meetings were sought to be disturbed with slogans like "Hang JP the traitor."

JP felt that the Kashmir issue was a black spot on the fair name of India. He was against forcible occupation of Kashmir. He wanted India to honour her commitment regarding deciding the fate of Kashmir according to the wishes of the people.

In 1965 after infiltration of Pakistani guerillas into Kashmir and the Indo-Pakistan war that followed, JP modified his political stand on Kashmir. By attempting to annex Kashmir by force, JP said, Pakistan had lost its position as a party to the Kashmir dispute. But he still acknowledged the right of the people of Kashmir to decide their future within the framework of the Indian Union. This stand too was unpopular with many Indians, who were against any negotiations with Sheikh Abdullah. On the other hand this stand did not come up to the expectations of the Kashmiri leaders.

Right to Secede

In 1968 Sheikh Abdullah invited him to inaugurate what was called Jammu and Kashmir State People's Convention. Being used to speak in unpopular language, he had not cared for cheap popularity in Kashmir either. He bluntly told a big audience in Hazoori Bagh, Srinagar, that even if he were the Prime Minister of India he would not be able to get Kashmir seceded from India. The only solution possible for the State was to seek appropriate status for it within the framework of the Indian Union. The Sheikh retorted sharply and questioned his Gandhian bona fides. For according to him he had deviated from his stand that the people alone were masters of their fate and could take any decision including a decision to secede from India. JP remained unruffled and participated in the convention, which gradually veered around much nearer to his stand.

Throughout this period, JP continued this efforts for a dialogue between Sheikh Abdullah and the Government of India. In 1964 he had blessed the idea of a confederation between India, Pakistan and Kashmir. It was this proposal that Sheikh Abdullah and his colleagues took along with them when they went to Pakistan in 1964 to discuss it with Pakistan's leaders. General Ayub Khan, the then President of Pakistan, dismissed these proposals straightaway. JP, however, continued his efforts for a solution of Kashmir problem within the framework of India on bilateral basis, that is, between Sheikh Abdullah and Government of India, eliminating Pakistan from the negotiations. He met Sheikh Abdullah at the Kodaikanal jail for this purpose. [I reported the dialogue between the two in a piece I wrote for *Opinion,* edited by AD Gorwala entitled "What Transpired between JP and Abdullah". JP was surprised by accuracy of my report and asked my source. I told him that I had known both of them for so long that I not only knew their views but also the words they used for expressing them. I wanted him to confirm whether my report was correct. He agreed.]

The Main Contribution

Though in final phase of the parleys between Beg and Parthasarthy, representatives of the Sheikh and Government of India, respectively, and later between the Sheikh and the Prime Minister, Smt. Gandhi, JP was not associated on account of his own confrontation with the Government of India, the parleys were more or less on the lines JP had advocated. He was, therefore, first to extend wholehearted support to the accord which was arrived at between the Sheikh and the Prime Minister in 1975. He also persuaded most of the political parties of India, excepting the Jan Sangh to welcome the accord.

JP's main contribution lies in winning back the people of Kashmir for India who had been alienated and offended by the actions of the Governments in state and at the centre after 1953. In essence his approach coincided with that of Mahatma Gandhi in 1947, who had won the hearts of Kashmiris and their loyalty against the appeal of Pakistan by asserting that the people and not the ruler had the right to decide the future of the state. Whatever be the modifications in the political philosophy of JP from time to time, it was basically ethical and humanitarian, on account of which he endeared himself with the people of Kashmir irrespective of the cost he had to pay in terms of popularity in the rest of India.

Support to Regional Autonomy

It is important to note that while supporting Kashmiri aspirations, JP was not oblivious of or indifferent to the aspirations of the people of Jammu. In a seminar on the Kashmir Problem which he convened at Delhi in 1966 he lent his unequivocal support to the idea of regional autonomy so that the apprehensions of the people of the Jammu were allayed. The J&K state People's Convention convened by Sheikh Abdullah two years later he and his colleagues accepted the idea of regional autonomy. Happily the question of Centre-State relations and inter-regional relations are being discussed on the lines suggested by JP years ago.

The basic approach of JP towards the Kashmir problem is thus marked by not only moral and human consideration but also reflects his sense of patriotism and faresightedness. He has helped not only in raising India's moral stature but has also served vital national interest by his contribution in solving one of the most critical and embarrassing problem of independent India.

Above all, JP has demonstrated that national interest, democracy and morality are not mutually contradictory.

(Based on a talk at the University of Jammu, given on JP's 75th birthday celebrations.)

2

JP's Role in J&K before Independence

Jayaprakash Narayan in Jammu

Jayaprakash Narayan visited Jammu and Kashmir state for the first time on 30 December 1946; in support of the Quit Kashmir movement that the National Conference led by Sheikh Abdullah had launched against the autocratic rule of the Maharaja. As the movement and the National Conference were mainly Kashmir based, they did not have much popular support in Jammu. The Congress, too, had a separate existence in Jammu. But as JP was the guest of the National Conference, it was not associated with his reception. Moreover, the NC alone was affiliated with the Congress sponsored All India State Peoples' Conference.

It was a period when the relations between Socialists and Communists were extremely strained on accounts of, inter alia, support of the latter to the war effort and opposition to the Quit India movement in which the Socialists had played a leading role. The National Conference organisation in the state in general and in Jammu in particular was dominated by the Communists who were not very enthusiastic in organising reception to the Socialist leader.

The responsibility for organising a public meeting to be addressed by JP was therefore taken up by me and my colleagues in Jammu Students Union; which was the strongest secular force in the region.

A few weeks earlier, another Congress Socialist leader Aruna Asaf Ali's public meeting at Ranbir Singh Pura, first station on the railway line from Sailkote in Punjab (now in Pakistan) to

Jammu, was sought to be disturbed by pro-government demonstrators. The volunteers of the Students Union formed a ring around Aruna and the people willing to listen to her and pushed the demonstrators away. Earlier the senior leaders of the National Conference had advised Aruna to cancel her meeting. But she accepted our advice and was happy to see that the noisy demonstration was turned into a receptive audience.

In view of this experience, we planned JP's meeting at RS Pura, a few days ahead of it. As we landed into the border town and sought shelter in a Sikh Gurudwara, along with the literature of the National Conference, we were asked to leave. But we argued that nobody was ever turned out from the house of God. After we were allowed to stay and after long discussions with the local prominent persons, they agreed to cooperate with the arrangements for JP's reception. However, the leader of the hostile demonstrators against Aruna Asaf Ali insisted on one "condition" that is JP and his colleagues should have Tea at his place. We happily accepted the "condition". The result was that JP addressed a large successful and peaceful public meeting on 30 December 1946 at RS Pura. I met JP for the first time on that day. (Ed.)

Letter to JP from Jammu Congress

30, December 1946

Sh. Jai Prakash Narain
C/o The National Conference,
Ranbir Singh Pura

Dear Friend,

The Congress workers of Jammu welcome you, the hero of the stormy days of 1942, on your first visit to their province. They wanted to receive you here at Ranbirsinghpora in a body and in a manner most befitting you, the galla fighter of the historic war of Indian Independence; but they regret that compelled by the circumstances and much against their wishes they are doing so in a different manner. They suspect a double edged conspiracy against them, and would thus beg to be excused for being not present in a body. But this in no way belittles the high esteem and respect that they possess in their hearts for you. State government on the one side and the Communist element in the National Conference on the other are doing all that they can to discredit the Congress.

Last time, too, when Shrimati Aruna Asaf Ali came, they tried to disrepute the Congress workers. The goondas backed by the government created a trouble and tried to disturb her meeting for which the heads of the citizens of the state hang with shame; and no repentance however great shall be sufficient to wipe away the ugly slur. The Congress Committee with all their good intentions, was dragged into this. We were blamed by our friends in National Conference for the ugly incident.

We have, much against our wishes, decided to keep away in order to avoid any misunderstanding. But shall be much honoured if you very kindly condescend to spare some time for us. We want to pay our homage to you, and thus the martyrs of 1942; to explain our view point and also to place our humble services at your disposal. We hope that you will accept our invitation and allow as to meet in a tea party at Jammu. Please intimate your acceptance and the time suitable to you.

Sd/-

(A.N. Vaid)

General Secretary Congress Committee

Jammu

(As JP was guest of the National Conference, he did not accept the invitation of the Congress Committee Ed.)

(Nehru Memorial Museum and Library, Teen Murty, New Delhi. Subject file No. 236)

Communalists and Princes Allies of British

Jammu, Dec. 31— Congress Socialist leader Jayaprakash Narayan addressed a public meeting at RS Pura, a border town, on Jammu-Sialkote (in West Punjab) road, on 30 December 1946. Munshi Ahmad Din, the Punjab Socialist leader presided. He said: "India does not belong to the Britain or the rulers of the states. It belongs to you and me. Jammu and Kashmir is a part of my country."

Referring to the hostile demonstrations against Aruna Asaf Ali, when she visited here some time back, he said it was shameful and those who did it demonstrated their culture. He drew the attention of the Prime Minister of the state in whose rule a great personality of the country was treated like that. He could not disbelieve the report of Aruna and the Punjab Socialist leader Mubarak Sagar who had briefed him about the incident.

He assured full support of the Congress to the National Conference which was affiliated with it. Congress did not recognise any other party in the state. He respected the Jammu Congress Committee but not at the cost of the National Conference. He conceded that there could be room for differences between the two. He himself had differences with the Congress working committee. Despite their differences with the NC, the Congress should support it.

He recognised only two parties. One that of princes and landlords and the other of working classes. If the government was sincere, it should then accept responsible government elected by every adult citizen so that people were satisfied and happy. The state had no other alternative, he said.

It was the first visit of JP to the state. He could not come earlier not because he was not interested in the state but because he was engaged in other activities. He was now closely associated with the politics of the princely states. He said the country was on the threshold of independence. It faced two main hurdles. One by the communalists and the other by the princes. The British government, according to him, repeatedly declared that it was ready to leave India within a day but to whom it should be handed over. On the other hand the viceroy through his political agents continued to conspire for creating hurdles. Continuing he said: "People of India, including princely states are so powerful today that they could throw the British out. In 1942, the youth and students had created a new enthusiasm in the country. Netaji's open war against the British had revolutionised the minds of the people. Today's India is much stronger than it was in 1942. The Britishers know that their rule cannot last longer. If Pandit Nehru and Qaid-e-Azam (Jinnah) jointly demand Lord

Wavel to quit, he could not stay a day longer. But Qaid-e-Azam does not join hands with the Congress which he calls a Hindu party; he joins the British government which had treated the Muslims in a worse way than the Hindus might do. We ask the Muslim League to at least fight for the independence of Bengal, Punjab, Sindh and Baluchistan. It begs the British rulers not to leave. They do not have their own power to stay on but are building up communal forces to do so. The Muslim League alone is not a communal party. Hindu Maha Sabha and Akali Dal are equally so. All of them are traitors to the country. When Pandit Nehru moved a resolution in the Constituent Assembly to declare India an independent republic, the opposition came from not only the Muslim League but also the princes. The people of the princely states want their representatives in the Consembly. The rulers are puppets of the British. If their representatives are in the Consembly that would mean that the British government had sent them. They would speak its language who will hold strings from behind the curtain."

He concluded that the Interim government and the Consembly are not going to succeed. The Interim government was paralysed the day when the League joined it. The League wants to prove that Indians cannot run their government and British should continue to have maximum interference in our affairs and to arbitrate in our disputes. The British would then say as the League and the princes are not with the Congress, why should they accept its decision. The Congress will then be forced to renew its struggle."

(Translated from original in Urdu from the Ranbir, Jammu dated 31 December, 1946)

In the end he cautioned the people to beware of the machinations of the Communists who often worked in disguise through other mass organisations. (The reference was obviously to the Communists working in the National Conference).

After JP's critical reference to the role of the Communists, the National Conference leaders cancelled the rest of the scheduled programme of his public meetings at other places in Jammu region. He returned the other day. (Ed.)

Kachru Writes to JP to withdraw in Favour of Abdullah for Presidenship of AISPC

All India States'
People's Conference
17, York Road, New Delhi

Dated: 7 March 1947

My dear Jaiprakashji,

Your name has been proposed for the Presidentship of the AISPC from the Punjab region. You will of course withdraw in favour of Sheikh Mohammad Abdullah and send me a telegram to say so. Please remember that the final date for the withdrawal of names is the 10th of March, and you will write to me before the 8th. Your statement should also come out either on the 9th or 10th. In your statement you will please give a brief review of the affairs of Kashmir. Your impression of the visit to Kashmir should also be given in this statement. You should deal at length with the present famine conditions in Kashmir and also with the hardships and sufferings of the political detenues in Srinagar Central Jail. The political detenues in the Central Jail, Srinagar tried for over a month to get their grievances redressed, but ultimately have decided to resort to hunger strike. They are now on hunger strike for the last 8 days. Just this morning Panditji sent them a telegram requesting them to abandon the fast. The Congress delegation is shortly visiting Kashmir and in your statement you should make some reference to this fact also.

In conclusion you should bring out the unity of interest and the solidarity of the States Peoples' struggle and the symbolic value which Kashmir has for this people's movement in Indian states. In suppressing the people's movement of Kashmir the political department and the Princes as a whole played an important part. It would therefore be an expression of our solidarity and unity of interest with the people of Kashmir, if we would elect Sheikh Abdullah for the presidentship of the forthcoming annual session of the Conference. Please remember that your statement should not come out before the 9th of March.

With regards,
Yours sincerely

Sd/-
(Dwarkanath Kachru)
Secretary to Jawaharlal Nehru

Shri Jaiprakash Narayan,
C/o Shri Purshotam Tricumdas, Bar-at-law,
Dilkush, 40, Ridge Road, Malabar Hills, Bombay.
(NMM&L New Delhi, File No. 236, PP 75)

JP's Withdrawal from Contest of A.I.S.P.C.

(In response to the letter of Dwarkanath Kachru, Private Secretary of Jawaharlal Nehru, Jayaprakash Narayan withdrew his name for the Presidentship of the All India State People's Conference in favour of Sheikh Abdullah who was unanimously elected when still in jail. He had succeeded Nehru. Ed.)

3

JP's Policy on Kashmir (1947–1953)

Non-interference in Kashmir Under Abdullah Government

I resumed my contact with JP, after his visit in Jammu in December 1946, around two years later in Delhi where I was a postgraduate student in 1948-49 and later also when I returned to Delhi for brief spells. Whenever he visited Delhi, I used to call on him to report to him my assessment of the situation in J&K state; in which he always evinced keen interest. When the Congress Socialist Party parted company with the parent organisation to form an effective opposition, I shared its belief that the role of an opposition party was essential for the growth of democracy in India. For the same reason, I suggested to him that Kashmir, too, needed an opposition. I pointed out authoritarian trends in Kashmir politics, which under a popular leader like Sheikh Abdullah and the well organised party like the National Conference, was leading to a regimented set up. For lack of democratic opposition, popular discontent in Jammu was being exploited by Hindu communalists and feudal elements and in Kashmir by anti-India elements. In this connection, I mentioned the role of Kashmiri leader Ghulam Mohiuddin Karra who was next in popularity to Sheikh Abdullah. Differences between the two leaders led to parting of the ways and persecution of Karra and his colleagues.

I pleaded the case of Karra who could possibly be accommodated in the opposition if Socialist Party extended its activities to the state. Though JP listened to my arguments with interest and despite agreeing with me in principle, said, "we should not interfere in the state till Kashmir problem was solved." I, on the other hand, envisaged "indefinite prolongation of

Kashmir dispute", (title of a statement at my first press conference in Delhi) and wanted India's Kashmir policy to be framed accordingly.

It will be pertinent to add that Karra, after five years of persecution and in sheer desperation, was the first political leader of consequence in Kashmir who gave a call for the state's accession to Pakistan in June 1953. It unnerved Sheikh Abdullah who in order to steal the thunder of Karra started equivocating on the issue of accession, though there were other factors also that influenced Sheikh's changing mood. It led to serious differences between him and Jawahar Lal Nehru and his removal from power and arrest in August 1953, which marked the first crisis in the internal politics of the state. However, Karra returned to the mainstream politics in 1977 to lead the Janata Party when he got a pro-India platform to oppose Sheikh Abdullah.

Despite the support of the socialists to Sheikh Abdullah's government in the state, he started campaigning for the Congress Party during the first election in 1951. I pointed out to JP the anomaly in the unilateral Socialist support to the National Conference. JP was equally upset about Sheikh's campaign for the Congress and accordingly sent the following Express telegram to him and a statement to the press on Ist December 1951. (Ed.)

JP objects to Abdullah's Campaign for Congress (Press Statement)

I was greatly surprised to learn that Sheikh Abdullah is coming to India to assist the election campaign of the Congress party. Sheikh Abdullah is not a Congressman nor is the Kashmir National Conference a part of the Congress organisation. What is more important, the Kashmir question has never been a party question in this country. The Socialist party, for instance, has been second to none in this country in its support to Sheikh Abdullah and the freedom struggle of the people of Kashmir both before and after the end of British rule. If Mr Nehru has not the strength to rise above petty party interests, I hope Sheikh Abdullah will not allow himself to be exploited in this manner. He would be doing incalculable harm to the cause of Kashmir if he did so.

(Statement issued from Patna on Ist December 1951)

(NMM&L, File No. 236, PP 77)

Upset about Sheikh's campaign for the Congress and accordingly sent the following Express telegram to him and a statement to the press on 1st Decemeber 1951. (Ed.)

Express Telegramme to Abdullah

Sheikh Mohammad Abdullah

Prime Minister

Government of Kashmir

Srinagar (Kashmir)

Amazed to learn your impending visit to campaign for the Congress party stop Other parties than the Congress have lent you full support stop Kashmir has never a party question stop You are not a Congressman nor Kashmir National Conference a part of that organisation stop The Socialist Party out of consideration for you and the National Conference has refrained so far from forming a party branch in Kashmir stop Advise you strongly to desist from identifying yourself with a single party stop You will do incalculable harm to Kashmir thereby.

Sd/-

Jayaprakash Narayan

Patna

1st December 1951

(NMM&L, New Delhi, File No. 236 PP 78-80)

4

Kashmir's First Emotional Rupture with the Rest of India (1953)

JP Accuses Kashmir Government of Criminal Negligence for Mukerjee's Death

Lucknow, July 7: Mr Jayaprakash Narayan, Praja Socialist leader, said here today that the Kashmir authorities were "criminally negligent" in looking after the health of Dr. Shayama Prasad Mukerjee (President Bhartiya Jana Sangh).

The Praja Socialist leader in a statement issued said "I regret deeply that the Prime Minister in his reply to Shri Atulya Ghosh, as reported in the press this morning, has stated so categorically that there was no negligence shown by the Kashmir government in the case of the late Dr. Shayama Prasad Mukerjee.

I cannot say what facts have been placed before the Prime Minister. But the facts as I know them lead to an entirely different conclusion.

I was at Calcutta only 3 days ago, when I took the opportunity of calling on Dr. Mukerjee's family to offer my condolences and my homage to the departed leader.

It was on this occasion that Mr Justice Rama Prasad Mookerjee told me the whole story, as he, a distinguished jurist, had been able to place together. The story left no doubt in my mind that the Kashmir authorities were not only negligent but criminally negligent in looking after Shyama Prasad Babu's health. I feel sure that the life of this great Indian could have been saved by better care."

Impartial Enquiry

Mr Jaya Prakash Narayan added, it seems to me that after such a national tragedy the least that the Indian government could do was to institute a proper and impartial enquiry into the whole affair. "In the meanwhile it does not seem proper for the Prime Minister to pronounce judgement on such a controversial subject and to attempt to whitewash the guilt of those who seem to deserve severe punishment."

Mr Narayan added that he had no intention to say anything about this matter. But he was afraid that the expression of the Prime Minister's opinion might lead to a grave injustice and he thought it was necessary to challenge it publicly - PTI

(Amrit Bazar Patrika, 8 July, 1953)

Nehru's Letter to JP on Mookerjee's Death

29 July 1953

My dear Jayaprakash,

I returned yesterday from Karachi and received your letter of the 25th July. Since yesterday, I have been thinking whether it will serve any useful purpose to send any immediate reply to you. It seems to be my misfortune that I get out of step with you however much I may try to do otherwise.

Some time ago we had talks when, without any mental reservations but only with the desire that we should come closer to one another in our work, I had made some suggestions. Those suggestions may not have been good enough and you were perfectly justified in not accepting them. But to my great regret I found that a controversy had arisen about it and motives were imputed to all of us, including you and me. The result was that instead of our coming somewhat nearer, we are pushed further away.

There was the case of the election at Purnea where, again, it was my desire as well as that of my colleagues to make a friendly gesture. That too failed and led to some amount of bitterness. Evidently some evil fate is pursuing us and I have begun to think that the safest policy might well be not to tempt that fate and to remain quiet.

I wrote to you, when I saw your statement in the Press about Dr Mookerjee's death, because I should indicate to you frankly what I felt. (Thereby I tempted fate again and I have had my punishment.) If you feel that I am behaving in this matter or on any other matter, like some High Authority which considers itself infallible, then, of course, there is nothing more to be said by me. If I have fallen from grace, nothing can justify what I do.

Some time ago, I received a letter from Dr. B.C. Roy about Dr. Mukerjee's death and the suggested enquiry. He had himself urged this enquiry publicly and privately. His letter, therefore, has some relevance. I am enclosing a copy of it for your information.

You refer to Indo-Kashmir relations. I presume you know that these relations for some time past have been very strained and difficult. Indeed it is not merely a question of governmental relations but popular reactions, more especially in the Kashmir valley. The Jammu agitation of the Praja Parishad and the Jan Sangh, whatever its local justification might have been, was carried on in such a way, both in Jammu and in some other parts of India, that it produced powerful reactions on the people of Kashmir generally. Naturally disproportionate publicity was given to that agitation by our opponents in Kashmir as well as in Pakistan. The Pakistan Press played it up greatly, realising that would do them good. The effect of all that was an increasing feeling among the people of Kashmir that the communal face of India was much bigger and more powerful than had been thought and that their future might well be imperilled by association with this. Their desire to remain with India became weakened and they tried to seek escape from it in other ways. That may have been foolish. But such was their reaction.

Unfortunately many statements and writings of some of our leading persons affected them even more, because they came from non-communal people. Kriplani's writing in the Vigil and some of his speeches hurt them very much. So did Lohia's. It is in this context that I would like you to consider your own statement in regard to Dr Mukerjee's death.

I am merely trying to analyses the situation not justifying or criticising. You may be right in what you say about Sheikh Abdullah. But that does not help much when large number of others feel with him. Since Dr Mukerjee's death, a frequent slogan in the Hindu Mahasabha and Jan Sangh meetings has been "Abdullah ko phansi do". Also "Dr Mukerjee ke kaun qatil - Nehru or Abdullah. Khoon ka badla khoon se lo". Thus Sheikh Abdullah and the Kashmir government have been put in the dock as murderers and the whole enquiry into Dr Mukerjee's death becomes a trial of Abdullah, etc for murder. That is how it appears to large number of people in Kashmir.

There has been a controversy about the measure of accession of the Kashmir state to India. That controversy has not ended. In the final analysis, we cannot hold any part of Kashmir by force of arms alone and without the wishes of the people concerned. If that is so, these reactions in the Kashmir valley have weakened our position terribly and for the first time I feel very doubtful about the future. No amount of strong speeches or statements here on this subject help, because ultimately the decision will be made by the people of Kashmir. They have been frightened and angered by much that has been said here and is being said. When there is so much controversy about the measure of accession, for us to impose an enquiry from above, which is clearly outside the subjects of accession, would immediately raise not only constitutional issues of importance, but passionate resentment. It would become an example, in many people's eyes, of how we treat Kashmir as a subject country. It would, in fact, put an end to such case we have had in Kashmir based on the people's goodwill.

As I have said above, I decided to write to you with some reluctance because you are the last person with whom I would care to have a controversy of this nature. But then I felt that I should at least place some facts before you because grave issues are at stake. The Kashmir issue is grave enough in all conscience. But, with that are tied up so many other issues in India. Kashmir has been a symbol to us of secularism, etc. If that is decided on a communal basis, then the reactions in India are likely to be far-reaching and unfortunate. Therefore, I have written. You need not trouble to reply to me in so far as this subject is concerned. If you hold a different opinion, you are at perfect liberty to do so. I received your telegram about Burnpur just before going to Karachi. Your letter came when I was at Karachi.

Before going away, I left instructions to delay any possible action at Burnpur and to wait for your letter. I understand that as a result of this, your advice was largely followed.

Yours affectionately

Sd/-

(Jawahar Lal)

Shri Jayprakash Narayan
C/o Dr Dinshah Mehta,
Nature Cure Clinic,
Little Gibbs Road, Malabar Hill,
Bombay.
(NMM&L File No. 240L PP5-7)

JP on Abdullah's Arrest

Apart from Jawaharlal Nehru's reaction to JP's demand for an impartial inquiry into Dr. Mukerjee's death in Kashmir jail, Sheikh Abdullah took a strong exception to it. In a statement, he had retorted that "a Hindu leader like JP has no right to interfere in the affairs of our state."

The events moved fast thereafter leading to dismissal from power of Abdullah and his arrest on 9 August 1953, whatever my difference with him might have been, I condemned this action unequivocally. For it was legally, morally and politically unjustified. He was dismissed by the Sadar-e-Riyasat (as the Head of the state was then called) when he still commanded majority in the legislature; on the ground that he had lost the confidence of the majority of his cabinet colleagues, which legally and politically, is an invalid ground. The indefinite detention of a popular leader who was the architect of the state's accession to India, without any trial, was bound to alienate his entire following in Kashmir.

I argued on these, lines with JP requesting him to condemn Abdullah's arrest. But he silenced me by quoting Abdullah's statement which had questioned his right to interfere in the affairs of the state. I did urge him to ignore the pettiness of Abdullah and consider taking a stand on the merit of the matter. He agreed to give a consideration to my request. Meanwhile I arranged to send a letter to Abdullah in jail explaining how important was the support of JP in any campaign against his arrest. I had enclosed draft of a letter addressed to JP which he should sign. That letter made an impassioned appeal to "the moral leader and conscience keeper of India," to whom Kashmir looked for support after Gandhi. The Sheikh promptly signed the letter which I presented to JP. His reaction to Abdullah's earlier indiscretion had already been mellowed. He condemned the arrest though not dismissal of Abdullah. (Ed.)

Abdullah Should be Tried or Set Free: JP

Cultack, April 24: Praja Socialist leader Sri Jayaprakash Narayan criticised the detention of the Kashmir leader Sheikh Abdullah. He said, "as far as he has been able to understand the Sadar-e-Riayasat (as head of the state was then designated) was justified in dismissing Abdullah but no convincing case had yet been made for his arrest and continued imprisonment."

Whatever might be the political consequences of setting Sheikh Abdullah free, he added, he had no doubt that he should either be tried in an ordinary court or be set free without delay.

The PSP leader, presiding over the fifth annual conference of the All India Civil Liberties Union here today, strongly condemned the extension of the Preventive Detention Act and of the Press Act.

(Amrit Bazar Patrika, Calcutta, 25 April 1954)

Nehru's Letter to JP on Situation in Kashmir

New Delhi,
May 3, 1956

My dear Jayaprakash,

Your letter of May 1. I well remember your mentioning to me about filling Narendra Deva's seat in the Rajya Sabha. I passed on this message immediately to the A.I.C.C. Office. I confess that I forgot about it afterwards. Normally I have nothing to do with these elections or the choice of candidates except that some kind of a final reference is made on the very last date usually. The normal procedures were later followed and the U.P.P.C.C. sent their recommendation. Even then I had pointed out that you had said to me. But I was told that it was too late then to make a change. Personally I would have welcomed Farid

Ansari or Shakuntala. But I have seldom and in fact never interested with the selections of the U.P.P.C.C. or indeed normally with any other.

About Kashmir, it is difficult to discuss the situation in a brief letter. But I am absolutely convinced that your information about 95% Kashmir Muslims is completely wrong. It is difficult for anyone to express a firm opinion about this matter. If one takes the population of the whole of the state, apart from the part occupied by Pakistan, I think it is rather doubtful which way a majority would lie. I think there is a fair possibility of the majority being in favour of India. If you take Kashmir proper only, the probability is that the rural areas would be in favour of Bakhshi Government. In some of the urban areas there will be a marked divisicn and it is possible that in two or three of them the majority may be against Bakhshi. It is rather difficult to say what might happen in a plebiscite in Kashmir proper. Much depends on how this question is raised. If it is made a communal issue, then it is probable that a majority of Muslims might vote against India. If the issues are purely political, different voting would take place. But all this is guess work and people's opinions vary from time to time and are affected by some occurrence.

At the present moment there is a rather small group which is carrying on an agitation against the Bakhshi Government. That group itself is a small one, though it may have the sympathy of many others. Most of the people in this group are very irresponsible.

Apart from these questions, I am sure that any change in the present position in Kashmir would lead to dangerous consequence, large migrations, great bitterness between India and Pakistan and probably war.

You might be interested to know that some time ago Fatima Jinnah went to Azad Kashmir. She returned rather disgusted and said that Azad Kashmir would vote for India if they had a chance. The fact is that the people in Azad Kashmir are in a miserable condition and they look with great envy on the much better conditions on our side. Also Kashmiris proper (excluding others in the state who are not Kashmiris) have always had no great love for the Punjabis.

This applies to both Hindus and Muslims as the Punjabis were looked upon as exploiters in Kashmir. This is the reason why Kashmiris who are in Azad Kashmir now are distrusted by the Pakistanis and are in a particularly bad condition.

I have written to you briefly about this matter. The story is a long one and a very complicated one. But it seems to me clear that your sources of information are not good.

Yours affectionately,
Sd/-
Jawahar Lal Nehru

Shri Jayaprakash Narayan,
C/o Mahila Charkha Samiti,
Kadam Kuan,
Patna.
(NMM&L File No. 240, PMH/56 No. 933)

Letter from Mridula to JP

81/48, Diplomatic Enclave,
Kastaliya Marg, New Delhi,
March 20, 1958.

My dear Jai Prakash Ji,

Herewith a copy of the letter that I wrote to Justice Das, President of the All India Civil Liberties Union. I understand you are the Vice-President of this organization and therefore, I wanted to see and consult you on the question mentioned in the attached letter. Unfortunately this did not happen. So I have talked to Shri Ashok who is meeting you tomorrow at Banaras and requested him to discuss the question with you and advise me accordingly.

I had learnt that some members of the Civil Liberties Union like Shri Mani and other were going to move a resolution on Kashmir in the coming Civil Liberties Conference. I met him and suggested that instead of passing a resolution the best would be for the Civil Liberties Union to send two or three expert lawyers and others to Kashmir on a study tour of the Civil Liberties problems that face the people of the state. They should go to Jammu, Rajouri, Poonch and Kashmir, assess the problems and report to the President. May be some of the problems are such which should not be given publicity but should be brought to the notice of Shri Jawaharlalji and the authorities, while some could be publicly discussed. Later on when the criminal cases against nationalists wrongly involved in the Hazratbal incident of 21st February begin it will be necessary to help them get lawyers. After fact finding, the Civil Liberties Union may consider it desirable to take up their cases. If this happens I have no doubt that it will go a long way in creating popular goodwill towards India provided, of course, the whole thing is not marred, by political considerations.

In 1954, a few days before the death of Kidwai Saheb, under his advice I had contacted Shri Vaziruddin of Civil Liberties Organisation at Bombay. At that time they did not consider it desirable to intervene, specially, as I was told, members like Pandit Kunzru have been opposed to it. In view of all this cross-currents I apprehend difficulties even this time, unless well wishers of Kashmir like you take an interest in this matter, and advise them and also me and my colleagues as to whether one should expect any concrete help from the Civil Liberties Union.

In 1954 from the secretary Civil Liberties Union office, for the first time I learnt that since 1947 the Congress was averse to it and there was some directive to the Congress members against associating themselves with it. So I informed the Congress President, at that time Shri Jawahar Lal Ji, about the action that I had taken in contacting the Civil Liberties Union. He did not like the idea and strongly reacted against it. There was no question of my persuing the matter as the Civil Liberties Union were themselves reluctant to do anything. However, the question before me is to urge all, progressive forces in India including the Congress to assist the people of J&K state to secure justice from Indian sources and thus meet the challenge of vacuum that might be filled up through other intervention if we fail. I am not sending you the literature except the latest on Hazratbal incident to give you an idea of the foul ways and means adopted by the ruling party to involve political opponents in serious criminal litigation. This has increased bitterness.

With best wishes,

Yours sincerely,

Sd/-

(Mridula Sarabhai)

(NMM&L, File No 238 PP7)

5

Theft of Holy Relic in Kashmir

Disappearance of Holy Relic in Kashmir

Towards the end of December 1963, the relic of prophet Mohammad kept in the famous Hazratbal shrine of Srinagar mysteriously disappeared. As it was regarded by Kashmiri Muslims as their most sacred and precious possession, its loss caused an unprecedented shock and anger throughout the valley. People had no faith in the state government and sought personal intervention of the Prime Minister and the President of India. The holy relic was recovered as mysteriously as it was lost. People demanded that its genuiness be verified by religious leaders and the culprits be identified.

I rushed to Delhi and called the Home Minister Gulzari Lal Nanda for an immediate appointment. He wanted me to explain the matter. I hold him there was an excellent opportunity for the government of India to win over the goodwill of the people but his ministry had bungled. He asked me how? "Should I explain the entire list of my complaints on phone?", I asked. Thereupon he asked me to come to his office immediately.

He repeated my complaints against his officials who were handling (or, according to me, mishandling) the situation in Kashmir to the Home Secretary Vishwanathan on phone. I pointed out glaring loop holes in his explanation. He again called Vishwanathan who had meanwhile left his office. Then he asked Director of Intelligence Bureau B.N. Mullick to come to his room immediately and confronted him with me. I said that the holy relic was a Muslim property and was to be handed back to the community soon. If that was not verified properly, and was displayed to Muslim congregation, which was bound to be largest which was the scheduled day of Deedar (display of the relic), even a handful of persons could challenge its authenticity that could cause an explosion. Mullick tried to assure Nanda and me that adequate arrangement had been made to face the explosion. I said, "it was neither bravery nor wisdom to first create an explosion and then try to face it."My alternative proposals were dismissed by Mullick with the remark that there were certain matter of national interest which could not be revealed." Thereupon I said in a rather angry tone, "Nanda ji, have you called me to get a lesson in national interest from a person who had served British masters when we were fighting battle for freedom?" Nanda tried to pacify me and promised to find a way out. However, I managed to convey my views to Nehru. He had suffered first serious illness when all his engagements and appointments were suspended. My letter was delivered to him in his bed room by Ashoka Mehta, the then Deputy Chairman of the Planning Commission. Acting on my advice, the Prime Mininster deputed Lal Bahadur Shashtri, a cabinet minister of his government, to go to Kashmir where he was able to resolve the problem to the satisfaction of the people.

Meanwhile, I had written the following letter to JP on the same subject: (Ed.)

Letter to JP on Relic Agitation in Kashmir

A-4, Model Town,
Delhi - 9
January 26, 1964

My dear Jayaprakash ji,

Apropos our very brief talk on Kashmir, I am enclosing a note on the current handling of the situation as also a copy of my letter to Nandaji.

My purpose in acquainting you with the situation in Kashmir is not merely using your good offices with the authorities. I also seek sympathy and understanding for the current popular movement in Kashmir from Indian leaders. If justice cannot be done to the people of Kashmir, there should at least be a few Indians who share their demand for justice. For while it may never be possible to fully satisfy them - as also any other people, surely adequate outlets for dissatisfaction could be provided.

Expectations from you in this respect are not improper. For free from considerations of chauvinism, government and party interest and with your status, you are in a unique position to influence the climate of opinion in the country as also in encouraging the secular and healthy trends in Kashmir politics. It is really not too much to expect a word of support from you for the current movement in Kashmir and even a visit to the valley during its hour of anguish. After all you do take interest in the problems of other parts of India and Kashmir's problems have repercussions not only beyond the borders of the state but also of the country.

I hope I am within my limits in writing you a letter like this.

With kindest regards,

Yours sincerely

Sd/-

(Balraj Puri)

Shri Jayaprakash Narain
Kadam Kuan,
Patna (Bihar).

JP on Theft of Sacred Relic

(Statement published in *Sarvodya*, Vol XIII, April 1964)

Shri Poorna Chandra Jain, Shri Ahad Fatmi and Shri Krishnaraj Mehta, who went to Srinagar on behalf of the Sarva Seva Sangh and the Shanti Sena Mandal, have returned after spending nearly a week in that city of turmoil. In their stay they met a number of people of different communities and persuasions and tried as dispassionately as possible to understand the situation there. Having heard their report and discussed the matter with them, I feel called upon to make a few observations for the attention of both the Government of India and the people at large.

First of all I should like to emphasise the remarkable communal harmony among Muslims, Hindus and Sikhs throughout the anxious days since the theft of the sacred relic on December 27 and the public deedar on February 6. I am afraid this fact of harmony between the communities, has not been fully appreciated in India and abroad. In the face of this every sensible person in the world should regret that some leaders of Pakistan and its press tried to give the whole affair the colour of deep and intense communal ill-will and discord. I feel proud to be able to congratulate the people of Kashmir, irrespective of communities, upon their exemplary unity.

In view of the intense excitement which prevailed in the state it was remarkable that along with communal harmony the people were able on the whole to remain peaceful. The few instances of arson and rowdyism must be unreservedly condemned. It must also be regretted that the police had to fire on two occasions, causing a few deaths and many other casualties. The popular demand for a judicial inquiry into the firing deserves the sympathetic consideration of the Government of India, which has already wisely conceded the demand for an outside judge to try the cases if those arrested for the theft of the holy relic.

Secondly, praise is due to Central Intelligence officers for acting so promptly and efficiently in tracing the stolen relic. It is regrettable that there was initially so much hesitation and delay in identifying the relic, and this unfortunately raised unnecessary doubts and worsened the situation in the state. It was therefore good that Shri Lal Bahadur Shastri went to Srinagar, where he handled the situation with wisdom, courage and foresight.

Kashmir Government

Thirdly, there is evidence that Kashmir Government does not enjoy the confidence and support of the people of the state. This is a dangerous state of affairs and must be mended as soon as possible. The same kind of wisdom, courage and foresight are necessary to deal with the situation as were evidenced in the matter of deedar. No doubt every course that is open involves an element of risk. But the present course is fraught with greater risk. In determining the future line of action it would be advisable to consult informally all sections of public opinion in Kashmir and Jammu. I need not point out that formal and institutional expression of opinion, as through party-based, elections, is often unrepresentative and misleading, particularly when civic freedom is strictly restricted either by law or actual practice as has unfortunately been the case in many democratic countries.

Fourthly, any dispassionate study of events since the theft of the holy relic and its recovery and public display would establish the great and widespread popularity of Sheikh Abdullah. Any political settlement in Kashmir would therefore be inadvisable without him. Fair minded people in India and abroad have watched with dismay the strange progress of the Sheikh's trial, which I am sorry to say is a blot on the otherwise bright record of Indian justice. Moreover Sheikh Abdullah has already been in detention or prison for nearly ten years. But he cannot be held prisoner indefinitely. Whatever the legal or other difficulties, statesmanship demands that the trial be forthwith ended and the Sheikh set at liberty. Only when he is free could a political approach be possible to him. Finally, in view of the emergence on a considerable scale of harmony and peace in Kashmir, it seems a very favourable moment for the Sarvodaya movement to turn its attention to that state and launch a well-planned programme of constructive work. Its extreme poverty and pervading unemployment cry out for widespread development of handicrafts and cottage and small- scale industries. Many of the peace volunteers who made their appearance in the period of turmoil could be converted into a stable and trained band of Shantisainiks, I hope the Sarvodaya movement is able to face up to the challenge.

6

Abdullah's Release (1964)

Abdullah's Letter to JP

Camp Batote,
April 15, 1964

My dear Jayaprakashji,

I am very happy to receive your thought provoking telegram on my release.

Earlier, I had also received your kind letter on the eve of my release.

I have no doubt that with the blessings and cooperation of friends like you, "Kashmir can become a bridge between India and Pakistan instead of being a dividing wedge between the two."

I am reaching New Delhi on or about April 26 and will be there for a few days. I hope it will be possible for you to give me the pleasure of your company at that time.

Meanwhile, you may perhaps help in maintaining a proper atmosphere in Delhi which has been vitiated a little by hasty unfavourable comment on my speeches by some responsible Indian leaders.

Please convey my best regards to Prabhavatiji.

Yours sincerely
Sd/-
(Sheikh Mohd Abdullah)

Shri Jayaprakash Narayan
Kadam Kuan,
Patna - 3 (Bihar)

Please excuse bad stationery. I am on my way to Srinagar and not have proper secretarial assistance. With kindest regards from me and my wife.

S.M. Abdullah.

(NMM&L, File No. 86 PP 173)

The Need to Rethink: JP

(Hindustan Times, 15 May 1964)

My recent article on Kashmir has provoked a rather fierce controversy. That is good, because after the emotional catharsis tempers should cool down, allowing for a more reasoned approach to a question that has plagued the subcontinent for the last 17 years. There is urgent need for rethinking on this question, and all I did in my article was to plead for this. It is to be regretted therefore that most of those who thought it necessary to preach angry sermons to me on patriotism refused to look squarely at the truths I had drawn attention to.

Yet I have no desire to prolong this controversy, because I believe it would help if everybody concerned kept his own counsel for a while. But in recent days there have been some amazing statements revealing a dangerous state of mind. It seems necessary to deal briefly with some of these matters which cause anxiety and point to a constructive way out if possible.

When I wrote about the ballyhoo in my article I little imagined that there had been such a vast, organised attempt to work up a state of mind which was hysterical and closed to reason and intolerance to a violent degree of all dissent. The public temper in Delhi at the time of Sheikh Abdullah's arrival reminded one of the days when the Father of the Nation was sacrificed at the altar of a similar synthetic hysteria. Regrettably Parliament itself helped to create that spirit of violent intolerance: recall- to give only one example-the shouting down of Mr Frank Anthony.

A rather mortifying example of the mental state of some members of Parliament was provided by Mr A.P. Jain, president of the UP Congress and one time Union Minister. He is reported to have said in New Delhi that there were men who held a different opinion from mine on Kashmir who had voluntarily imposed upon themselves "extreme restraint," but that "if provocations of the type that Mr Narayan is making continue their patience might be exhausted."

I have no idea what Mr Jain means by that threat; perhaps he and his friends would have me put away in prison. Personally I would welcome that as an opportunity to snatch some rest and do some reading. But the crucial point to ponder is that irate young men go about muttering about assassination if a person in Mr Jains's position utters threats in this manner?

The pity is that when I referred to this mass hysteria at a public meeting in New Delhi some friends in the Rajya Sabha turned it into an issue of personal security-I am in no need of protection-rather than give serious thought to the dangers of the situation that had developed. May I say with due respect that in order to remedy the situation members of Parliament might well begin by practicing a little more patience and tolerance themselves?

Importance of Human Values

Of all the amazing statements made in the course of this controversy the one by 27 Congress MPs (including the secretary of the Congress Party and other important members) easily takes the prize. First, there was the astounding assertion of the primacy of law over moral and human values. As legislators the MPs should know the nature and limitations of law as they are making and unmaking laws, even amending the constitution, all the time. In human affairs law no doubt has an important role to play, but it has its limits. Morality and human values transcend the limits of law and take precedence over it.

Nor is it a question of " anyone's personal views of what is moral." It is not at all difficult to identify what civilization in this age considers moral and human. Mahatama Gandhi devoted his whole life to spiritualise politics. It is sad to find that in a decade and a half leaders- one hopes their number is limited- of the organization he built have come to sneer openly at morality and humanism.

Coming to Kashmir, this is how they authoritatively summed up the position: "You can no more talk of self-determination in the case of Kashmir than in the case of say, Bombay of Bihar." Further on they said: "After the Americans attained independence was any state allowed to exercise the so called right of self-determination?" Surely Congress MPs know better. Then why this deliberate obfuscation? Is the answer far to find?

Lest the public, which has a proverbially short memory, should be led to believe that the idea of self-determination for Kashmir was a creation of Jayaprakash Narayan and his ilk, let me try to put the record straight. When partition was agreed upon it was decided that what was known as British India would be divided according to Muslim majority and Hindu-majority areas without a referendum, and that in princely India the princes would have the option to accede to India or Pakistan. Thus there was no question of any referendum in Bihar or Bombay.

History of Partition

As to the princely states, the accession of the princes was to be final. So when Maharaja Hari Singh of Kashmir acceded to India that should have set the matter beyond doubt for all time, as indeed in strict law it actually did. But there was a snag: the accession had to be accepted. And it was precisely at that point that the idea of a referendum or self-determination in regard to Kashmir was injected into the course of events. After accepting the Instrument of Accession of October 27 1947, Lord Louis Mountbatten, wrote the same day to the Maharaja as follows: "In the special circumstances mentioned by Your Highness, my Government have decided to accept the accession of Kashmir state to the Dominion of India. Consistently with their policy that, in the case of any state where the issue of accession has been the subject of dispute, the question of accession should be decided in accordance with the wishes of the people of the state, it is my Government's wish that, as soon as law and order have been restored in Kashmir, and her soil cleared of the invader, the question of the state's accession should be settled by a reference to the people."

A few days later (November 2,1947) Mr Nehru underlined in a broadcast the assurance given by the Governor-General in these clear words: "We decided to accept this accession and send troops by air, but we made a condition that the accession would have to be considered by the people of Kashmir later when peace and order were established. We were anxious not to finalise anything in a moment of crisis, and without the fullest opportunity to the people of Kashmir to have their say. It was for them ultimately to decide."

"And here let me make clear that it has been our policy all along that where there is a dispute about the accession of a state to either dominion the decision must be made by the people of that state. It was in accordance with this policy that we added a proviso to the Instrument of Accession of Kashmir."

Later in the same broadcast the Prime Minister declared to all the world: "We have declared that the fate of Kashmir is ultimately to be decided by the people. That pledge we have given, and the Maharaja has supported it, not only to the people of Kashmir but to the world. We will not, and cannot, back out of it. We are prepared when peace and law and order have been established to have a referendum held under international auspices like the United Nations. We went it to be a fair and just reference to the people and we shall accept their verdict. I can imagine no fairer and juster offer."

In view of this crystal clear position it is amazing that such frantic efforts should be made to cloud the issue.

At this point it might help to clarify matters to consider another variation of the theme, though this was not the theme of the 27 MPs. Briefly it is this: there was a proviso to the Instrument of Accession, but that has already been given effect to and there is nothing further to be done about it. The proviso was carried out, it is said, when the Kashmir Constituent Assembly adopted in 1956 a constitution which declared that "the State of Jammu and Kashmir is and shall be an integral part of India." That was three years after Sheikh Abdullah's arrest, but that may not be considered very important. The really important point is that a decision of the Constituent. Assembly cannot be equated with a referendum, which the Prime Minister had solemnly pledged.

Statement of Sheikh Abdullah are bandied about to prove that he himself had accepted accession. But there never was any question about this. After the Maharaja's legal act of accession, the Sheikh and the National Conference endorsed and explicitly accepted accession, and on many subsequent occasions their acceptance was reiterated. All this is incontestable, the proviso remained and had to take effect. Neither the National Conference nor Sheikh Abdullah could take the place of the people of Kashmir, whose will had to be ascertained, and not the Sheikh's or that of the National Conference.

Still another argument is that since Pakistan joined SEATO and CENTO and USA supplied it with arms and other things happened the situation became so transformed that the offer of a referendum stood no longer. But it is forgotten that it was not to Pakistan that the offer or pledge was given but to the people of Kashmir. There is no justification for punishing the Kashmiris for Pakistan's actions.

In view of all this it appears to me that the right and constructive approach is not to deny Kashmir the right to self-determination, or to assert that the right has already been exercised, but to show rationally how impractical and imprudent it would be to exercise that right now.

The following considerations might be put forward: First, there is the hard fact of aggression by Pakistan, which it shows no intention of vacating; second, a referendum might have serious consequences for the minorities both in India and Pakistan; third, a referendum might lead to further disintegration of the State of Jammu and Kashmir; fourth, the effect of the foregoing would have serious consequences for India's defence. There may be other factors, but these four are weighty and reasonable and neither Sheikh Abdullah nor any other Kashmir leader would brush them aside because they are as much concerned with India's good as with that of Kashmir.

Search for Settlement

My humble plea is that we put aside all this heated controversy about the accession having been final and irrevivable and sit down with the Sheikh and discuss practical ways of achieving a settlement. If according to us the only way is for Sheikh Abdullah to accept the finality and irrevovability of accession, we might as well send him back to prison; he will never agree to that position. But to find a mutually acceptable solution it is not necessary for either side to give up its position. The important thing is for each to understand that merely by asserting one's own position and sticking to it the problem is not solved. No matter how aggressively we affirm that Kashmir's accession to India is final and irrevocable the world does not accept it, the "azad Kashmir" area remains under Pakistan, the cease-fire line remains, the two armies remain facing each other, the minorities in both India and Pakistan continue to live in fear, discontent in Kashmir simmers and might have to be put down by force. So what have we gained, or hope to gain in the future, by our insistent unilateral assertion? On the other hand if Sheikh Abdullah continues to press for the right of self-determination and circumstances do not permit it to be exercised what good does it do to him or anybody else?

So let each hold on to his position, but put it aside and get down to brass tacks to find a practical solution. Let it be recalled that there were three referendums in Alsace-Lorraine, and now who cares to whom it belongs?

I do not think anybody knows what the solution can be. Yet a few positive things might be stated about it. One, that there must be an honest desire on all sides to find a solution. Two, it should be remembered, as an English statesman said, that nothing is settled unless it is settled right. Of course it is not easy to know what is right in a complicated situation, but one test may be that it gives satisfaction to all concerned. Therefore the third point about the solution is that it must be such as to satisfy India, the people of Kashmir and Pakistan.

Sheikh's Stand

Sheikh Abdullah's insistent stress on Indo-Pak understanding as a part of any solution of the Kashmir question has irked Indian public opinion, and many have read into it his predilection for Pakistan. This however is a complete misreading. Sheikh Abdullah sees, as everyone else should, that there could be no settlement if Pakistan were not a party to it. The Kashmir question came into being on account of Pakistan, and India made it a party to the dispute at the UN. Apart from Kashmir, Sheikh Abdullah also sees that the future of both India and Pakistan depends upon whether they are friends or enemies.

This is a view that will not be seriously contested in this country, and it has the support of no less a person than the Prime Minister. In a courageous and statesmanlike speech in the Lok Sabha, in reply to the foreign affairs debate, Mr Nehru was reported to have said that "he would have hoped that India and Pakistan would come together closer, even constitutionally, but that would annoy the Pakistan authorities." So he would content himself to declare: "There is no other way for us except to live in peace." When it is recalled that the speech was made at a time of intense communal feeling its courage and wisdom become still more impressive.

I might remark here parenthetically- though this is not the place for it-that the Prime Minister's speech was equally remarkable for its responsive approach to the inquiry made by the Prime Minister of Ceylon. I should add however that it is not for China to make a "proper approach" to us as the Prime Minister said. How that both sides have been sounded, it is for the mediators, the six Colombo Conference powers, to make the proposal in a formal manner to both governments. That would amount to a mutually agreed amendment of the original Colombo proposals and enable India and China to meet at the conference table.

But to return to Indo- Pakistan relations and Kashmir. The reference by the Prime Minister to some kind of constitutional link between the two countries is particularly interesting in the present context. And it need not be assumed that Pakistan would always oppose such an idea. After all every country is concerned about its security and economic development. Can there be any doubt that a constitutional link between India and Pakistan would go a long way to guarantee their security as well as economic progress? Moreover the fact that Sheikh Abdullah is also thinking on similar lines introduces a fresh element of hope into the situation. So if rigid positions are kept out of the way there is every hope that a constructive approach will be agreed upon that might lead ultimately to a solution at once satisfying to India, Kashmir and Pakistan. Here is a task of statesmanship of the highest order.

Hindu Communalism

Before concluding I wish to take a look at our secularism in relation to Kashmir. Apart from other considerations Kashmir is deemed of great value to us because we wish to hold it up as an example of our secularism. I wonder if the spokesmen of secularism are aware of the irony of the present situation. The same Kashmir that is supposed to be an example of Indian secularism has occasioned a nasty upsurge of Hindu communalism. It is not easy to discern this process because it is happening under the cover of nationalism. India being a Hindu-majority country, it is not difficult, as has been remarked by many observes, for Hindu communalism to trot out in the garb of Indian nationalism. Therefore it is all the more urgent for those who believe in a truly secular and composite nationalism to be on their guard.

What is meant by Kashmir being an example of Indian secularism? It means I believe that the people of India have given such proof of their noncommunal outlook that the Muslims of Kashmir, even though they are in a majority there, have freely decided to live with India, which is a Hindu-Majority but secular country, rather than with Pakistan, which has a Muslim majority but is an Islamic state. But suppose we had to keep the Muslims of Kashmir within India by force. Would that also be an example of our secularism? The very question exposes its absurdity. And yet how wide-spread is the mentality today that in order to defend the secular basis of our nation we must keep Kashmir, if necessary by force, within the Indian Union.

I therefore wish most seriously to plead with the Prime Minister, the Congress president and other Congress leaders to look carefully at the cancerous process that is taking place within their party. As things are moving there will soon be little to choose at least in this matter between the Congress and the Jana Sangh. Shallow and timid Congressmen feel that the Jana Sangh is stealing their thunder. But by and large people's minds are sound, and they would rally round Pandit JawaharLal Nehru- as they have always known him- if he were to give a clear and bold lead. And so would all the faint-hearted Congressmen who are eager to ride to victory on the communal wave. If some such event does not happen, I am afraid the secular base of our nation will be vitally damaged.

7

Post-Nehru Kashmir Policy

Shastri's Letter to JP

7th June 1964

My dear Jayaprakashji

I have your letter of the 22nd May. I think your idea of visiting East Pakistan is a good one. Apart from giving your on opportunity of judging the actual situation of the Hindus and other minorities in East Pakistan, your visit will, I hope, have a beneficial effect on the relations between India and Pakistan. Anything that can contribute to a betterment of our relations is welcome. I have there will be no difficulty in the grant of a visa to you by the Pakistan High Commission.

I trust you are in good health

Your sincerely
Sd/-
Lal Bahadur

Shri Jayaprakash Narayan
Kadam Kuan,
Patna-3

Accord on Kashmir
JP: Situation Favourable

Madras, June 26 (PTI): Mr Jayaprakash Narayan, Sarvodya leader, said here today that the present situation was more favourable for a solution to the Kashmir problem than it had been for many years past.

At the same time he added it would not be very easy to find a solution because it must satisfy India, Pakistan and the people of Kshmir. "But I am sure if the problem is trackled with patience and preserverance this seems to be the best time for a solution to be found."

When his attention was drawn to the unhelpful attitude of the Pakistan Press and certain of its leaders towards a solution to the Kashmir problem, he said: "That is all politics and should not be exaggerated. However, I am afarid that the section of the Pakistan Press does not want a solution."

(Hindustan Times, 27 June 1964)

JP's Letter to Sayeed Ayyub

Sokhodeora.
June 7, 1964

Dear Ayyub Saheb,

I have been deeply moved by your letter of May 18. I agree with you that only a miracle can save the sub-continent. If present trends are at all portends, we may hope that the miracle might indeed be in the making. The exchange of compliments between president Ayyub Khan and Prime Minister Lal Bahadur Shastri is a promising beginning. In the meanwhile let those few individuals on both sides of the border who have humanity and courage do whatever possible to keep down the monster of hate and violence.

Regarding Shrimati Maitri Devi, I have myself been rather struck by her work, and I would be happy to take her along with me when I go to East Pakistan. I am not quite sure now (because of Pandit Ji's death) when I should go. It may not be possible before July.

With all good wishes,

Yours sincerely,
Sd/-
(Jayaprakash Narayan)

Mr.Abu Sayeed Ayyub,
5, Pearl Road, Calcutta- 17
(NMM&L, File No. 86 PP 146)

JP's Letter to Tyabji

June 10, 1964

My dear Tyabji Saheb;

I was very happy to read your letter of May 15. It is difficult to say after the great tragedy that has befallen the nation what will happen to the Kashmir problem. I shall surely persevere in my endeavor to persuade my countrymen to bring reason and humanity to the solution of this problem, but how the Government of India will handle it now is difficult to say. I have no doubt that the new Prime Minister's head and heart are in the right places. But he does not have the same authority as Pandit Ji, and his colleagues and party might prove to be too much for him. The recent exchange of compliments between him and president Ayub Khan is indeed a good augury for the future, and we shall do our best to help them both. You too must play your constructive role in this problem- in your own way.

I am glad you liked my article so much.

With kind regards,

Yours sincerely,

Sd/-

(Jayaprakash Narayan)

Mr. Badr-Ud-Din Tyabji,
Vice- Chancellor,
Aligarh, JP.

(NMM&L File No. 86, PP 142-43)

Constitutional Integration without Emotional Integration Meaningless: JP

It is saddening beyond words to find the same old policy of confusion and ambivalence being again pursued in the case of Kashmir. Deeds do not seem to correspond with words. Even the words of different spokesmen appear contradictory. On the one hand, it is stated that there would be no change in the present status of Kashmir and on the other, that eventually it would be brought in line with the other states of the Union. Again, on the one hand, it is emphatically reiterated that we are keenly desirous of friendship with Pakistan, and on the other, we deliberately launch upon a policy that cannot but worsen the already strained relationship. I think it is time that the Government made up its mind. The present policy of indecision and lack of direction and purpose is doing this country incalculable harm.

The question we must squarely face is whether constitutional integration of Kashmir with India is more important in the national interest than friendship with Pakistan and justice to the people of the Valley of Srinagar. Legal technicalities will not provide the answer. What is needed is a mature and realistic reckoning. As far as I can see, the disadvantages of the present policy far outweigh the advantages.

Let me take up first the issue of justice to the people of the Valley. There has been no credible proof yet that they have freely accepted the legal fact of accession. Constitutional integration has little meaning in the absence of emotional integration. In this age and time, it is impossible to hold down by force any sizeable population permanently. If we continue to do it, we cannot look the world straight in the face and talk of democracy and justice and peace. Nor, on account of the historical circumstances, can we take shelter behind the internationally recognised limitations of the right to self-determination. Perhaps the most harmful consequence of the policy of forcible integration would be the death-knell of Indian secularism and enthronement of aggressive Hindu communalism. That communalism is bound in the end to turn upon the Hindu community itself and destroy it.

As for friendship with Pakistan, let us calculatedly determine how dearly we need that friendship. No country can afford to buy friendship at any cost. So let there be a reckoning of gains and losses. First of all, let us be mature enough to understand that if we persist in our present Kashmir policy, there can be no friendship with Pakistan. The leaders of that country have not left us in any doubt on that score. If we disbelieve them, we shall have only ourselves to blame.

Here is the pricing of Indo-Pak friendship as it appears to me. First, if Pakistan turns hostile, as I fear it would if we persist in the policy of full constitutional integration, the defence of the country would become a hundred-fold more difficult. Certain parts of it, such as Assam, NEFA and Nagaland would be next to impossible to defend. Indo-Pak amity on the other hand would automatically result in large scale dis-engagement, thus strengthening considerably our defence capability. Our communications too would be automatically strengthened ten-fold. As far the defence of Ladakh, I am sure any amicable settlement of the Kashmir issue would make a provision for it.

Second, both history and geography destined the subcontinent of India to play a key role in South and South-East Asia. But as long as India and Pakistan remain at loggerheads, India's, as also Pakistan's capacity to manoeuver in this area-remains drastically restricted. No initiative taken by India can have the same value and attraction for the countries of this region unless India and Pakistan moved jointly. At present, they cancel out each other, creating a power vacuum that no one but China can fill effectively.

Third, what is true of the South-East Asia region is very largely true of the world. India's posture on the world stage is very considerably determined by her obsession with Kashmir and her consequent relations with Pakistan. In the Afro-Asia world, this quarrel between the two big Asian countries has cost both heavily in prestige and influence and diplomatic effectiveness.

Fourth, there is the vast economic harm the quarrel is causing both countries. It is beyond doubt that the development of each would have been much faster had there been cooperation between them in the economic field.

The last and in some way the most disastrous consequence of the quarrel is its human and moral cost and the alienation of peoples that it threatens to bring about. If the quarrel continues, Muslims in India and Hindus in Pakistan would continue to live under the shadow of suspicion and suffer severe spiritual unrest. The danger of communal rioting would be ever present. These conditions would be sure to cause mass human degradation on both sides. The political division of the sub-continent cannot hide the fact that the peoples of India and Pakistan are really one people. This is not the first time that India has been divided politically. But there had always been a feeling of oneness and identity among the people divided between kingdoms and republics. Today, the Bengalis of the West and East are one people, irrespective of region; so are the Punjabis. In like manner, the Bengalis and Punjabis and Sindhis and Pathans and Jats and Rajputs and others of both countries make up one single Indian people, who are distinct from all other peoples of the world. States are passing shows, but the people are eternal. Therefore, I would consider this alienation of the people of India and Pakistan from one another to be the most disastrous consequence of the present quarrel.

This briefly is the balance-sheet as I see it. Let logic and reason rather than childish emotion guide the debate and the ultimate decision.

I am aware that settlement of the Kashmir issue would not in itself mean establishment of firm Indo-Pak friendship, but it would certainly remove the greatest obstacle on the way and create the necessary psychological conditions. I am also aware that friendship is not one-sided. But I am convinced that friendship is as precious for Pakistan as for India and they will be found to be as keen for it as we persuade ourselves to be.

A last word to the leaders of the government. At this critical moment in the country's life, it is their duty to lead and not to be led. The crippling fear of public opinion and party rank and file is only a reflection of the leadership's own weakness and division. It is for the leaders to shape public opinion and educate the back-benchers. If they fail in this, they will do disservice to the country in this hour of decision.

(Press statement released from Calcutta on 18 December 1964)

(NMM&L. File No. 86, PP 89-92)

8

On Indo–Pak Relations

Indo-Pak Conciliation Group

(*Letter from British Labour Party Leader)*

26, Bon Accord Road,
Swanage, Dorset
28.2.1964

Dear Jayaprakash,

A few weeks ago I was put in touch with a Pakistani at present working with the United Nations at Geneva, who has a strong conviction that something needs to be done to get Indo-Pakistan relations onto a quite new basic. He sent me a copy of the first outline he has prepared of the book he wants to write, and asked for my comment.

His general approach seems to me to be so right-minded that I have not attempted to criticise this draft in detail. As a result of further correspondence he now encourages me to send you this draft, so I am doing this, and at the same time I enclose the second letter he wrote me, as I think this may help you to get an impression of the man. I have not met him.

I have discouraged him from trying out his ideas in the Observer or any other paper at present. I wish you would find time to write to him and advise him how to proceed. From what he says in other letters, I gather that he has friends among Pakistani officials and others, so if before long he returns to Pakistan, he might help to bring into being the kind of group you had hoped to work with.

I wonder how you feel about the present Indo-Pakistan situation. To me it looks worse than ever. The discussions in

New York can hardly have helped at all. Is it not possible to forget the past and try to begin again without harping on past failure of one side or the other? I wish Sheikh Abdullah could be released. I hope that the release of Abdul Ghaffar Khan by Pakistan might hasten the release of Abdullah.

My recollection is that you told me you had hopes of good things if Shastri became the successor of JN. I gather that now he is in effect the nominated successor; but for the time being I presume that Nehru is still the effective Prime Minister.

With warm regards,

Yours sincerely

Sd/-

(Horace Alexander)

(A leader of the British Labour Party)

(NMM&L. File No. 86, P 178)

JP's Letter to Pakistan High Commission

Varanasi

July 31, 1964

Dear Arshad Hussain Saheb,

Many thanks for your letter. I was happy that the fruits were found enjoyable.

As you will see from the enclosed letter, which I request be sent on to the President, we have finally decided to visit Pakistan in the first part of September. We are planning to leave Delhi on September 1 or 2 for Karachi and to spend a week to ten days in West Pakistan, and thereafter to visit East Pakistan. (The delegation to East might be differently constituted).

In West Pakistan, we would want to visit, besides Karachi, Rawalpindi, Lahore and Peshawar and meet leading personalities in different walks of life. But our main objective would be to have as much time as possible with the President, Mr Bhutto and other Ministers. It would also be our endeavors to persuade like-minded personalities to form a group similar to ours so that our combined efforts might help in bringing about understanding between our two countries.

The members, besides myself, of the delegation to the West Pakistan would be: Shri J.J. Singh, secretary of the Group, Shri B. Shiva Rao, Shri S. Mulgaokar.

I shall be thankful for an early reply so that we might finalise the arrangements for the visit.

With kind regards,

Yours sincerely,
Sd/-
(Jayaprakash Narayan)

Mr. Arshad Hussain Saheb
Pakistan High
Commissioner in India,
Pakistan High Commission,
New Delhi

(NMM&L File No. 86, PP 125)

JP, Ayub Hold Frank Talks on Indo-Pak Ties

From Anand Swarup
Hindustan Times Correspondent

Rawalpindi, Sept 6—Great cordiality and warmth marked the start of talks here today between President Ayub and the five-member Indian goodwill delegation headed by Mr Jayaprakash Narayan.

The delegation includes Mr S. Mulgaokar, Mr B. Shiva Rao, Mr J.J. Singh and Mr Radhakrishan, secretary of the Sarvaseva Sangh.

The president honoured his guests by arranging an unscheduled luncheon meeting in the President's House so that he could carry on discussions with them informally.

The talks were held in a free, frank and informal fashion and covered a wide range, embracing not only Kashmir and other outstanding Indo-Pakistan problems, also but the larger and more fundamental question of future relations between the two countries and collaboration between them in socio-economic and cultural spheres.

Two Meetings

President Ayub Khan and the delegation leader, Mr Jayaprakash Narayan, had two meetings today lasting more than two hours.

They met for 25 minutes at the beginning, while the Pakistan Law Minister, Mr Khurshid Ahmad, discussed general scope of improving relations between India and Pakistan with other members of the mission, according to informed sources here.

Later President Ayub and Mr Jayaprakash Narayan joined them.

During the morning session, Pakistani Foreign Secretary Aziz Ahmad was also present.

Mr Narayan and four other members of the mission are due to arrive in Karachi tomorrow evening. They will hold talks with the Foreign Minister, Mr Z.A. Bhutto, in Karachi on Tuesday.

Mr Narayan told newsmen on arrival here yesterday that Pakistan President Ayub Khan has been invited by Prime Minister Shastri to visit India at his earliest convenience.

Mr Narayan and his colleagues were given a warm welcome on their arrival at Chaklala airport in the evening for talks today with Marshal Ayub.

Mr Narayan said that his delegation would discuss with Marshal Ayub not only Kashmir and other disputes between India and Pakistan but also the positive question of future relationship between the two countries and constructive cooperation between them.

Private Citizens

The delegation was received on behalf of Marshal Ayub by Raja Hasan Akhtar, president of the West Pakistan Muslim League, and Mr Kaiser Rashid, Deputy Chief of Protocol. The delegates then posed for pictures. They are staying in the State Guest House here as Marshal Ayub's personal guests.

Mr Narayan said: "We are all private citizens and hold no official position. We represent no one but ourselves in the India-Pakistan Conciliation Group. I am, however, confident that we do represent the general desire of the people of India to see an end to the disputes and differences of the past 17 years. I am sure this desire is reciprocated by the people of Pakistan."

He added: "We are aware that the task is going to be difficult and complicated one. We would consider our visit worthwhile if it takes us one step forward towards the solution of difficult and complicated problems."

He hoped the group would have the goodwill of Pakistani Press and public as also their co-operation in making its mission" as much of a success as a non-official mission can be."

No Commitment

Asked if his mission had the blessings of Mr Shastri and his government, Mr Narayan said: Yes. We have the sympathy and cooperation of the Indian government, though it is in no way committed to our mission, just as we do not expect anyone here to be committed to our mission.

"As to the possibility of an early Shastri-Ayub meeting, Mr Narayan said: "I am bringing with me the request from Mr Shastri that President Ayub should respond to India's invitation to visit that country at his earliest convenience."

Mr Narayan declined to be drawn into any discussion of the Kashmir problem at this stage but in a reply to questions from Pakistani newsmen, he said: "We (he and his group) are doing in India whatever is possible to solve the Kashmir problem. We also want our position to be understood in Pakistan."

Asked whether he was hopeful about the success of his mission, Mr Narayan said: "Any one who believes in conciliation and works for it is away hopeful. No one can start with a lack of hope".

Mr Narayan thanked the people and Government of Pakistan for their welcome at Lahore and Rawalpindi.

PTI adds: Pakistan newspapers have given prominence to Mr Jaya Prakash Narayan's Press statement in Rawalpindi yesterday that his mission was aimed at creating a congenial atmosphere for "positive cooperation" between India and Pakistan.

(Hindustan Times, 7 September 1964)

JP: Real Possibility of Indo-Pak Amity

Work on 'New Ideas' to be Continued on Return

Rawalpindi, Sep. 7—After his two meetings with President Ayub, Mr Jayaprakash Narayan said here today that "a real possibility exists for evolving a workable approach to the solution of the outstanding disputes" between India and Pakistan, including the Kashmir dispute.

The Sarvodaya leader, who is leading a five-member unofficial goodwill mission, in a written statement to newsmen said he found "an encouraging response" from President Ayub to the cause of advancing friendship between the two countries.

He said many useful ideas had been thrown up during his talks with President Ayub which he described as "constructive and unusually frank."

Mr Narayan added significantly: I shall work on those ideas when I go back to India and I hope some of them will bear early fruit."

Text of Statement

Following is the text of Mr Narayan's statement:

"I am very happy to meet President Ayub after three years and to find him as genial and warm as before. I was also very happy to see that he was in excellent health."

"There have been in recent months many indications both in India and Pakistan of a desire for a new relationship of co-operation and good neighbourliness. We came here to explore the ways in which this desire could be consolidated and the cause of friendship advanced.

"We have found an encouraging and statesmanlike response from President Ayub and we believe that a real possibility exists for evolving a workable approach to the solution of the outstanding disputes between two countries, including the one relating to Kashmir.

"The task will not be an easy one and the ground for a new relationship of trust and confidence will have to be prepared with care and patience. But the road ahead no longer seems dark and uncertain as it has seemed during many periods in the last 17 years. And with God's grace and the help of men of goodwill in both countries the end of the road will not be far off.

"To say more at this point will not help. Many useful ideas have been thrown up during the talks I had with the President which were constructive and unusually frank. I shall work on those ideas when I go back to India and I hope some of them will bear early fruit."

The members of the delegation have formed the definite impression that the President's attitude towards the Indo-Pakistan problems is not rigid.

When a correspondent asked him to elaborate the "useful ideas" that had emerged from his talks with President Ayub and whether this meant the possibility of an early summit meeting between President Ayub and Prime Minister Shastri and cessation of day-to-day border incidents along the ceasefire line in Kashmir, Mr Narayan remarked: "Gentlemen, I do not want to be drawn into a discussion on this point. I should leave it at that."

Mr Narayan told Pakistan corespondents that in India some of the recent statements by Mr Bhutto had caused "a lot of anxiety."

He added that he was not saying this in the sense of any criticism of the Foreign Minister.

Mr Narayan told the correspondents that he had no intention of joining the Congress.

Basic Democracies

He said this when Pakistani correspondents asked him to confirm reports in certain sections of the Press in India and Pakistan about his joining the Congress and returning to active politics.

Mr Narayan said: "I have no plan to join the Congress, I have no intention of joining any party to fight elections or to participate in the struggle for power."

He added: "I may be able to do more from outside."

When asked whether he had studied the village development programme in Pakistan and whether he would visit Pakistan again specifically for this purpose, Mr Narayan said: "I am very much interested in this programme and in seeing the working of the basic democracies. But this must wait for another visit."

Mr Narayan said: "if we succeed in organising a conciliation group here we will invite it to Delhi."

He said he hoped to visit East Pakistan in October.

This morning Mr S. Mulgaokar, Mr B. Shiva Rao, Mr J.J. Singh and Mr. Radhakrishnan called on Home Minister Habibullah Khan who is convalescing in a hospital here. Later they visited Islamabad, the new developing capital of Pakistan.

Last night Raja Hasan Akhtar, president of the West Pakistan Muslim League, gave a dinner in honour of the delegation. Among the guests was Mr Ghulam Abbas, former president of "Azad" Kashmir government who exchanged views with the delegation on the Kashmir problem.

(*Hindustan Times,* 8 September 1964)

JP Pleads for Negotiated Settlement on Kashmir

New Delhi, Sep. 15—Mr. J.P. Narayan told a gathering here today that he had never advocated a plebiscite in Kashmir in the present circumstances.

He also denied that he had at any time suggested that the Kashmir valley should be handed over to Pakistan.

Such insinuations had been made by interested parties who called him a traitor. He had told President Ayub Khan in clear terms that there could be no plebiscite and that India cannot give up the valley.

He said he had informed the Pakistan President that even if he (JP) were the Prime Minister of India, such a transfer could not take place because the Government would be thrown out by the people.

When a restive, demonstrative audience heard these views of Mr Narayan, they gave up their attempts to heckle him and preferred to listen to what he had to say. Mr Narayan was addressing a meeting on Indo-Pak relations in Lajpat Bhawan.

The hecklers created enough disturbance at one stage to make a section of the audience swarm round the dais. Security men moved in to restore order.

Mr Narayan began by saying that during the past few months misconceptions had been created about him by piecing together his utterances taken out of context to call him a traitor.

The trouble-makers took their cue from this and began chanting: "Desh ke gaddar ko, nahin sunenge, nahin sunenge."

Mr Narayan called out to them and said those who did not want to hear him could go. Slogans would not solve the Indo-Pakistan dispute.

Mere Slogan

Mr Narayan indicated that just as plebiscite was a slogan in Pakistan, "final and irrevocable accession" had become a mere slogan here.

He posed the question why Sheikh Abdullah was allowed to go to Pakistan if the Government was so sanguine about the finality of the accession issue. Why was the Government striving for an "honourable and equitable settlement", he asked.

The seeds of the current problem, he maintained, had been sown in the proviso added to the instrument of Accession. It gave the assurance that when the raiders were driven out, the issue of accession would be referred to the people.

That was the basic mistake, he said. A heckler shouted: "Are we to stand by the blunders our leaders have made in the past."

Mr Narayan warned that there may be a civil war or major unrest in the country if the dispute over Kashmir was not solved. What had been done so far were attempts to "stabilize the quarrel." There was the crying need for a new solution other than plebiscite or giving away the Kashmir valley to Pakistan.

"What solution have you found? If you have no solution, why have you come to address the meeting," another heckler shouted.

Mr Narayan maintained that he had not come back with a solution from Pakistan but there were "rays of hope" for a negotiated political settlement.

(Hindustan Times, 16 September 1964)

'JP Visit has not Changed Pak Stand'

Karachi, Sep. 18 (PTI)—The Indian Sarvodya leader, Mr Jayaprakash Narayan, was given no indication whatsoever of "any shift" in Pakistan's stand on Kashmir while he was on a goodwill visit to this country.

This was stated today by the Associated Press of Pakistan in a despatch quoting official sources.

The agency said: "Mr Narayan, since his return to New Delhi, has been trying to create the impression that while in Pakistan he had partially succeeded in talking Pakistani leaders out of the demand for a plebiscite."

It added: "Pakistan, it is pointed out, has emphasized over and over again that the Kashmir impasse could be resolved only through the implementation of the UNCIP resolutions which stipulate that the problem of Jammu and Kashmir be settled through the exercise of the right of self-determination by the people of the state to decide whether they would join Pakistan or India."

(Statesman, 19 September 1964)

JP's Letter to JJ Singh

Rajya Bhavan, Kohima,
September 29, 1964

Dear JJ,

I thank you for your letter of September 23. Only a few days ago I wrote to you and Malti. You should have received it by now.

Chaudhari Khaliquazzaman's letter has disappointed me but not overmuch. I shall write to him in a day or two.

I should like to know if Mr. Qasuri had any thing of interest to say.

Bakshi's arrest certainly came with a surprise to me. I am afraid, Government of India will have to continue to take irrational and immoral action in Kashmir until her policy comes to be based on reality and justice.

The peace talks with the underground have unfortunately been dead-locked these last six days. But hope has arisen today of the dead lock being broken, in which case the talks might be resumed tomorrow.

Prabha arrived here on the 25th. She joins me in sending you both all our affectionate regards,

Yours Sincerely
Sd/-
(Jayaprakash Narayan)

(NMM&L.File No. 86 PP 113)

I B Minister Seeks Clarification of JP's Statement

New Delhi
25th November, 1964.

Dear Shri Jayaparkash,

The press has given publicity to a statement supposed to have been made by you in East Pakistan in September last, to the following effect:-

"Mr. J.P. Narayan warned India that there may be a Civil war or major unrest in the country, if the Kashmir dispute is not solved. He asked how it could be possible for President Ayub to visit India when Indian leaders continue to repeat their slogan of the so-called finality of accession of Kashmir".

This statement attributed to you has caused misapprehensions in many quarters and I shall be personally grateful if you could kindly let me know whether the alleged statement as reproduced above, was madė by you at all; if not, the necessary corrective statement may be issued by you or we may have a clarificatory handout issued through our Press Information Bureau.

I shall be grateful for favour of a very early reply.

With regards,

Shri Jai Prakash Narayan Ji, Sd/-
Kadam Kuan, (C.R. Pattabhi Raman)
Patna.

(NMM&L File No. 86, PP 100)

JP's Clarification

Camp: Peace Centre,
Kohima
December 11,1964

Dear Friend,

I am most thankful to you for your letter of November 25 which reached here only today.

Of all the misrepresentations of which I am a frequent victim the statement as quoted in your letter is a particularly daring one. As you know, I differ sharply with Government's policy in regard to Kashmir; but unreservedly repudiate the statement alluded to me. I shall be thankful for clarification by the P.I. Bureau.

With warm regards,

Yours sincerely,

Shri C.R. Pattabhi Raman, Sd/-
Deputy Minister, (Jayaprakash Narayan)
Information and Broadcasting,
New Delhi, India.

(NMM&L File No. 86, PP 99)

Khushwant Singh's Letter to JP

Baikunth
1-A, Janpath,
New Delhi - 11.
9th January, 1965

Dear Jayaprakashji,

I received your note with the enclosures- clumsily opened and re-sealed by the censors as no doubt this letter will be.

I am seeing J.J. today and will get the group together for briefing. Unfortunately members of Parliament are not in town.

I am not quite clear about the way of handling the material you or Michael Scott give me. Unless J.J. has clear notions on the subject I will await guidance from you.

I agree with every word you have said about Kashmir. My only regret is that I am unable to do something concrete in forwarding the great work you are doing for your country. Future generations of Indians will bless you.

Yes, I will be in Delhi till the Ist of March and will look forward to another meeting.

Yours
Sd/-
(Khushwant Singh)

Mr. Jayaprakash Narayan
Kadam-Kuan, Patna-3.

(NMM&L. File No. 86, PP 88)

JJ Singh's Letter to JP

101, Friends Colony,
New Delhi - 14.
January 10, 1965

Dear J.P.,

Thank you for your letter of January 4.

I can quite see that you must have felt very low after your talk with Shastri ji.

The Kashmir situation continues to be confusing. On the one hand, the Kashmir government with the full approval of the Central government, arrests Bakshi Sahib and alleges that he is responsible for all kinds of crimes, yet on the other hand, the

Prime Minister, the Vice President and other ministers call upon him. Of course, the latter could be on purely humanitarian grounds. All the same, it creates a question mark.

I went to see Bakshi yesterday and he told me that he thought that one of the main reasons for arresting him was because he had met you and as a result had seen Sheikh Sahib twice. That seems rather exaggerated to me.

Shri Mulgaokar told me that Michael Scott is here but I have not heard from him. Khushwant Singh is supposed to bring the documents that were left with him by Michael.

We had lunch with Gaganvihari. He was to have a preliminary meeting on the 7th of this month - we returned to Delhi on the 5th - with some of the people of India-Pakistan conciliation group. Noorani was also at the lunch and he is still very enthusiastic that a group in Bombay should be started and he has quite a few ideas about bringing out certain pamphlets - one of them entitled "JP on Kashmir." He has all kinds of cuttings and he feels they should be put together for people to see what exactly you have said on this subject on different occasions.

I hope I will hear from Gaganvihari by tomorrow or the day after about the meeting on the 7th. If not, I will write to him to find out what transpired at the meeting.

Before going to Bombay, I wanted to get together with Mr Rameshwar Thakur but he was out of town. We have fixed up to meet at Shri's office on Wednesday, January 13th.

I have noted from your programme that you will be in Delhi on January 22. Are you going to be here only for a day? I am sure you will let us know the date and the time of your arrival here.

With affectionate regards from Malti and myself to Prabha ji and you,

Yours as ever,

Mr Jayaprakash Narayan — Sd/-
Kadam Kuan — (J.J. Singh)
Patna -3, Bihar.

(NMM&L. File No. 86, PP 101-102)

JP on Question of Minorities and Kashmir

While everyone in India and elsewhere would condemn the ghastly treatment of the minority communities in East Pakistan it would be self-defeating to slur over the events in West Bengal. Comparisons between the degree of suffering inflicted in both countries upon innocent human beings, or the attempt to belittle or explain away what happened in our own country as being a mere reaction to the events across the border, are dangerous tricks of the mind which cannot but have disastrous consequences.

It is therefore heartening to learn from the Indian Home Minister that all political parties in West Bengal are unanimous in their determination to see that no harm in done to a single member of the minority community.

I express my happiness at the firm declaration of Shri Gulzarilal Nanda that the question of exchange of population could never even be contemplated as a solution of Indo-Pakistan communal problem.

Indo-Pak Amity

Notwithstanding all good resolutions of parties and citizens and pronouncements of high official policy, the human mind being what it is bound in moments of stress to plunge into irrational courses. It is my conviction that neither in Pakistan nor in India are the minorities safe, nor is peace and tranquility and healthy inner and outward growth assured to the peoples of both the countries unless their leaders agree to sit around a table with the honest and firm determination to settle all outstanding disputes, including the dispute over Kashmir.

Turning to Kashmir, I disagree with those who speak and act as if the Kashmir issue has been settled once and for all and that the people of Kashmir have put their seal of consent upon that settlement. The very "hellfire," to use the expression of Shri Nanda, through which the minority community has recently passed in East Pakistan bears tragic testimony to the fact that the issue is far from settled. If we do relate these facts we are behaving like ostriches. He said the problem was not legal, nor was it so much a question of facts and of apportioning praise or blame. It was a human and political problem and had to be approached in that light. What was needed was fearless application of those high political and human principles to which this country has been devoted from the beginning.

Referring to the present situation in Jammu and Kashmir, I commend the remarkable communal harmony which obtained in the recent anxious days in the state. I praise the wise and courageous manner in which Shri Lal Bahadur Shastri handled the situation. But I regret the lack of similar policy in dealing with the political issues which the situation in the state has thrown up. It is widely felt that the Kashmir Government does not enjoy the confidence and support of the people of the state. Delay in correcting the situation is fraught with great risks.

(JP's speech at the annual conference of the West Bengal Gandhi Samarak Nidhi on 31 January, 1965).

9

Debate on JP's Views on Kashmir

Puri-Noorani Discussion on JP

I published my comments on JP's New Initiative on Kashmir, (as published in the *Hindustan Times)*, in the socialist weekly *Janata*. My first contention was that he need not have posed his views as "lacking in patriotism". Secondly while endorsing his critique of the Kashmir policy of the Government of India, I also suggested that on account of his reputation as a friend of Pakistan and people of Kashmir, it is also his responsibility to give healthy advice to both of them; so that a person of his eminence could play a more effective role.

My article became a subject of debate between AG Noorani and me in the columns of the *Janata*. Later, after the Indo-Pak war of 1965, for which JP and Noorani held Pakistan to be responsible and hence they changed their views on the solution to the Kashmir problem. Obviously none of them had anticipated it. But JP gave precisely the same advice to Pakistan and Kashmiri leader Sheikh Abdullah that I had suggested.

I had reproduced our debate in a cyclostyled pamphlet, for private circulation only and had sent a copy to Noorani. But on his request I withheld its circulation. For it could possibly have caused an embarrassment to him. But as by now he is a respected commentator on political affairs, and as some of the articles on our debate are available in collection of writings of and on JP, I do not think publication of our debate can do any harm to his well established reputation.

It may also throw some light on how sharply the opinion on a subject like Kashmir was then divided. For while Noorani found my views no better than those of Hindu chauvinists, many a nationalist accused me of being a champion of Pakistan's case.

Incidentally I was shocked when Noorani was arrested during 1965 Indo-Pak war. I launched an active campaign with the Government of India and with the Maharashtra government and through public protests for his release. For I firmly believed then as now that his patriotism is beyond doubt. On the day of his release, I greeted him at his Mumbai residence. (Ed.)

The Challenge of Jayaprakash Narayan

Balraj Puri

Shri Jayaprakash Narayan's current political positions and an almost crusading campaign for them have given a visible shaking to the nation. He has been hit back no less violently. But the challenge he poses is rarely met in all its dimensions and at its appropriate level.

When the Sarvodaya leader insists on his right of expression, he is on invincible grounds. No sensible Indian can fail to agree with Shri Morarji Desai that a challenge to this right would cut at the very roots of democracy. Those who indulged in hooliganism at JP's meeting thus not only threatened Indian democracy but also exposed their weakness in meeting his challenge at the level of arguments.

Tolerance apart, as a mature nation we should be able to debate delicate nuances of all the issues confronting the nation internally or externally. To always accept or reject in toto political or diplomatic suggestions of a leader is not the quality of a discerning nation.

Meaningful Debate

Is J.P. wrong in his ideological postulates, political assessment or practical prescriptions? Is he wrong all along the line? But can he be wrong on all the points and in the same degree? Should not we try to locate the precise points on and the extent to which he does go wrong? Not just to be fair to an outstanding Indian. In the interest of the health of the nation, the near hysterical reactions need to be channelised into a meaningful debate, however fierce.

What are the theoretical objectives of JP? What position a nation should aspire? Morally perfect, militarily invulnerable, materially prosperous, culturally rich, international prestige? More pertinently, what is the order of priorities? JP's vision of

India does clash with that of many of his country-men. He seems to reject self-interest as the guiding principle of national policies. If his country is in the wrong, he may not hesitate to say so. While calling it a lie that the people of Kashmir had already decided to integrate themselves with India, he admits, "I may be lacking in patriotism or other virtues." If truth and patriotism are in conflict, his choice is clear.

JP's Troubles

Exclusive pursuit of self-interest is certainly the cause of strife between nations as also individuals. Nevertheless there is no nation - and only a few individuals - which has given up this pursuit altogether. If the choice is posed - as JP does in the statement quoted above - Indian nation would not choose in a very different way than any other nation in the world. By hinting at a dichotomy between truth and patriotism, JP does compromise his competence to lead the country; though not his position as her conscience keeper.

However, he does not press the point further. His Aksai Chin formula is, for instance, not based on moral considerations. Latterly he developed the thesis that India could not fight at once on three fronts - poverty, China and Pakistan. He wanted the people of the country to decide what they wanted first. Again, his own choice is clear. Poverty is enemy number one. And to wage an effective war against it, let us settle on the other two fronts.

If it boils down to a choice between patriotism and material well being, to many Indians choice would not appear to be as easy and virtuous as to JP.

Perhaps a part of JP's troubles is due to his unreal posers. By merely speaking the truth, according to his lights on Kashmir, why should he feel that he lacks in patriotism? The dichotomy between self-interest and moral obligations is really not so inevitable. In fact, every nation in the world is obliged to maintain a moral pose; sometimes taking recourse to rationalisations and ideologies. India's glorious debut in the comity of nations and her rise, for a while, to an eminent role, second only to the two leaders of the power blocs, was in no mean measure due to the moral halo she had acquired. Her later plight could also be attributed, at least partially, to her failure to live up to the professions of a moral leader of the world; though diplomatic and military reverses also contributed to it. Now diplomatic and military manouvres alone cannot help in salvaging India's position unless her moral image also revives its glow.

A moral case at the cost of self-interest and a selfish course, without a moral cover, real or illusory, are seldom accepted by a nation. One suspects that JP is asking the country to do it. To expect the people to support his Kashmir policy merely on moral grounds, is to expect too high an idealism on their part. But to expect them to revise their attitude to China and Pakistan merely to be able to fight poverty is to betrary too poor an opinion of the Indian people.

Not of JP's Creation

Solution of Kashmir problem should also serve the national interest. An a settlement with China should also be defensible on non-material considerations. While popular reaction of a proposal must depend upon its presentation, its essence is more important. Essentially JP purports to point a non-chauvinistic and realistic way out from the impasse in the creation of which he had no hand. We cannot afford the matters to remain as they are either in Kashmir or in Nagaland. We cannot remain content with our present international position, further threatened by growing Sino-Pak alliance.

The nature of our relations with other countries and the degree of tension with our adversaries need not be determined by reflex reactions. Let us resume the initiative in shaping those relations; launching friendship offensive where necessary and lowering or raising the key of other offensive according to our convenience.

A school of thought in India does consider tension with Pakistan a guarantee for keeping anti-imperialist character of the country, while amity with Pakistan is thought to serve American international strategy. Those who are not solely guided by this objective would not share this attitude to Pakistan. However, if the recent Russian overtures are any guide, it would seem that they are no less interested than Americans in weaning Pakistan away from China. The only way of weakening Sino-Pak alliance is improving Indo-Pak relations.

It is unnecessary to resist pressures of world powers. For tension with Pakistan scarcely serves any Indian interest. It may be necessary for Pakistan to use the tension as a cementing force between its two parts and justify her alliance with China. But why should we be keen to oblige her?

Kashmir and Nagaland

Friendship and appeasement are not synonymous. Nor is friendship exactly proportional to the degree of concessions. Nevertheless a price has to be paid. Pakistan has certainly inflated her price following India's troubles with China and exposure of her internal weakness in Kashmir.

In the interest of a settlement with Pakistan on reasonable terms, a certain relaxation on the northern front may be necessary. Whatever be our long term objectives about China, we are hardly in a position at the moment to launch an offensive to drive her out from our area under her occupation. Meanwhile, we should seek to adjust the current tempo of tension, according to exigencies of the international situation.

The above outline of foreign policy objectives and strategy do not seriously contradict JP's position. In any case theoretical considerations can be discussed more rationally than practical proposals. The latter may in fact be left to the official negotiators who could, of course, be helped. In case of Nagaland, JP failed even to get the broad approach endorsed by the parties while his offer to China is too concrete.

While JP has simultaneously taken up a number of unpopular causes, their logical connection is not explicit. Are his policies towards Pakistan and China interrelated, apart from common theoretical considerations of good neighborliness, say, in the sense discussed above?

JP does stress a close connection between communal situation and his Pakistan Policy, Indo-Pak amity would certainly reduce communal tension. But it is not only gross over simplification but also dangerous to treat, as JP implies in his statements, attitude to Pakistan synonymous with attitude towards Muslims. He apprehends civil war and killing of Muslims if Kashmir issue is not solved.

Already much damage has been done to the cause of secularism by making anti-Pakistanism a test for the secularity and loyalty of the Indian Muslims. To make pro-Pakistanism a test for the secularity of Hindus would be no less disastrous. There are many secular Indians, Hindus as well as Muslims, who do not like Pakistan for her theocracy or militarism, for right or wrong reasons. Whatever be the communal overtones of Indo-Pak relations, friendship with Pakistan must be defensible on grounds other than the fate of Indian Muslims. And every Indian Muslim must be perfectly safe whatever be our relations with Pakistan.

Fear of Civil War

Many Indian leaders have expressed fears that civil war or communal conflagration would break out if Kashmir's position as a part of India is disturbed. JP reverses the logic and apprehends civil war if the status quo continues in Kashmir. Indian secularism did draw strength from Kashmir at a very critical period. Kashmir can equally be a liability for the cause of secularism. But to stress a direct causal relations positive or negative, between Kashmir's political status and Indian secularism is not only logically deficient but also a disservice to the cause of secularism.

Perhaps it is JP's pose on Kashmir that strains the susceptibilities of the nation most. For all these years the country had been led to believe that Kashmir had become irrevocable part of India. The emphatic assertions of the leaders remained unchallenged even in Kashmir (whatever be the devises to silence the dissent) and even by JP. As long as the people suffered under a corrupt and tyrant regime in Kashmir, JP refused to visit them and lend a helping hand to their resistance. When, during the last winter, people of Kashmir, particularly the Muslims, were stirred to the core of their heart over the loss of the holy relic and had revolted against the local administration, JP hardly expressed a word of sympathy for them or support for their demands. Only when the movement acquired a distinct secessionist character that the weight of JP's personality seems to have been added to it. This indeed may not be deliberate. Nor past mistakes can be used to condemn current policies. But the past in this case does help in partially explaining the popular reaction to JP's views on Kashmir.

These views, in essence, require India to honour her commitments - by which she refuses to be bound now. On purely moral grounds, JP's attack on India's official position is quite devastating. While lapses of others do not exonerate India, why does not JP remind them of their commitments? The leadership of Kashmir is today repudiating all its agreements with Indian government and public pledges about the future of the state. Likewise, Pakistan-having committed aggression according to all canons of international law-has hardly any superior moral position on Kashmir.

JP seems to be too conscious of being an Indian (and a Hindu) and concerned with protecting the moral image of his country (community). He perhaps does not feel equally qualified to advise Pakistan, Kashmir or Muslims and concerned about their moral position.

A Non-partisan Role

In another respect, however, JP assumes a non-partisan pose. He suggests that claims of Kashmir, India and Pakistan should be reconciled. These claims, it may be pointed out, have been fluctuating. There was indeed a time when Pakistan was not enthusiastic about a plebiscite and made far less demands than she is insisting on today. Popular leaders of Kashmir for a while did press for finalisation of accession with India. Their terms for settlement with India also varied from time to time. Again, the amount of concessions that India was willing to give to Pakistan and Kashmir, too, have not remained constant.

That JP chose this particular moment in history to take upon himself the task of solving the Kashmir problem may not be dictated by the consideration that India's bargaining position is weakest today. But his contribution to work the agreement that Kashmiri leaders willingly entered into with the Indian government bears no proportion to his current campaign for a settlement with Pakistan.

If India's image has been darkening in Kashmir over all these years, partly it is because JP surrendered his claim (to which he is eminently entitled) to represent it. His role of a self-conscious Indian and a non-partisan perhaps inhibits his thinking and action.

A cosmopolitan and a rational outlook need not compromise one's position as an Indian or a Hindu. If JP is a friend of Kashmir – as he certainly is acknowledged by most of its people –, he should not shirk his responsibility to guide, advise and criticise its leaders and politics.

Whatever a good Indian's attitude towards Kashmir may be, whatever a democratic conscience may expect in Kashmir, JP's current role would demand certain corrections in Kashmir politics.

His aim of Indo-Pak friendship would be harder to fulfil, if Kashmir refuses to be a fit instrument. The politics of Kashmir needs to acquire a more sober and responsible tone. Its commitment to secularism must regain its own old firmness. The political virtues should cease to be measured by the length of a lathi or the size of a crowd.

Kashmir has to make a long leeway to live up to Gandhi's expectations and JP's ideals. The extent of his lack of understanding with the leaders of Kashmir is further indicated by the fact that while he rules out plebiscite, a major section of the latter is organised in the form of Plebiscite Front.

Statesmen of JP's courage of conviction, humanitarian outlook and eminence are indeed rare. It would also be a pity if his critics do not accept his challenge at his level.

(Janata, 28 February 1965)

In Defence of Jayaprakash

A.G. Noorani

It is always a pleasure to read Balraj Puri, particularly when he writes on Kashmir, a subject on which he is an acknowledged authority. I dissent from his stimulating analysis of Shri Jayaprakash Narayan's role published in Janata of February 28, 1965 with the utmost diffidence.

Shri Puri recognises that "we cannot afford the matters to remain as they are either in Kashmir or in Nagaland." and that "the only way of weakening the Sino-Pak alliance is improving Indo-Pak relations. For tension with Pakistan scarcely serves any Indian interest." But he argues that "solution of the Kashmir problem should also serve the national interest". Unexceptionable enough. But is it fair to say, "a moral case at the cost of self-interest and selfish course without a moral cover, real or illusory are seldom accepted by a nation? One suspects that JP is asking the country to do it?"

Power Balance

Reading of the very first of JP's famous articles in the Hindustan Times suggests that JP advocates a solution on both grounds, moral and material, after disposing off the stock arguments against a settlement, JP wrote: "Neither India nor Pakistan can live and grow unless there is friendship and cooperation between them. The lack of such relationship between them has, among other things, upset the power balance in South and South East Asia, depriving the sub-continent of the role that history and geography had destined them to play."

Shri Puri's basic criticism, however, appears to be that JP admonishes India alone and ignores Kashmir and Pakistan. "On purely moral grounds, JP's attack on India's official position is quite devastating. While lapses of others may not exonerate India, why does not JP remind them of their commitments? The leadership of Kashmir is today repudiating all its agreements with the Indian government and public pledges about the future of the state. Likewise, Pakistan - having committed aggression according to all canons of international law - has hardly any superior moral position on Kashmir."

Let us take Kashmir first and next Pakistan. Shri Puri takes Kashmir leaders to task thus: "Popular leaders of Kashmir for a while did press for finalisation of accession with India." Yes indeed but what happened? As Jawaharlal Nehru declared at a press conference on June 21, 1952, "When the Constituent Assembly met in Kashmir for the first time it was its intention to pass a resolution forthwith confirming the state's accession to India. We asked it not to do it so as not to be embarrassed before the UN" (India had assured the Security Council, earlier, that the Assembly "is not intended to prejudice the issue before the Security Council or come in its way.").

The Kashmiri leaders did not repudiate their obligations. But faced with the finality of our stand that Kashmir is an open question they set up an eight-man committee, of which Sheikh Abdullah, Mirza Afzal Beg, Maulana Massodi, Bakshi Gulam Mohammad and GM Sadiq were members, to consider alternative solutions. Indian leaders were apprised of its deliberations and objected not. Indeed, Indo-Pak negotiations were on - and on the basis of plebiscite. Suddenly Sheikh Abdullah was dismissed from office, arrested on one set of charges, tried on another and then released. I prefer to withhold comment on this entire episode, save to point out that the charge of Kashmiri volte face is groundless. Incidentally, the only man prepared to talk about that committee has been Sheikh Abdullah. Sadiq only limitedly in defence, Indian leadership has been discreetly quite.

Plebiscite Agreements

Pray, what justification can any Indian leader now have to ask Kashmir to treat the accession as a closed chapter?

As for Pakistan, the issue surely is not aggression. Well after that even agreements for plebiscite were entered into with her. They were not implemented. Whatever be the obstacles in their way, surely it is another matter for India to repudiate the basic agreement to hold a plebiscite?

But is plebiscite the issue of today? "There was time when Pakistan was not enthusiastic about a plebiscite and made far less demands than she is insisting on today." Shri Puri unfortunately does not mention the earlier period. However, the record shows that, since its Foreign Minister's major policy speech on 12, 1960, Pakistan has been willing to consider alternatives to a plebiscite. General KM Cariappa reported a year back that President Ayub was prepared to come to India to negotiate "if India offered fresh alternative plans for resolving the Kashmir issue, if India ruled out the holding of plebiscite". Have we cared to evolve any alternative save that we hold what we have?

Soon after Nehru's death, there was published a significant news item with a Rawalpindi dateline to the effect that Pakistan was prepared for "a working agreement on Pakistan's relationship with India, without waiting for close friendship presumably conditioned on a Kashmir settlement, but provided that meanwhile India shows readiness for shift, however, small it may be, in her basic attitude towards the Kashmir issue." In September, JP found "a ray of hope" after a plebiscite is out of the question. One may be sure he saw some flexibility in their stand which warranted hope of a via media. If again he still finds fault mainly with India, it is because the basic hurdle is India's stand that Kashmir is a closed chapter. Expressions of willingness to negotiate are ludicrous against the background of such a stand.

Shri Puri comments on the "extent of his (JP's) lack of understanding with the leaders of Kashmir" is indicated by the fact that, while he rules out a plebiscite, they agitate for it. However, only last month, speaking in New Delhi (February 10), Sheikh Abdullah said that, if a plebiscite would release the forces of disruption and communal disharmony, it could be ruled out but some way had to be found to ascertain the wishes of the people of Kashmir. As he said, there could be no rigidity in regard to the manner of exercising the right of self-determination.

Out of Proportion

Shri Puri in perhaps the most critical para of his article writes, "That J.P. chose this particular moment in history to take upon himself the task of solving the Kashmir problem may not be dictated by the consideration that India's bargaining position is weakest today. But his contribution to work the agreement that Kashmir leaders willingly entered into with the India government bears no proportion to this current campaign for a settlement with Pakistan". I have already commented on the charge of volte face by the Kashmiris.

But the reason for India being singled out is apparent if one reflects on an interesting comment by Shri Puri himself. "He suggests that claims of Kashmir, India and Pakistan should be reconciled. These claims, it may be pointed out, have been fluctuating." The reason why India is singled out is because the fluctuation in its stand had led to a hardening, not a softening, of its position.

Pakistan is officially committed to a plebiscite, but since 1960, has consistently been prepared to discuss alternatives. Kashmir's leaders, once told their Assembly had no power to ratify an accession ratifiable only by plebiscite, thought of plebiscite for various solutions but are now prepared to discuss alternatives.

Only India once pledging to hold a plebiscite argued over its modalities, meanwhile changing emphasis from the provisional character of the accession to its legality, hoping it secured permanence, seizing on US arms aid as a ground to rule out plebiscite, next arguing a la Menon that even mediation is unacceptable. Even so Krishna Menon still swore by U.N. resolutions. In 1962 they were dubbed "Obsolete" There is surely a pattern in this, and, if JP "chose this particular moment in history to take upon himself the task of solving the Kashmir problem," it is not for the reason Shri Puri faintly hints but because he believes and rightly, that Sheikh Abdullah's release afforded a fine opportunity for reversing a trend in Indo-Pak relations that could not fail to prove suicidal to both. If in the process he has criticized India more, it is because he feels, I submit rightly, that the major obstacle is India's stand that the state's accession is irrevocable and the ball is, therefore, very much in its court.

(*Janata*, March 14, 1965)

Who is Right on Kashmir?

Balraj Puri

After a vigorous defence of the position of Pakistan and Kashmir leaders, A.G. Noorani concludes (*Janata*, March 14, 1965) that the ball is very much in India's court. To be sure, there are more persons in Pakistan and Kashmir as well as in India who defend their respective stands almost equally vigorously. I am incapable and unwilling to discuss the issue with that vigour and at a plane where Noorani has tried to drag me-viz., who is guilty and who is innocent, who is black and who is white.

The comfortable and categorical position that Noorani has managed to take is, if I sum it correctly, based on the fact that, while India has repudiated her commitment of a plebiscite, leaders of Pakistan and Kashmir are still bound by the commitment and are willing to consider alternatives. As I pointed out in my article, under discussion, the enthusiasm for a plebiscite by the parties concerned has been varying. Pakistan's original aggression and obstacles in the way of a plebiscite are no less responsible for the complications of the problem than India's present intransigence. I do not hold that the former justifies the latter. But if you are keen to apportion responsibility, let the record be straight.

No Moral Sanctity

"But is plebiscite the issue of today?" Noorani rightly doubts elsewhere. His grudge is, "Have we cared to evolve any alternative? Is he sure no alternatives were ever mooted? What else do the Swaran Singh - Butto and Nehru-Abdullah talks signify? Apparently, the alternative offers fell short of the expectations of either Bhutto or Abdullah.

There is hardly any moral sanctity of a particular level of expectations which have been fluctuating. Noorani quotes my statement to this effect to single out fluctuations in India's stand-that "has led to hardening of its positions".

I, however, also discern a shift in Pakistan's position from Ayub's offer of joint defence, partition proposals to its latest reported insistence on getting the whole state minus a district of Jammu. Abdullah who offered to abide by all his agreements made with the Government of India till August, 1953 (*Hindustan Times*, April 17, 1964) now adds another rider-viz., a resolution must be acceptable to Pakistan also.

India did change over the period, particularly since the exit of Krishna Menon. From liberation of Azad Kashmir, status quo, to offers (informal, of course) of more territory was one line of concession. The process of integration of Kashmir with the Union was for a while halted to consider restoration of the pre-1953 status or so. The removal of Bakshi, demolition of the entire edifice of repression, restoration of civil liberates, freedom of Press and platform and release of Abdullah and his colleagues, were indeed courageous advances on another front. The willingness to consider the confederation proposal - comprising India, Pakistan and Kashmir - which Ayub rejected outright, reconciled the new approach on both the fronts.

Triumph and Despair

There has been a panicky retreat from that policy for the last few months. I do not condone it. But I am not convinced that New Delhi alone is responsible for it. To be fair, each had its compulsions. Presidential elections in Pakistan, Mirwaiz Farooq's challenge to Abdullah in Kashmir, an unsure new leadership in India.

For Noorani it may be possible to find only a uniform pattern in India's stand which has continuously been leading to a hardening of its position. Having invested the best part of my life in the cause of satisfying the aspirations of Kashmir, I could not escape the tormenting experience of hanging between triumph and despair during the last year. As the situation started deteriorating, irreversibly, I anguishedly, of course vainly, wished (through my article) perhaps Shri Jayaprakash could rescue it.

It was in this context that I felt a better understanding between him and Kashmir leaders would have helped both of them as also the wider cause, I do miss the understanding that Noorani is able to see.

The political organisation which Sheikh Abdullah blesses is called the Plebiscite Front. Its president, Mirza Mohammad Afzal Beg, declared in a statement published in the official organ of the party, the *Front* (December 9, 1964): "As far as the Plebiscite Front is concerned, the only method to end the Kashmir dispute is through a plebiscite". If the name of the party, resolutions passed by it, slogans invariably raised in all its public meetings and innumerable statements and speeches by all ranks of its leaders do not seem at a variance with the declared position of JP that rules out a plebiscite, I really do not know how to carry the argument further.

At the ideological level, the gap is more conspicuous. For the first time in the political history of Kashmir, Jinnah is sought to be rehabilitated and gets tributes on the pages of the Front. When the communal situation is already tense, the emphasis of the Front leaders changes from secularism to Muslim grievances in the services exclusively to Muslims.

JP's love for Pakistan has, on the other hand, never led to a concession to its philosophy or that of its founder. His commitment to Gandhian ideals is too categorical to permit equating them with those of Jinnah.

Disturbing Developments

Only a true friend of Kashmir can feel disturbed over these developments. Kashmir has been almost the most secular state of India. It cannot afford to lower its standards if it aspires to any great role in the sub-continent. I do not deny that stupid and communal elements in other parts of the country often provoke it. But that hardly justifies a suicidal course on the part of Kashmir leaders.

If the leaders and people of Kashmir who willingly became a part of India in 1947 feel reasons to change their mind, they do not need to repudiate the heritage of common values. Nor can they dispense with the goodwill of the people of India as also of the non-Muslims of the state.

I am amazed at Noorani's forthright assertion that leaders of Kashmir have not changed their mind. The leaders do not make that assertion. They only try to justify the change in their position. The reference, otherwise pointless, by Noorani to the eight-man committee appointed by Abdullah to consider alternative solutions only contradicts him. For it indicated a process of change from the original categorical position of Kashmir's remaining a part of India. Noorani asserts that Kashmiri leaders did not repudiate their obligations. His sole reason is Kashmir was an open question. So what? If you change sides in the midst of an open debate that change matters all the more. Nor is a change no change if its responsibility can be shifted. Noorani tries to absolve Kashmir leaders on the ground that the Government of India did not allow the Constituent Assembly of Kashmir to finalise the issue of accession.

Those who now criticise India for not honouring her commitment of a plebiscite cannot criticise her for not dishonouring it before 1953 i.e. when Abdullah was in power. JP and the Front leaders have taken the position that the Assembly verdict could not be a substitute for a plebiscite. Afzal Beg went to the extent of saying that "the issue of accession was not within the scope of the Assembly... it had no business whatsoever to take a decision on accession." (*The Front*, December 9, 1964).

Idealism - or Lack of it?

Noorani may be right Afzal Beg may be wrong. The leader and the president of the Assembly did indicate that it would decide the question of accession. It was never prevented from taking the decision. The Government of India simply stated that the decision would be further ratified by a plebiscite. This stand was never opposed by Kashmir leaders.

But is it Noorani's contention that Kashmir leaders changed their decision to remain a part of India simply because India insisted on a plebiscite? I do not rule out the possibility. But that only means that he accuses India of too much idealism. His criticism of the later conduct of India implies that she lacks that idealism. If idealism is as bad as lack of it, what should one do?

I, however, believe that the reasons for the change are weightier. Let Abdullah state his position and the reasons for changing it. In a statement at Cairo, published in *The Indian*

Express of March 8, 1965, he says, "There was an understanding between me and Government of India that, if it stuck to its promises and did not interfere in our internal affairs, then at the time of referendum I would support accession to India. This was a contract between the people of Kashmir and the Government of India. My misfortune is that one party has broken all its pledges. It interfered with our internal autonomy. It says there is now no need for a plebiscite. You cannot now ask the other party to stand by the agreement."

Who broke the contract first is a moot point. But does Abdullah demand that India should now unilaterally stand by the agreement, from the obligations of which he would continue to be free? Is not it on a par with India's position vis-a-vis Pakistan? Since Pakistan did not fulfil the conditions of a plebiscite, India no more feels bound by the obligations. Supposing Pakistan now agrees to meet the conditions, shouldn't India honour her commitments? If India now agrees to implement the contract with Kashmir, should not Abdullah and his followers stand by their part of the agreement-viz, to support accession to India?

Simple Solution

The problem should be much simpler - morally and politically- if each one of the parties returns to its original commitments. Abdullah has hinted that the situation has changed. I agree it has. Not only for him but also for the other parties. So let us start discussing new alternatives without a self-righteous pose, appreciating one another's difficulties.

I admit the Government of India encroached upon the autonomy of the State against its solemn pledges. I further admit that it imposed on the people of the State a regime of intolerable corruption and tyranny. An Indian who loved his country and moral principles, should have supported Kashmir's struggle in defence of its autonomy and liberties and should have helped to work the agreement between the leaders of Kashmir and the Union. I do not think J.P. ever seriously tried that role or even demanded a trial of that agreement.

However, he has a right to transcend the role of a mere Indian and pass judgement on the collective failure of the country as a non-partisan, objective observer with belief in high moral principles. But in that role he is obliged to pass similar judgement on non-Indians also.

The Role of JP

It was precisely this question that I posed in my article on JP. What role he chooses to play, as an Indian, good, conscientious, moralist and patriot - or a non-partisan cosmopolitan? Both have their respective obligations. I mentioned Kashmir in the article only to see if JP meets either of the obligations. And I expressed my misgivings. I did not intend to discuss JP's views on Kashmir as such. It was a general criticque of his approach with the sole desire to add a little more coherence to his thinking and effectiveness to his practice. I wish Noorani had subjected my main thesis to his critical judgement and not just drawn me into this discussion of some aspects of the Kashmir problem - which I join only in self-defence. For I do not have illusions about my defending capacity, which has not helped me from becoming lonelier and lonelier. It was a consolation to learn, in the opening sentence of Noorani that there was at least one person who got pleasure in reading me. I wonder if I am still entitled to that consolation.

(*Janata,* 11 April, 1965)

The Kashmir Dispute

A.G. Noorani

Shri Balraj Puri (*Janata*, of 11-4-1965) takes issue with me for writing that the ball is in India's court in regard to the Kashmir settlement. I had argued that both Pakistan and Sheikh Abdullah were prepared to consider alternatives to a plebiscite, but that India had not cared to evolve any alternative save that we hold what we have."Shri Puri fortifies me in this opinion when he asks." What else do the Swaran Singh - Bhutto and Nehru - Abdullah talks signify?

In the former, India's concessions were all based on the status quo. The Nehru-Abdullah talks were in an exploratory stage. Their result was the Abdullah mission to Pakistan and the Nehru-Ayub agreement to summit but before Shri Nehru could meet President Ayub he passed away. There was a flicker of hope; more cannot be said.

What has happened since gives little ground for thinking that we have evolved any other alternative. President Ayub repeated his offer of joint defence in London last July. We cared not to take it up. His latest reported insistence "on the whole State minus Jammu" follows the Shastri government's unfortunate measures last December. Do we, indeed have any alternative to the plebiscite other than the status quo today.

Shri Puri is less than fair when he writes that "*Abdullah, who offered to abide by all his agreements made with the Government of India till August 1953 (Hindustan Times, April 17, 1964) now adds another rider, viz, a solution must be acceptable to Pakistan also.*" (Bold mine).

Just two days after his release last year, Sheikh Abdullah declared that there were three parties to the dispute; India, Pakistan and Kashmir. He had expressed similar views on his release in 1958. Indeed, the suggestions of the eight-man committee were based on the proposition that Pakistan is very much a party. It is not an after-thought by Abdullah as he tries to make it.

As to the *Hindustan Times* report, it quotes the Sheikh as saying he did not disown responsibility for what he did in 1947. "Nor do I repudiate my subsequent agreements with the Government of India". Sheikh saheb then proceeds to give the reasons; India's volte face regarding the Constituent Assembly's powers and the coup of 1953.

"I am amazed at Noorani's forthright assertion that leaders of Kashmir have not changed their mind." I had written; "The Kashmiri leaders did not repudiate their obligations. But faced with the finality of our stand that Kashmir is an open question they set up an eight man committee... to consider alternative solutions". After mentioning the aftermath of Sheikh Saheb's dismissal in 1953, I wrote "the charge of a Kashmir volte face is groundless".

The very obvious point I made was that the Kashmir responded to India's volte face, not the other way about. I prefer to let the reader judge whether Shri Puri's interpretation and the reaction of amazement are fair.

He is, of course, at liberty too make the most of the Plebiscite Front's insistence on a plebiscite. Presumably the Front is expected, in so many words, to abandon this once agreed solution and then be told that the alternative remains the status quo. Anyone seriously interested in the quest for a compromise can read the repeated pronouncements of the Front's acclaimed guide, Sheikh Abdullah, that he is prepared to consider alternatives.

As an instance of the "ideological gap" and a lapse from secularism are cited the Front's grievances in regard to the Services. No one who can read the tell-tale figures cited in the Front's resolution on the subject can fail to be impressed by the genuineness of the grievances. Pandit Prem Nath Bazaz, who wishes the Sadiq government well, has written only recently that "inadequate representation of Kashmir Muslims in Central government departments is not an unreal grievance."

This is a lapse from secularism, not its criticism. Of course, "only a true friend of Kashmir can feel disturbed over these developments."

Shri Balraj Puri's expressions of dislike for a black or white approach would have been more credible if he had not tried to depict that "since Pakistan did not fulfill the conditions of a plebiscite, India no more feels bound by the obligations". This is demonstrably wrong. As early as 1950 Sir Owen Dixon records Pakistan as having accepted his proposals and opined of India's rejection that "in the end, I become convinced that India's agreement was never to be obtained to a demilitarization" which would ensure a free plebiscite. Of course, Pakistan, too, at times has obstructed plebiscite but India's obstruction is simply not a response to them. All that would take one back to the entire barren record.

I, therefore, entirely agree "let us start discussing new alternatives without a self-righteous pose, appreciating one another's difficulties". Is it, then, realistic to believe that the status quo can be such an alternative, or that ignoring Pakistan can help as Shri Puri seems to think. It is particularly here I find Shri Puri most disappointing. He can contribute a lot if only he would care to.

It is, because JP has and, more, he has courageously pinpointed the hurdles that I think Shri Puri's criticism of him is misplaced. It is pointless to deny that he intended to "discuss JP's views on Kashmir as such." The sheer length of the discussions of JP's view on Kashmir in Shri Puri's article belies this.

Shri Puri wonders if I shall continue to read him with pleasure, as I said I did. Of course, I will. But that, I must point out, depends on him. If he writes of himself and of other in the strain he has, he will be read with amusement. Sample these; "For Noorani it may be possible to find only a uniform pattern in India's stand which has continuously been leading to a hardening of its position. Having invested the best of part of my life in the cause of satisfying the aspirations of Kashmir, I could not escape the tormenting experience of hanging between triumph and despair during the last year. As the situation started deteriorating, irreversibly, I anguishedly, of course, vainly, wished (through my article) perhaps Shri Jayaprakash could rescue it" and "For I do not have illusions about my defending capacity, which has not helped me from becoming lonelier and lonelier".

(*Janata*, May 16, 1965)

Kashmir, Abdullah and JP

Balraj Puri

A.G. Noorani concludes his latest rejoinder to me (Janata, May 16, 1965) with the remark that if I write in the strain I have (*Janata*, April 11, 1965), I would be read with amusement. He merely confirmed the apprehension I had expressed about his possible attitude to my further writings on Kashmir.

As each side to the dispute was tending to be more rigid and dogmatic, I doubted my own capacity to carry conviction with either of them and escape becoming lonelier and lonelier on the issue. I further failed to share Noorani's assertion that "fluctuation in India's stand has led to a hardening, not a softening, of its position." The fluctuation, I had submitted, was not continuously hardening. In the earlier part of 1964, it reflected a softening of the position, from which later on there was panicky retreat. In view of my own involvements with the developments in and about the State, these fluctuations kept me hanging between triumph and despair.

I have reproduced those samples of my writings, with slight elaboration, that have amused Noorani. I do not know how far my loneliness and despair should be source of amusement even to an unsympathetic critic. But the reference to them still does not seem to be entirely pointless to me. For when Noorani insists on repeating the same arguments that I have already tried to answer, it could, on the one hand, imply a reflection on my capacity to express myself and also indicate, on the other hand, my isolation even from those who are supposed to know me or the problem better.

Clean Chit to Pakistan

I make another attempt to take the debate a point further with the hope that Noorani is a little more helpful and his further reaction to what I write might not be worse then even amusement.

I have been raising my feeble voice against the Kashmir policy of the government of India, on moral and political grounds, ever since the problem started. In the current debates too, I have not justified that policy. But, when I fail to join Noorani in giving the cleanest chit to Pakistan or Abdullah, he does not forgive me. What is worse, he uses the arguments of the official and nationalist policy to defend Pakistan or the Plebiscite Front against my criticism. At that level, the debate is already going on and Noorani could get more appropriate replies from Hindu chauvinists. Likewise he could have left their counterparts across the border to defend their case.

Even at that level, a fruitful discussion is possible if there is respect for facts and appreciation for each other's position. But I had earnestly believed that my debate with Noorani could transcend that level. My difference with him is indeed not sufficient ground for his suspicion of my earnest and strenuous efforts to be objective about facts.

Unnecessary Refutation

My dislike for a black-and-white approach does not seem credible to Noorani because he thinks I have tried to depict that "since Pakistan did not fulfill the conditions of a plebiscite, India no more feels bound by the obligations". After refuting this statement, in a full para, he concludes "It is particularly here I find Shri Puri most disappointing".

The refutation and disappointment are unnecessary. For I have myself refuted the argument, in most unambiguous terms, that Noorani credits to him. I did say, "Pakistan's original aggression and obstacles in the way of a plebiscite are no less responsible for the complications of the problems than India's present intransigence." I, however, categorically added, "I do not hold that the former justifies the latter." This was merely to put the record straight and refute the claim that one side was entirely black and the other entirely white.

I reverted to the argument in another context. Sheikh Abdullah did not feel bound to honour his agreement with India because the latter had broken its pledges on autonomy, etc. I put it at par with India's position vis-a-vis Pakistan. My statement that Noorani had quoted and criticized is in this context. I justify-morally speaking-neither India nor Abdullah for not honouring their part of the agreement because the other party did not honour its part. My further questions make my own position clear beyond doubt. I ask, "Suppose Pakistan now agrees to meet the conditions, shouldn't India honour her commitments? If India now agrees to implement the contract with Kashmir, shouldn't Abdullah and his followers stand by their part of the agreement?" I am, however, willing to concede that, if the situation has changed, it has changed for all the parties.

Finality of Stand

I really wonder how on earth it was possible to misrepresent such unequivocal statements. I do hope it was not deliberate. Perhaps he did not appreciate my failure to be convinced by his use of the same logic for proving two contradictory positions, pointed out by me above.

Noorani still insists that leaders of Kashmir have not changed their mind. "The very obvious point I made was that Kashmir responded to India's volte face, not the other way about," he adds. The point is unfortunately not so very obvious to me. The essence of his explanation of India's volte face is "the finality of our stand that Kashmir is not an open question."

When did India take the stand of keeping the question open? It was certainly not in 1953 or after, when the Kashmir leader is supposed to have responded to India's so-called volte face. Ever since Kashmir acceded to India in 1947, Indian leadership, of which Kashmiri leaders formed a respectable part, treated the issue as open.

A thousand and one declarations, at home and at international forums, by the leaders of Kashmir, linking their destiny with India once for all, were never subject to the condition that the issue be closed or be decided by the Constituent Assembly. Now the burden of the criticism of the same leaders against India is that neither should the issue have been closed nor have been decided by the Assembly - "which did not have the mandate to do so."

Double Logic

Noorani has used the following arguments in almost so many words: "India was not right in keeping the issue open. She is wrong in closing it. The Assembly should have the power, to finalise the issue of accession to India and a plebiscite should not have been insisted on. Going back from the commitment of plebiscite is immoral and the Assembly's decision was no substitute for it."

I crave forgiveness of my dear friend Noorani if I am unable to reconcile these arguments with one another and appreciate his compulsions to use double logic as often in what, at least for me, is a friendly discussion and an occasion to learn from each other.

He clearly exceeds his brief when he maintains on behalf of the leaders of Kashmir that they have not changed. For they no longer take that position. But why then does he proceed to justify the change?

The very appointment of the eightman committee, by Sheikh Abdullah, to consider alternatives in 1953, is sufficient proof of the change in his unequivocal stand on the issue of accession to India. The coup of August 1953, however unjustified in itself, cannot retrospectively justify the change that had already taken place in Abdullah's mind.

Noorani is hardly fair to me in suggesting that I am less than fair to Abdullah in saying that he now does not stand by his offer (made in April, 1964) to abide by his agreements with India till August 1953. The emphasis that he has added on "now" is misplaced. My point is not that he changed only after April, 1964. I merely submitted that each party to the dispute has been fluctuating in its position. April-May, 1964 was the period when once again all the parties had moved closest to each other.

Plebiscite Demand

I am accused of taking a liberty in making the most of the Plebiscite Front's insistence on a plebiscite - "this once-agreed solution". I have yet not discussed the merits of this mode of solution. I had merely contended that this was at variance with the declared position of Jayaprakash Narayan that ruled out plebiscite.

Noorani defends the Front insistence on plebiscite on the fear that it might then be held the alternative was the status quo. Jayaprakash challenges the status quo without insisting on a plebiscite. Noorani himself says that plebiscite is not the issue and makes most of Sheikh Abdullah's and Pakistan's willingness to consider alternative. Then how would the status quo be guaranteed only if the Front gives up its exclusive adherence to plebiscite?

The chauvinistic frenzy aroused around the exclusive slogan of plebiscite, "the only method to end the Kashmir dispute," circumscribed the manoeuverability of Sheikh Abdullah and weakened the hands of Jayaprakash and all those who were in search of alternative solutions. The rigid and uncompromising attitude of the Front on the means of solution provoked equally rigid reactions in the rest of the country and thus became the single greatest stumbling block against attempts to change the status quo.

Communal Representation

Noorani has picked up only a minor instance of the gap that I pointed out in the ideological position of Jayaprakash and the Front. I had referred to the change in the emphasis of the Front leaders from secular problem to Muslim grievances in the services and elsewhere. Noorani is impressed by the genuineness of the grievances. He quotes Prem Nath Bazaz to show that the representation of Kashmir Muslims in the Central services is inadequate. I would be happier than Bazaz and Noorani if that representation improves. But the controversy over whether the share of Hindus in the services of the state is declining or increasing is definitely harmful in the already communally tense atmosphere and hardly contributes to the far bigger and important issues facing the state. There is much to be said about the futility of this debate, in which extreme Hindu and Muslim communalists of the state were engaged. But that would divert my attention from the more important issues I have in mind.

In an honest debate you do not choose the most minor point and ignore the main issue. I had accused the Front leaders of seeking to rehabilitate Jinnah for the first time in the political history of Kashmir and pay him tributes on the pages of their official organ. So far even the pro-Pak parties of Kashmir had claimed to be Gandhian. I had also accused the Front leaders that their appeals were exclusively addressed to Muslims. I further accuse them of giving up their socialistic red banner in favour of a green flag, officially interpreted as a symbol of Islam, with a white stripe for minorities. Can those who consider Muslims of Kashmir to be a nation - and consequently Hindus of Kashmir as another nation - still claim to belong to Jayaprakash's philosophical camp?

Instead of denouncing me for pointing out the gaps between Jayaprakash and the Kashmir leadership at the ideological and political levels, if Noorani had contributed a little to bridging them, he would surely have done better service to them and could also count on my humble support.

Concessions

I am also one of those who had believed that in any settlement, it is India that must offer concessions to the Pakistani and Kashmiri sentiments. If efforts of persons like me - including Jayaprakash - have not succeeded, it is not entirely due to resistance in India. I share this experience with "S.M" of the Hindustan Times (April 15, 1965) who admitted that "Pakistan and Sheikh Abdullah between them have succeeded in putting Indians like me, who had often found Indian politics narrow and ungenerous, more completely in the wrong than the most militant Hindu communalist." I am not authorised to quote other members of this tribe, who suffer a similar agony and who are likely to be the targets of Noorani's criticism like me.

He has not appreciated my own reluctance in discussing Kashmir in this manner-being under cross-examination on points of his choice. For in every answer I have to take care to refer to the proper perspective, which the space of the Janata may not always permit. Moreover, as a co-sufferer and friend, Sheikh Abdullah has always treated my private criticism and advice with the utmost consideration and respect. However, as my private and public positions are exactly alike and as I should be read in the context of my general view-point on the subject, I hope, I should escape being misunderstood. Now after I have taken the risk and have agreed to join issues with Noorani on issues of his choice, it is futile to count the sentences of my original article and quote their contents to argue with him whether my primary intention was to discuss Jayaprakash's general approach, his views on Kashmir, the problem of Kashmir or Sheikh Abdullah.

The ingenious imagination with which Noorani puts India in the dock and lumps together Abdullah, extremist Kashmiris and Pakistan in the prosecution counter, pushing Jayaprakash into that counter, if possible, otherwise representing him as a prosecution witness, might be good tactics in a diplomatic war against India. But it hardly serves the purpose of bringing the parties to the dispute nearer and making Jayaprakash a more effective mediator.

Complicating Factor

One of the complicating factors in the situation, in fact, is that Abdullah and Pakistan want to extract concessions from India in different directions. Noorani again misquotes my question, "What else do the Swaran Singh - Bhutto and Nehru - Abdullah talks signify?" To fortify his opinion, which is: "India had not cared to evolve any alternative save that we hold what we have."

What is the basis of his interpretation of those ill-fated talks? The alternatives to plebiscite which Pakistan was willing to consider and for which Noorani gives her so much credit, included, according to the press reports in India and Pakistan, insistence on getting the entire catchment area of the Chenab and Jhelum rivers (Pran Chopra in the *Stateman* of February 10, 1963). She conceded only one district of Jammu, namely Kathua, to India. Pakistan thus demanded 83,000 square miles out of the State's total area of 84,000 square miles (*Hindustan Times*, April 29, 1963). Somehow, Noorani confidently reports that Ayub's insistence on "the whole State minus Jammu follows the Shastri government's unfortunate measures last December (i.e. 1964)." I do not have any source to verify if after these "unfortunate measures" Ayub has become more generous than he was in 1963 and is now willing to concede the whole of Jammu to India.

Collapse of Statesmanship

What is more significant is that I then personally conveyed to the late Prime Minister Nehru the considered opinion of the leaders of Kashmir, inside and outside the jail, that India was going too far in her concessions to Pakistan at the cost of Kashmir.

In 1964, Pakistan's stand, on the other hand, was that concessions to Kashmir by India would not satisfy her. Sheikh Abdullah had felt that a basis existed in India for a kind of settlement he was working for (*Stateman*, May 13, 1964). There was, he had said, no basic differences between him and the Prime Minister; "differences existed only in the imagination of some people." (*Stateman*, May 4, 1964). The specific proposals that he had taken to Pakistan at the advice of men like Jayaprakash and consent of Jawaharlal are known to have been rejected by Ayub.

I have discussed elsewhere (*Economic Weekly*, May 15, 1965) how India's statesmanship collapsed in dealing with Abdullah or Pakistan in the crucial year of 1964.

But there I am concerned only with pointing out the complexities of the problem and the three widely divergent approaches to it. Noorani hardly helps the delicate task of bridge-makers by singling out India for the blackest paint and being so self-righteously indignant against anybody who does not completely agree with him.

(*Janata*, June 13, 1965)

From Many Angles
Observer

Kashmir and the Sheikh are becoming many things to many men and it is not strange that outside India they are major points for denouncing India. In the *Janata*, however, they are fast becoming the measure of the degree of friendship existing (or not existing) between Shri Balraj Puri and Shri A.G. Noorani. I believe the second round between these two stalwarts is just over. What is strange is that both appear to be anxious to see a change of policy towards Kashmir, a reconciliation with Pakistan and a settled South Asia - the major difference being whether it can be done around (since it can no longer be done through) Sheikh Abdullah or independently of him. Shri Balraj Puri is almost fastidious in correctly repeating what he said before and in insisting on what he meant. The figure of Jayaprakash Narayan, always a trifle shadowy, is beginning to recede from prominence it once had in this controversy.

The service such devoted protagonists render to us lesser men is in making us think again over many questions on which we had long made our minds up. Take Kashmir, for instance: I had always held the view that nothing could have been more injurious to the Kashmiris, to Indians, to Pakistanis and to the rest of the world than a prolonged unsettled controversy over the status of that state. It has never been clear to me - in spite of Lord Mountbatten, Jawaharlal Nehru and the constitutionalists - why India had to insist on the formal accession of Kashmir before going to help of the Kashmiris against tribal attacks. It is not yet something I can grasp that the position would have been worse had we acted on humanitarian grounds without either Kashmir or India being committed. As a matter of fact, I can see the advantage in a loose arrangement because both sides could have extricated themselves easily. I am not able or anxious to read what was in other people's minds but the Indian government's insistence at the time on the accession being tentative seems to suggest dissatisfaction with the earlier insistence on formal accession. However, two mistakes do not mean a rectification. Nor did the third one of talking loosely of plebiscite improve matters.

When I consider the matter of plebiscite, there is another aspect that baffles me: Many foreigners and some Indians, attach a sanctity to the plebiscite proposal, contending that the references to a suitable atmosphere are so many evasions. I think I have mentioned this before but it can bear repetition. This attitude reminds me very much of that of a young woman - was it in a story by D.H. Lawrence or Erskine Cauldwell or neither? Who plagued a man into marriage with the reiterated accusation, "But you touched me". No one seems to think of the other implied promise in the very intervention to Kashmir and its people to preserve it whole and to afford some assurance of good government. This and the Union government's failure to fulfil it seem much more serious to my mind. And, if I might presume to raise my small voice against the loud clamour of the "friends of Kashmir" from Shri Jayaprakash to the debaters in the Janata, attention to this issue will be far more productive of results than harping on a plebiscite, which no one seems to want and no one of the government's critics seems quite prepared to let go off. Again, it seems to bordering on the indecent to keep on predicting reproachfully a different turn of events had Jawahar Lal Nehru lived a year longer.

(*Janata*, June 13, 1965)

Kashmir Obsessions

A.G. Noorani

Balraj Puri's rejoinder (*Janata* of June 13) contains more of the something which makes a detailed answer unnecessary. I had written, "The Kashmiri leaders did not repudiate their obligation" and "the charge of a Kashmir volte face is groundless." To Balraj Puri's expression of amazement at this I replied, "the very obvious point I made was that Kashmir responded to India's volte face, not the other way about."

Apparently, Shri Puri regards any denial of "repudiation of obligations." or of a "volte face" as denial of any change at all. Else, it is difficult to see why he harps "Noorani still insists that leaders of Kashmir have not changed their mind" and so pathetically remarks "the point is unfortunately not so very obvious to me."

Balraj Puri avers that "ever since Kashmir acceded to India in 1947, Indian leadership, of which Kashmiri leaders formed a respectable part, treated the issue as open. "True, but all I had written was that "faced with the finality of our stand that Kashmir is an open question" the Kashmiri leaders set up an eight man committee to consider alternative solutions. I fail to see how any-one could have construed me as suggesting an abrupt Indian decision to treat the issue open which prompted the Kashmiri leadership to take a hand in mooting solutions.

"In an honest debate you do not choose the most minor point and ignore the main issue, "writes Puri. Why then does he so studiously ignore Sheikh Abdullah's repeated offer to consider alternatives to a plebiscite and talk about "the rigid and uncompromising attitude of the Front on the means of solutions."

As recently as February 10, 1965, Sheikh Abdullah said, "If the fear is that the method - the mechanism of plebiscite - may create or encourage forces of disruption and discord, let us think of an alternative mechanism." A constructive publicist would note this and not ignore it, and, worse, contend to the contrary.

I had hoped an exchange would be along the lines Shri Puri had suggested "let us start discussing new alternatives, without a self-righteous pose". The hope has been belied.

Shri Puri writes, "I am also one of those who had believed that in any settlement it is India that must offer concessions to the Pakistani and Kashmiri sentiments, but we note that during the Swaran Singh - Bhutto talks Puri "personally conveyed to the late Prime Minister Nehru the considered opinion of the leaders of Kashmir, inside and outside the jail, that India was going too far in her concessions to Pakistan at the cost of Kashmir," a venture with a touch so characteristic he described as "what is more significant is that I then personally conveyed." Nothing in Sheikh Saheb's remarks over since his release would support this statement of Shri Puri and it is idle for him who threw his weighty support against concessions to read homilies on "bridge building".

As idle also to identify his position with that of "S.M." who wrote his very understandable criticism on April 14, after Sheikh Saheb's talks with Chou En-lai and the remarks he made thereafter. Shri Puri's criticism, such as they are, were well before that and were peculiar to him.

It is surely absurd of him to talk of "efforts of people like me - including Jayaprakash." The fact is that JP did find a "ray of hope" after his talks with the Pakistani leaders, and is not oppressed by their pronouncements, whereas Shri Puri deliberately judges them solely by the positions they took during negotiations with an India unprepared for a basic change and conveniently finds Pakistan adamant. Even the hints they have publicly and repeatedly thrown are lost on him. The Indian alternative to a plebiscite is nothing but a slight modification of the status quo. Shri Puri may be happy with it, but it is no basis for a settlement.

As for the "Hindu chauvinists" with whom he tries to frighten me, they would make no worse accusations than does Shri Puri himself - conducting "a diplomatic war against India", "singling out India for the blackest paint", defending "the Pakistani counterparts of "Hindu chauvinists" and the like. Only, the chauvinists would not in that event call me "dear friend" as Puri does.

One notes that "as a co-sufferer and friend, Sheikh Abdullah has always treated my private criticism and advice with the utmost consideration and respect". Why, then does Shri Balraj Puri lament his "loneliness" and his despair? Surely even Shri Puri cannot have it both ways.

"I do not know how far my loneliness and despair should be a source of amusement even to an unsympathetic critic" writes Puri with the same lofty indifference to the record. I had written "if he writes of himself and of others in the strain he has, he will be read with amusement." The samples from Puri I cited there speak for themselves. They have increased in the latest missive. For good measure his venture in diplomacy is thrown in. "I would be happier than Bazaz and Noorani if that (Muslim) representation improves". Any thing you can do, I can do better, is the constant refrain.

(*Janata*, July 25, 1965)

Abdullah's Drift from his Ideals

Balraj Puri

I wonder if we - Noorani and myself - have not already exhausted the limits of indulgence of the readers of the *Janata* in using its space for carrying on a debate over Kashmir, Abdullah, J.P. etc. I discern a mild snub to both of us - not entirely unmerited - in Observer's note, in the *Janata* of June 13. He has raised his "small voice against the loud clamour of the friends of Kashmir, from Shri Jayaprakash to the debaters in the Janata." The point he has voiced, however, is unexceptionable viz the intervention in Kashmir (by India) implied a promise to it and its people to "preserve it whole and afford some assurance of good government." This, to him, is more important than "harping on a plebiscite."

The "loud clamour" of J.P., Noorani and myself, it should be clear from the present debate, is not for plebiscite. The observer has, however, some further difficulty in discovering the difference between my position and that of Noorani.

On the other hand, Noorani thinks it absurd of me to talk of "efforts of people like me - including Jayaprakash". For him it is equally idle to identify my position with that of S.M. of the *Hindustan Times*. In fact, he finds the Hindu chauvinists no worse than me (*Janata*, July 25).

I do not insist on getting my position accepted as better than that of Noorani or the Hindu chauvinists. I primarily aspire to be understood. I do realize that in a rigidly polarised situation, as obtains today, even well defined positions can fail to be properly appreciated. I had welcomed Noorani's joining issues with me in the hope that it would help in defining our respective positions, knowing the extent of our agreement and demarcating our precise points of difference, which if possible could be reduced through a further debate.

I discover by now that what we are up against is essentially a problem of communication. As I am not occupying an extreme position and an vulnerable "from many angles" - the apt title of the Observer's note (*Janata*, June 13) - my job is more difficult. I was "almost fastidious", in observer's words, in repeating what I said and really meant. Unfortunately Noorani, too, had to do the same. But that hardly helped.

When I doubt my own capacity to carry conviction with him, he considers it a source of amusement. When I concede that Muslim representation from Kashmir, at the centre should increase, (and that I would be happier if it is so), he called it my "venture in diplomacy". When I submit that arguments of Hindu chauvinists are not my arguments and cannot be used in answering my criticism against Pakistan or Plebiscite front leaders, he accuses me of frightening him with Hindu chauvinists. He scorns at my reference to him as a "dear friend." The objectives he chooses for my statements include absurd and pathetic. My pleadings for respect for facts and appreciation of each other's position, for transcending the level of chauvinist debaters, and for discussing alternatives without a self-righteous pose perhaps deserved a better response.

The subject at issue is grave and personalities involved are important, and, on the whole friendly to me. I cannot, therefore, be easily provoked to join in a debating bout for the sake of it. Further I believe in the possibility of a fruitful and courteous discussion even with those with whom my differences are far winder than those with Noorani. So far, to my misfortune, I did not have much success in persuading him to be less angry and more understanding.

Pakistan not Cent Per Cent Right

I conceded a large measure of agreement with Noorani's criticism of the Government of India and the general nationalist line. This is not a matter of any satisfaction for him in the current chauvinistic climate. In fact he does not take any note of points of my agreement with him; simply because I do not cent per cent share his complete justification of the stands of Pakistan or Kashmiri leaders in opposition to India. While he is touchy about my disagreements with them, he does not care to answer substantial points of my criticism.

I gave a list of the lapses from the celebrated secular stand of the Kashmiri leaders. Starting from the removal of the photos of Gandhi, Nehru, Azad and Abdul Guffar Khan - that had adorned the Mujahid Manzil, the political head quarters of Sheikh Abdullah, for decades - to the eulogies of Jinnah in the official organ of the Plebiscite Front, I had described the process of shift that was taking place in the ideological complexion of this section of leadership of Kashmir, which I once described as the most secular state of India. The only point Noorani makes in this context is that the representation of Kashmiri Muslims at the centre is inadequate. I readily concede the point and add that I would be happier than him if it improves. For this audacity I am subject to 10 lines of ridicule.

But what has this point to do with my charges? Does he seriously maintain that the precious heritage of secularism, democracy and broad egalitarian values of socialism, that Kashmir shared with the rest of India under the influence of Gandhi and others should be thrown away simply because its share at the centre is inadequate?

My contention was, firstly, that these developments are not in the interest of Kashmir and, secondly, that a lack of J.P.'s understanding with Kashmiri leaders at theoretical and practical levels makes him less effective.

As an illustration of divergence at practical level, I quoted the political position of the Plebiscite Front. Noorani chides me for ignoring Sheikh Abdullah's offer of February 10, 1965 to consider alternative mechanism to plebiscite. I indeed welcomed it. But by the same token the frenzy aroused around the slogan of plebiscite in the valley, categorical and repeated official reiteration by the Plebiscite Front about "plebiscite as the only method to end the Kashmir dispute," Abdullah's own insistence on plebiscite on other occasions and the very name of the Front should be equally unwelcome. How does Noorani expect me to appreciate two completely different position merely because they are held by the same group.

I agree with Noorani that it would be "idle and absurd" for me to identify my position with that of S.M. of *Hindustan Times* or J.P., if it were a question of level and magnitude of effort. But I could legitimately share their experience at my own level. It is immaterial whether my criticism of Sheikh Sahib preceeded that by S.M. For his statement that I quoted exactly echoes the feelings I have been trying to express on the subject in the current controversy. Noorani thinks that S.M.'s criticism of Abdullah has something to do with his meeting with Chou-En-lai and his remarks thereafter. Actually there is no reference to the Chinese leader in the entire note, though that too would have been quite in order and I would share also with S.M.

Likewise J.P. has never approved the ideological shifts in the camp of Abdullah away from the values to which he is so categorically committed. Nor has he ever come out with such righteous defence of the positions of either Pakistan or Abdullah as is done by Noorani. It is no secret that efforts to set up an Indo-Pak conciliation group in Rawalpindi and Srinagar, on the pattern of the group he heads in Delhi, were disfavoured and sabotaged by the leaders of Pakistan and the Plebiscite Front.

J.P. found a ray of hope in Pakistan, says Noorani, whereas I "deliberately" judge her soleby by the position she took during negotiations. Of course J.P. had an access to the leaders of Pakistan which I do not and I think even Noorani does not have. Still Noorani judges Pakistan by the reasonableness that he supposes to exist in the inner mind of its leaders, while he judges India by the position of its extremist sections. However J.P.'s expectations from Pakistan at that time were matched not only by his expectations from Shastri but also of Sheikh Abdullah from India, who had found an atmosphere of amity in New Delhi, a little before J.P.'s visit to Pakistan. Earlier he had discovered in India the basis of settlement for which he was working.

If I go back further, I would even say that India's response was poor to the hand of friendship that President Ayub had extended at the time of his first seizure of power. Since then, more particularly after the entry of China on the scene, the role started reversing. Last year it was, again, Nehru's initiative and courage that had raised fresh hopes.

To describe what happened then, let me quote S.M.: "The climate for fruitful negotiations of the outstanding disputes between the two countries, including the Kashmir dispute, looked ripe at this time last year. Now it is completely hopeless and many of Pakistan's actions in the intervening period have given little indication that in Rawalpindi there is much faith in the method of negotiated settlements." (*Hindustan Times,* April 14, 1965).

It is really as idle, as Noorani suggests, for me to identify my position with that of S.M. It could only be in the sense that I was a little milder in my criticism of the responsibility of Pakistan and I had not exonerated Indian statesmanship.

If S.M. and J.P. can be subjected to such gross misrepresentation by Noorani, surely I should not expect more mercy at his hands for me. But unfortunately his worst victim is Sheikh Abdullah. In his over anxiety to prove India as the sole villian of the piece, he unfairly and constantly brackets Abdullah with Pakistan.

In my last note I had dwelt at length on the divergence between the positions of the two. It was in that context that I referred to the reactions of the Kashmiri leaders to the possible concessions India might give to Pakistan during Swaran Singh - Bhuttoo talks, which I conveyed to the late Prime Minister Nehru.

I miss the implied satire for whatever is meant in the repetition by Noorani of a part of my statement viz. "What is more significant is that I then personally conveyed." The real significance lies in what I conveyed. That I did it is an evidence which Noorani is at liberty to disbelieve. For he avers; "nothing in Sheikh Saheb's remarks ever since his release would support this statement."

Even in his last statement, before his latest internment, made at Jeddah, the Sheikh had said that "Kashmir question concerned neither India nor Pakistan" and that "Kashmir belonged to its people". He has made it clear time and again that any settlement of Kashmir that does not take into account the aspirations of its people and ensure its entity would not be acceptable to him.

Swaran Singh - Bhutto talks seemed to be proceeding in the direction of dividing the state between the two countries, with third parties mooling proposals regarding a possible line of demarcation somewhere in between the positions of the two parties. Whatever be the degree of concession that India might have eventually agreed would have been at the cost of the entity of Kashmir, which understandably upset the entire leadership of Kashmir.

Noorani pooh-poohs my "homilies on bridge building" when I had thrown my "weighty support against concessions" by India. Firstly, I did agree with Sheikh Abdullah that the aspirations of Kashmir should also be taken into account in any final settlement. Secondly, Pakistan, which is reported to have officially claimed an area of 83,000 square miles of the state out of its total area of 84,000 square miles was hardly likely to be satisfied with what India was willing to cede. In view of this wide gap between the two parties, I did think that the task of bridge building would be better served by a sort of tripartite appraoch to the problem. Indian concessions on two fronts, viz to the aspirations of Kashmir and to the claims of Pakistan, did seem to have a better chance of success. It was precisely this approach in April-May last year for the first time raised hope for a possible settlement.

In any case to suggest that Sheikh Abdullah was for ceding of a larger area to Pakistan than Swarn Singh was authorised to offer is a gross injustice to him. I wonder if Noorani continues to advocate his case, he (Abdullah) would really need all the enemies that he does have in the country.

My position as a co-sufferer and friend of Sheikh Abdullah comes for a comment by Noorani. I do believe that an essential role of a sincere friend is to criticise and I would not like to deprive the Sheikh of my friendly criticism whatever be its worth.

But what has it to do with my loneliness - a recurrent source of amusement by Noorani? The respect and consideration that I get from holders of various view points on Kashmir, including the Sheikh, does not bind them to the acceptance of my advice and need not make me less lonely in my political role. If Noorani thinks complete agreement is the only condition for mutual respect and consideration, I would beg to differ.

Noorani again raises the question of India's volte face to which Kashmir responded. This time he draws a distinction between volte face and change. As I miss the distinction, I am accused of "harping upon Noorani's denial of change in the mind of the leaders of Kashmir". Dictionary defines volte face as sudden and abrupt change. But Noorani "fails to see how anyone could have construed me as suggesting an abrupt Indian decision to treat the issue open which prompted the Kashmiri leadership to take a hand in mooting solutions."

Could not Noorani take a little trouble in defining what he really meant by volte face? When did it take place? In an earlier article Noorani quotes Sheikh Saheb on India's volte face regarding the Constituent Assembly's powers and the coup of 1953.

The Indian volte face, which occurred after 1953, and the coup had followed and not preceeded, and therefore do not justify the appointment of the 8 man committee, the proposals of which did constitute a volte face on the part of the Kashmiri leadership, if the phrase has any meaning at all.

Noorani repeats "Kashmiri leadership did not repudiate their obligations". What were those obligations? There are hundreds of statements made by them at the United Nations, in the constituent assembly and public platforms irrevocably committing themselves to remain a part of the Indian Union. Whatever the rest of India might do, Sheikh Abdullah had once said, Kashmir would cling to it as a child clings to his mother, who may even maltreat him.

Those obligations and commitments were without conditions. Even if they were subject to a plebiscite, as it is made out now (although the Kashmir leaders are on record having insisted finalisation of accession without a plebiscite) consistent and logical stand would require of them to at least declare that they would vote for India in the event of a possible plebiscite.

I have already conceded that new compulsions might have made it difficult for the Kashmiri leaders to honour their obligations and commitments. India, under her own compulsions, has already taken that position. Likewise Pakistan may no longer feel bound by the terms of settlement she was once willing to accept. Nevertheless the case for friendship with Pakistan and satisfaction of Kashmiri aspirations can be strongly made on its own merits.

But by passionately persisting in trying to establish a spotless moral position for Pakistan and Kashmiri nationalists and complete synonymity in their interests and claims, Noorani not only flouts elementary standards of objectivity and logic but hardly contributes to the success of a good case. I am inclined to add that it would be unfair to judge the position of the Kashmiri nationalists by the way it has been advocated by Noorani, who, in my humble position, not only exceeds his brief but does injustice to it.

Finally, mere ridicule and condemnation are not enough to convince me - and perhaps also the readers of this journal that what I say is not correct. Nor do they automatically establish whatever case Noorani intends to defend or expound.

If he finds my position on Kashmir indistinguishable from that of the Hindu chauvinists, should not he tell us what precisely he considers to be a non-chauvinist or liberal Indian position? Would that position satisfy those whose cause he is pleading? Should not they, too, be liberal enough? Or, does he really believe that rulers of Pakistan and secessionist leaders, of Kashmir are already sufficiently liberal; more than the Indian leadership.

Why does not Noorani clear his own ambivalence on Kashmir? Once he refers to plebiscite as "once agreed solution", and takes the critics of plebiscite to task. Then he asks "is plebiscite the issue?"

Is Noorani for a plebiscite in Kashmir? He accuses India of not suggesting an alternative? What alternatives would he suggest either as an Indian - which is his obligations as a responsible citizen of the country - or as a defender of the cause of the other two parties to the dispute? If he considers the modifications suggested by India do not go far enough, how far should they go?

If there is a plebiscite - or any other alternative is agreed upon through his efforts or otherwise - what would be his advice to the people of Kashmir?

What is Noorani's position on the ideological shifts in the leadership of the Plebiscite Front, which is relevant to the controversy that he started with me? Does he also believe religion as the basis of nationality as was implied in the passport applications of Abdullah and Beg? What would he say of the Front paper's attitude to Jinnah, political system of Pakistan, conditions in Azad Kashmir? Does he approve of substitution of socialist slogans of Naya Kashmir and socialist red banner by religions slogans and an Islamic banner? What does he think of Abdullah's conduct abroad?

I avoid temptation to repeat all my criticism of the leaders of Pakistan and the Front. But I regret he criticises me for my criticism without answering it. Attack may be the best defence in a political or any other war. But I repeatedly pray that we should treat it as an exchange of views. Let not, therefore, Noorani attack me on the few points he chooses, convenient to him. But let him also explain his own position as well as get my explanations of the relevant issues involved. I can assure him that I would go on conceding whatever he can convince me about.

(*Janata*, August 29, 1965)

Postscript to the Debate on Kashmir

Balraj Puri

The "drastic pruning" of my last letter in the series of my debate with A.G. Noorani only confirmed my apprehensions with which I had prefaced it. For I was afraid we had already exhausted the limits of indulgence of the readers of the Janata in using its space. In view of that as also of the new context of the situation, the debate might come to a close, at any rate through the medium of this journal. I, however, offer to continue it through, say, correspondence and would request the editor of the Janata to send to Noorani the full text of my letter. My only plea to him would be to carry the further discussion with less passion and heat. I am still willing to be convinced him but not through contempt and ridicule of which he makes so much use.

In postscript to the present phase of the debate, may I say how unhappy I am to be so completely vindicated by the current developments in Kashmir - on the following main points that I had raised:

1. India's efforts at settlement with Pakistan that started in 1962 and culminated in the bold and imaginative measures taken by Mr Nehru in the last few months of his life were responded by Pakistan with growing toughness till, in the world of S.M. (S. Mulgaokar) of the *Hindustan Times*, her

actions gave little indication that "in Rawalpindi there is much faith in the method of negotiated settlement." Has Noorani or anybody else still any doubt that it is Rawalpindi and not New Delhi that believed in negotiations, unless bullets were also considered a medium of negotiations (as armed infiltrators had attacked the state at many places, followed by regulars of Pakistan army).

2. The ideological and political gap between Jayaprakash Narayan and the Plebiscite Front (or the Action Committee) leaders was becoming wider. The latter not only did not condemn the raiders and infiltrators from Pakistan but also felt disillusioned with J.P. for doing so.

I admit that I had made my statements much before Pakistan provided a glaring confirmation of them and a little before the disillusionment of S.M. with Pakistan and of the P.F. leaders with J.P. But is that enough to condemn me? Is it a reflection on the confused politics of the state, level of our debate on the subject or my bad luck that while Noorani finds Hindu chauvinists no worse than me, (*Janata*, July 25), observer brackets me with the "the friends of Kashmir, from Jayapraksh to the debaters in the Janata." (June 13). He could not distinguish my position from that of Noorani while the latter thought it absurd on my part to identity myself with S.M. or J.P. on any point.

(*Janata,* September 1965)

10

Re-Arrest of Abdullah

Letter from Kashmiri Students to JP

Dear Sir,

Ours is an organization of the students and youth of Jammu and Kashmir State. The aim of our organization which came into being in March, 1964 has been to create a feeling of discipline and responsibility among the students and work for the benefit of student community in general. In addition to this, we have been carrying on a peaceful struggle for securing ourselves the basic right- The Right of Self Determination. The whole Kashmiri nation is struggling for the right of self determination under the able leadership of Sher-e-Kashmir Sheikh Mohammad Abdullah. We being a part of our nation, have every right to do the same.

But the government has always taken an aggressive attitude towards us. It has always tried to crush us by all possible means. A large number of our students including the president Mr. Sheikh Ghulam Mohammad, the chief organisor, Mr. Abdul Rashid Kabli and the president of Sopore zone Mr. Abdul Rashid Shaheen are in jail. Others include league members from other units. These students are in continued detention under Defence of India rules for the last four months. Students in colleges and schools are being ruthlessly discriminated. Every institution is full of police and intelligence officers who continuously harass innocent students for nothing. Recently four office bearers of Anantnag unit including the unit president Mr. Bashir Ahmed Wani were arrested and subjected to torture for more than a week. They were ruthlessly beaten up by the police. They were asked to fill in Indian Congress forms and when they refused their tongues were pulled out and they were thrust into cells.

On one hand the Government alleges to follow a policy of liberalisation while on the other hand methods of German Gestapo are being used to crush the students, for simply demanding what is legally, constitutionally, and morally our right.

We are appealing to all right thinking people to take a stock of events and see for themselves what is really happening in OUR KASHMIR.

We demand the immediate and unconditional release of all our students and youth. Failure to do this may have very serious consequences whose responsibility will fully lie on the Govt.

Yours sincerely,
Sd/-
(M. Hussian)
Acting President
Jammu and Kashmir
students and youth league.

Dated Srinagar
13-4-1965.

JP's Letter to JJ Singh on Sino-Pak Collision

April 26, 1965

Dear JJ,

I felt very happy to read your letter in the Times of April 19 about Sheikh Saheb. I am sure you have spoken for all of us and I am glad that you have set the record right as far as we are concerned.

The Indo-Pak border clashes are being unfortunately represented as some kind of undeclared war and the leaders of the government seem to have taken more pleasure in establishing a Sino-Pakistan conspiracy than taking any diplomatic initiative to prevent the Pindi-Peking axis from developing any further. Russian friendship even if stable could hardly upset the danger of the Sino-Pakistan collusion against India. I should have thought that this should be made the corner-stone of long-term Indian diplomacy. But there seems to be little evidence of any such thinking in the South Block.

Yours, as ever
Sd/-
(Jayaprakash Narayan)

Mr. J.J. Singh
101, Friends' Colony,
New Delhi - 14.

(NMM&L File No. 86, PP 54-55)

Plea Against Arrest of Abdullah

New Delhi
May 7, 1965

Dear Mr Prime Minister,

We feel impelled to write to you as a result of ugly rumours that are going round that Sheikh Abdullah might be rearrested immediately on his arrival in this country late tonight.

We would not like to give credence to these reports which seem to us to be so basically contrary to the liberal and reasonable approach that you yourself have shown in matters of this kind. As far as we are aware, Sheikh Abdullah has not offended against the laws of this country nor done anything which should invite detention under the Defence of India Rules. As will be evident from Mr. Nuruddin Ahmed's statement in the press this morning, he has maintained his equilibrium while following his well-known stand in regard to Kashmir and has stood up for this country's treatment to its Muslim and other minorities during the last few days abroad.

In this context, Sheikh Abdullah's rearrest at this point of time appears to be a grave breach of civil liberties and the Fundamental Rights of which we in this country are so proud.

Apart from the question of principle, we feel that Sheikh Abdullah's rearrest at this juncture will be yet another mistake for which this country will have to suffer for many years to come as it will set in train, a chain of events and developments which will not be in the national interest.

May we therefore at least request that Sheikh Abdullah be allowed to land in India, to see you and other spokesmen of Government to explain his activities abroad and to make a statement to the people through the press and that it is only in the light of what he has to say publicly and to you that your government should define its attitude towards his further functioning?

Yours sincerely
Sd/-

Mr. Lal Bahadur Shastri,
Prime Minister,
New Delhi.

M.R. Masani, MP,
Kapur Singh, MP
Buta Singh, MP, J.J. Singh,
Pandit H.N. Kunzru

(NMM&L. File No. 86, P 48)

I
Letters from Mridula Sarabhai to J.P

31, Y Crescent, Rajdoot Marg,
Chanakyapuri, New Delhi-11.
May 26, 1965.

My dear Shri J.P

Since about the 19th of May no special event has been reported from Kashmir. The authorities have arrested some students of the Engineering College and are likely to try them for the destruction of Government property.

Youngmen's league is an organization which was started in Bakshi's time leadership of which consisted of some extremist boys of Government officers and B.B.C. (Bakshi Brothers Company) families. They have had no regard for Sheikh Saheb, Maulana Saheb or anyone else. Politicaly they are immature and call themselves extremist. Most of the arrested students belong to this organization. Most probably most of the student leaders in this case are going to be challaned.

During this upheaval some cases of molestation of women by police personnel have been reported. I am getting particulars from Srinagar and hope to write to you again.

Maulana Saheb wanted two or three women workers of Sarva Seva Sangh for a fact-finding mission in this matter. I have talked to Pooran Chandraji about this. Molestation of women by police has to be condemned with all the vigour that one has, specially when this happens as a part of law and order operation. It is not the question as to what is the number of such cases but the question is that even if one woman is molested or kidnapped, it is serious enough and must not be allowed to go unheeded. Otherwise all us would be unsafe if we are not going to raise a voice against this.

May I, therefore, request you to kindly convey this to Prabhavatiji also and help me to get some strong women workers of the Sarva Seva Sangh to go and find out truth after we receive some data about the cases?

A number of persons have started enquiring from Sadiq Saheb about police atrocities. Hereunder a sample of his stock reply:

" I am sorry to observe that responsible persons in our country should volunteer opinions without ascertaining the actual facts of the situation in Kashmir. The conditions in the Valley are completely normal and you can come and see things for yourself. The impression you have formed that there is some kind of a " reign of terror" here is totally unfounded and biased, perhaps, on interested propaganda stuff circulated by interested agencies. It is a fact that following the restrictions on the movement of Sheikh Abdullah some incidents were worked up by pro-Pakistani elements but the large mass of people has kept completely away from these. To deal with violent incidents and subversive activities law and order authorities in Kashmir took action and I do not think it is your intention to suggest that law and order should be given a holiday and pro-Pakistani elements allowed to hold people to ransom."

Herewith a copy of the *Hindustan Times* newsitem published on 25th may regarding Action Committee's proposed next step. I am awaiting details from Maulana Saheb. He has shifted from nursing home. Instead of going home, he went to the spot to control the situation and organize the movement, Maulana Saheb might like to contact you. So, will you please let me know your programme?

I had a meeting with the Home Secretary, Shri L.P. Singh.

Shri Balraj Puri returned from Srinagar two days ago.

With best wishes,

Yours sincerely,
Sd/-
Mridula
Sarabhai

Shri J.P.Narayan.

II

Alleged Cases of Molestation of Women by Police in Kashmir Valley

Confidential

31, Y Crescent, Rajdoot Marg,
Chanakyapuri, New Delhi - 11
June 7, 1965

In the recent post-Sheikh Abdullah internment demonstrations in the Kashmir Valley complaints have been received of molestation of women by police. The authorities have vehemently denied it; with same vehemence leaders repudiate the authorities. So, I sought Maulana Masoodi Saheb's help. His findings are that:

"Molestation of women has been reported at many places in the affected areas of the Kashmir valley and specially in the villages of Bomay, Dangerpora and Hajan.

"Even in Srinagar at some places molestation have been reported such as the following incident:

the sister and wife of Ghulam Mohiuddin Wani s/o Mohammad Sultan Wani r/o Babapora, Habbakadal, were molested and injured by the police. The report of this has already been given in the bulletin. In Kachgari Mohalla, Fatehkadal, police entered the house of Ghulam Hassan Khan S/o Noor Khan and molested his wife."

The police molested a nurse in the hospital, abused her and insulted her. Dr. Abdul Qayyum who was coming to the hospital protested. He was abused. This led to stoppage of work in hospital. The police in retaliation beat Habibullah Khan of Chhatabal, a student of Medical College. This led to students' boycott. The result was that all staff of the hospital and college suspended work. Mr. S.R.Kaul, Principal of the college called reinforcement of police and instead of protecting the students infuriated them further.

Sumbal: The Tehsildar, accompanied by 20 armed policemen, entered the village of Grattabal, Safapora, and frightened the people by opening fire in the air. Police entered various houses and molested women. The houses of Ghulam Mohammad Hakim, Abdul Ahad Butt, Mohammad Siddiq Butt and Subhan Wani were looted. In the day the people had taken out a procession protesting against the internment of Sheikh Saheb and some people had been arrested. The action of Tehsildar and police against the village during the night is both vindictive and barbarous.

The incident which had led to flare up in Hajan and details of which were suppressed for three days is that two Punjab Armed policemen entered a house and tried to outrage the modesty of a women who cried. Thereupon a person came there who overpowered the assailant. Another policemen who came standing outside fired at this man twice and killed him on spot. In the confusion which ensued, the women ran away and the villagers assembled and took out a procession. The procession was fired at resulting in the death of four more, causing injuries to a number of people. Total number of arrests is reported to be about 89. it is believed that a number of dead bodies were brought by the police from Hajin side and buried in the police lines, Srinagar.

In mohalla Killa in Bhaderwah the entire women-folk was asked to come out of the houses at midnight and maltreated by the police. Many of them were dragged and beaten.

In the villages of Bomay, Sopore the males had fled away. The police entered the houses of the people and harassed the women and insulted them.

So is the case of Hajan where the males out of fright had run away and the police entered many houses and molested the women.

Maulana Mohammad Saeed Masoodi Saheb suggests that let some independent persons, preferably women, visit these places and families and check up the truth.

Sd/-
Mridula Sarabhai

III
Fact-finding Party for Kashmir

31,Y Crescent, Rajdoot Marg,
Chanakyapuri, New Delhi - 11.
June 10, 1965

Generally the Kashmiris are terribly sensitive about talking about their women-folk and specially when anyone is molested, raped or harassed. They go to their own leaders and report but before others they remain silent unless somebody takes an initiative and asks about it. They have lost confidence and hence they do not include this in the list of complaints. They consider it humiliating and painful. Perhaps this is the reason why this matter was not brought to the notice of Pooran Chandraji and Trikhaji who were at Hajan only for two-three hours. Some incidents are reported to have taken place after their visit but I am not sure.

I am grateful to Shri J.P. for accepting the principle of sending a party for fact-finding in this case. I contacted Shri Ashadeviji on phone. She is lying ill and doctors have advised her not to undertake any journey or undergo any strain for sometime. I also talked to Shri Nirmalabehn at Lahore. First she was doubtful as to whether she would be able to go in view of the fact that the new term of the Shanti Sena Vidyalaya was starting from 14th June. I told her that she could go after a week after seeing the work settled down. I pressed her that she should go as there was no one else who could go. She said she would consult her colleagues and write to me. As soon as I receive her letter, I will send a wire.

If Shri Raghukul Tilakji is sent with Nirmalabehn, it would make a good team. At present he is in Mussoorie. His address is given at the end of this note.

Today I received a telephone from Shri Oak, Joint Secretary, Home Ministry, who is working as secretary to Nandaji, saying that Nandaji had enquired from Shri D.P. Dhar regarding complaint about molestation of women. Shri Dhar had flatly repudiated the story and said that it is false. In view of that Nandaji felt that this should be accepted. I appealed to Shri Oak to convey to Nandaji that in my letter to him I had stated that the state government were vehemently repudiating the allegation of molestation of women by police and that is why we had a right to appeal to him to intervene and allow fact-finding to be done. It was not in the spirit to ciriticse the Police but it is in the interest of all that this story should be investigated and if found wrong then repudiated but if found correct then appropriate steps should be taken to stop it. Shri Oak has promised to convey this to Nandaji.

As to MPs' visit, the hitch is that they belong to the Congress and whether they will be able to go or not is doubtful. They will have to consult their party leaders and at present Nandaji is the party leader and if his attitude is that no investigation is necessary, I wonder if he would like them to go for this purpose. So, it is the Sarva Seva Sangh which is the only organisation which can look into such difficult questions and get fair-deal and justice to the women.

If Nirmalabehn and Raghukulji go, then their estimated expenditure is enclosed herewith. They may be able to go by 22nd or 25th June, the latest. In case Nirmalabehn just can't go, then Ashadeviji has promised to suggest an alternate name but I doubt if there is anyone available with the necessary experience in this matter. Therefore, I appeal for sending Nirmalabehn and for considering this as urgent as one would if a riot had broken out and one was rushing Shanti Sainiks to the scene.

Situation in Bhaderwah and Doda districts is causing concern. It is an inflammatory atmosphere which can turn into communal disturbance at any time. Therefore, I had telephoned to Shri Balbhai and conveyed a message to Vinobaji to kindly release Achyutbhai for a month or two for working in Kashmir but whether this matrialises or not, I would request for sending Fatmi Saheb and Satyambhai to this area. Shri Om Prakash Saraf who has great influence will accompany them. This should be done without delay.

Sd/-

(Mridula Sarabhai)

(NMM&L. File No. 89, PP 1-2)

Estimated Expenses of Party of two who go to Investigate into Allegations about Molestation of Women in Affected Areas of Kashmir

Arrangements for Maulana Masoodi Saheb and others to play host to this party can be made but perhaps in interest of the mission it may be desirable that party makes its own arrangements. Regarding transport it will be supported by those who lend it, so no special cost is likely. If however, it is desired that the party should make its own arrangements then the possible cost is shown. If the party stays in Gandhi Ashram Karan Nagar - I do not know what charges have to be paid. Perhaps it will be possible to ask Gandhi Ashram to play host.

Railway fare has been estimated at the first class rate, third class charges are shown separately.

Estimated budget for sending party of two to Srinagar for investigation as per note.

For Smt. Nirmalaben	*For Shri Tilakji*	
Air Fare, Delhi-Srinagar-Delhi	Rs. 285.00	Rs. 285.00 (Return Fare)
Railway fare,	Rs. 129.80	Indore-Delhi-Indore (Ist Class)
Stay in Srinagar, independent arrangement for eight days	Rs. 200.00	Rs. 200
Transport common for one or two or three makes	Rs. 300	
no difference	Rs. 914.80	Rs. 485.00

JP's Letter to Shastri*

11 June 1965

My dear Lal Bahadurji,

You know how great a faith I have in personal contacts. The Commonwealth Conference will bring you and President Ayub together. This appears to me as a heaven sent opportunity, and I am writing to request you as earnestly as I can, to make the best use of it.

I would not have presumed to offer this advice, had it not been for newspaper reports emanating apparently from official sources that you would not agree to talk to the Pakistan President about Indo-Pak problems unless they had agreed first to the restoration of the status quo in Kutch as of January 1965. That is presented here as a posture of firmness. To my mind such a posture would do grave injustice to you, apart from unnecessarily prolonging a state of affairs that does inculcate harm to this country. Therefore, my humble and prayerful plea is that you yourself take the initiative to invite the President to a quiet lunch or dinner and pick up the threads of personal exploration and understanding that somehow were allowed to be suffered soon after your Karachi meeting.

Another matter. By separate urgent cover I am sending you a note on the Kutch dispute. That has been prepared at my request by a friend and relation of mine, Dr. Bimla Prasad, Reader, Indian School of International Studies. I hope you will have time to glance through this revealing document. Many things contained in it, you are no doubt aquainted with but I am sure it also brings out facts that might not have come to your notice - at least, no awareness of these facts could be discussed in the Parliament debates on the subject.

It is so pleasing to find you in such fine health despite the heavy strain on it.

With affectionate regards,

Yours sincerely

Sd/-

(Jayaprakash)

(NMM&L. File No. 86. pp 35-37)

P.S. : I am also writing to President Ayub Khan

* Hand written

Letter to Pakistan President

New Delhi
11 June, 1965

Dear Mr President,

During the recent critical months, I often wished to write to your Excellency, but desisted because I was not sure if that would have helped or harmed. But on this occasion I have no such doubts.

I consider it to be God's design that you and Sh. Lal Bahadur Shastri would be brought together at this time. I am a great believer, as you know, in personal contacts. The first such contact between the two of you at Karachi had remarkably succeeded in establishing a bond of mutual regard. Unfortunately, that bond has been dissipated in recent months. In a natural manner, the Commonwealth Conference has offered an excellent opportunity for repairing and strengthening that bond. I feel confident that once that had been achieved, it would be easy for your Excellency and the Prime Minister and your advisors to find a way out of the present rather petty squabble.

With deep personal regards and all good wishes for your Excellency's health,

Yours sincerely

Sd/-
(Jayaprakash Narayanan)

Field Marshal Mohd Ayub Khan
President of Pakistan,
Karachi.

(NMM&L. File No. 86, pp. 35-37)

Mridula's Letter to JP

31, Y Crescent, Rajdoot Marg,
Chanakyapuri, New Delhi-11
June 25, 1965

My dear Shri J.P.

Last night I received a wire from Vimalaji enquiring about her Kashmir programme. Earlier in the evening I had received a letter from Pooran Chandraji dated 23rd June written from Bombay. In this besides other things, he said:

जे पी के जाने के बाद श्री मनमोहन, नारायण, कर्ण भाई आदि कुछ साथी जो यहां थे उन सब से बात हुई। ये साथी इस राय के हैं कि सर्व सेवा संघ की ओर से जांच वगैरह के कार्य को हाथ में नही लेना चाहिए। वहां कार्य का (शांति सेना आदि का) आधार बन सके ऐसा कुछ कार्य कम ही उठाना चाहिए, उसके बगैर कुछ हो ही नहीं सकेगा, इत्यादि। कर्ण भाई आदि हम दो तीन व्यक्ति जुलाई में किसी समय कशमीर जावें: ये भी सोचा है। जयपुर २५ से २६ की शाम को पहुंचुगा तब तक एक पत्र और आप को दूगा वर्ना जयपुर से टैलीफून करूंगा।

(After JP left, some talk was held with M/s Manmohan, Narayan, Karan Bhai and others who were here. In their opinion, Sarva Seva Sangh should not take up the matter of inquiry. If basis could be laid for Shanti Sena, some activity could be undertaken but nothing beyond that. Karan Bhai and others two or three persons would visit Kashmir some time in July. I will reach Jaipur on the evening of 25 or 26. I'll send another letter or telephone you.)

I urge that the original proposal of sending trusted women workers to enquire into incidents in Kashmir should not be given up but if Sarva Seva Sangh is not prepared to do it, it is no use pressing them to do so because it will only mean half-hearted approach to the problem as we found in the other case.

I, therefore, plead that Vimalaji and Smt. Kulsum Sauani be deputed for an enquiry by you. We have already approached you with these cases and it is but fair that you get these enquired into before coming to any conslusion.

I hope this will meet with your approval or something else could be decided upon.

With best wishes,
Yours sincerely,
Sd/-
(Mridula Sarabhai)

Shri J.P. Narayan,
C/o Mahila Charkha Sangh,
Kadam Kuan,
Patna.

Mridula's letter to JP

31, Y Crescent, Rajdoot Marg,
Chanakyapuri, New Delhi-11
July 19, 1965.

My dear Shri Jayaprakash Ji,

I do not know where and when this letter will reach you. So, this is only to keep you informed as to what has happened in these days.

On 15th July I learnt that Beg Saheb's health was causing concern to the authorities and that it had deteriorated. So, on 16th I went to Ooty, reaching there on the 17th. The authorities were good enough to allow me to meet Beg Saheb in the presence of an officer. So, I was with him for a few hours.

I found his health deteriorated and causing deep concern to his brother and his son, who is a doctor. We decided that his brother and I should return to Delhi immediately and bring all this to the notice of Lal Bahadurji and others. So, we returned last night and started making representations to all concerned this morning.

Newspapers say that Beg Saheb might be transferred to Srinagar but simultaneously there is a news that he was O.K and they have transferred him back from the hospital to the place of internment. It is very difficult to know what really is brewing except that even though publicly whatever the authorities might be saying, they are concerned about him but perhaps they are not conscious of the seriousness of the situation and how much time factor counts.

A word from you to Lal Bahadurji will be very helpful. If you consider it desirable, kindly do the needful.*

Vimalabehn and Kulsumbehn are expected here today. If they get plane reservations, they will come. Vimalabehn will stay with Shri J.J Singh and Kulsumbehn with one of her friends-Dr. Sen.

With best wishes to you and Prabhavatiji,

Yours sincerely,

Shri Jayaprakash Narayan, Sd/-
Patna. (Mridula Sarabhai)

(NMM&L. File No.89)

*PS: * This is now not necessary. Home Ministry's Secretary informed me that the authorities are considering Beg Sahib's* *request and our representation and by 20th, i.e. tomorrow, some action will be taken. They realize the urgency to transfer him so that he can have treatment from doctors of his choice.*

11

After Infiltration from Pakistan and War

Massive Infiltrations in Kashmir

(The following statement was released by JP on 5 August 1965.)

I have watched with dismay the violent course of recent Pakistan policies towards India culminating in massive infiltrations into Kashmir across the cease-fire line in an effort to spread subversion and sabotage.

The plea that Pakistan has nothing to do with these activities and that they are the concern solely of "Azad Kashmiris" is unworthy of any government which wants its bona fides accepted by the world.

It is the plain duty of the Government of India under these conditions to eliminate this threat from Pakistan by all means at its command, and I fully support the measures that have been taken to this end.

It is a matter of deep regret to me that the promise contained in the Kutch agreement of a new beginning in the settlement of Indo-Pakistan disputes by the method of peaceful negotiation has been wantonly cast aside by Pakistan's adventurist action in Kashmir, and I recognize that the cause of friendly relations between the two countries has received a major setback.

At the same time I am convinced- no matter how realistic it may appear now-that if India and Pakistan are to avoid self-destruction they must return to the path of conciliation. The interests of both countries demand a relationship based on trust and good neighbourliness.

This relationship can only emerge from a mutual readiness to settle all outstanding differences in a spirit of justice, cooperation and mutual accommodation. This objective cannot be achieved without a reciprocal effort from Pakistan, and I venture to appeal to all men of goodwill in that country to help in this endeavour by urging restraint on their government.

In conclusion I do earnestly hope that the Kutch agreement which for the first time in the tragic history of Indo-Pak relations has opened the way to an equitable and honourable settlement of a dispute, will not be repudiated by either party, for in that case both would either drift willy nilly into a disastrous war or their festering sores would eventually lead to their national debilitation and decay. It is clear that the beneficiary of either of these eventualities can only be China.

(*Nation Building in India: Jayaprakash Narayan* Edited by Brahmanand, P 265)

Mridula's Letter to JP

81/48, Diplomatic Enclave,
Kautilya Marg,
New Delhi
Camp : Srinagar
16 August 1965

My dear Shri JP,

I thought I would be able to go to Delhi today to consult you but Maulana Sahib feels I should not do so for various reasons. Firstly I have started contacts with authorities, Dr. Karansingh and some officers for breaking the ice between them and the people's representatives. In a day or two the results will be known. A grave situation has arisen since two days. There are controversial versions about the causes of Batmallu fire. It is Sadiq Sahib and Karra's area. People say that some in authorities are responsible for it. The authorities have also not taken effective steps to ease the emotions of the people. So a conflict between them may arise if not averted. Unfortunately the popular impression of the functions of the authorities is so adverse that if nothing is done immediately to put things right, situation may worsen by people's desperation. We all know the techniques of "war fare" of the present Govt of India. Hyderabad and Goa are a good indication of it. Glimpses of that have taken place here and may flare up unless some one takes action. I therefore sought Dr. Karansingh's intervention and am going to pass on to him some popular suggestions. There is lack of tact in ruling party camp and such protection fobia that no one who counts is available to deal with people's problems. Sadiq Sahib has lost all ground because of the policies of his security getting first priority. Perhaps this is not to his liking but it is official policy and underneath 'leadership' race is going on amongst them.

The way matter has been handled until now has unfortunately created a feeling in some sections that genocide of Muslims is also at work under the cover. The Bihar police is reported to be cruelly behaving.

Regarding molestation of women report of Kunti ji and Kulsum behn, I hope you will please do needful with Lal Bahadur ji and others and got a definite policy taken against it. I had talked to Smt. Raksha Saran and some others. They are also prepared to take the line as advised by you. If you find it advisable to call her and ask her to talk to Kusum and Mrs Laxmi Menon to mobilise women workers. She will do the needful. Ashadevi ji will also be staying in Delhi for some time. So she can do the needful on your behalf. Even now such things are happening like rough handling of women. On 10th & 11th night in panicky shooting by the concerned authorities in Srinagar, some women were wounded. They were shot at while they were standing at their windows. Vimla ji has created extremely good impression. Can she change her programme and come here to work? Anapurna ji will also be very useful. We want the women's movement to be started through your lead. Maulana Sahib and I await suggestions as to what you would desire us to do here.

All send their best wishes to you, JJ and Malati ji.

Any direction and a letter for me or Maulana, which can be given to Shaffi Sahib and he will arrange to send them to me. Today and yesterday's letter to you are also meant for Shri J.J. If Mulgaokarji and JJ do this needful with their friends in authorities, much can be avoided.

Yours sincerely

Sd/-

(Mridula Sarabhai)

(NMM&L. File No. 89, PP 1-2)

Mridula's Letter to JP

Camp: Srinagar
24 August 1965

My dear Shriyut J.P.

Hope this finds you Ok. Shri Nath Pai ji and Roopnarayan's visit has been helpful. I think they have got the gist of the problems that face Maulana Sahib, Karrasahib, (the Sheikhities) and to some extent me also. I have already given you, (in my letters) the gist of the problem that face us. Even Maulana Sahib has done the same in his letter to you. Nath Pai Ji tried to change the attitude of the law and order agencies towards local population. This process has to continue. We can't do much here, you all have to do it from Delhi. Read your statement of the 19th August. While I am generally in agreement with it, I think your saying that

"It is the duty of the govt of India under these conditions to eliminate this threat from Pakistan by all means at their command and I fully support the measures that have been taken to this end", gives opportunity for misrepresenting and distorting your stand. It has been misunderstood here. Those who know that I have been keeping you informed of the developments and Maulana Sahib also had written to you asking your help and good offices feel aggrieved at this catagorical support. Why this? Becausc under the cover of operation against the infiltration, the following is also going on:-

1. Ruthless repression on the people for their sulleness and effort to show that their will be kept under force even or through annihitation if need be.
2. Communal approach.
3. Declaring that the attack is on sovereignty of the country and the operations are must to protect it, means that the authorities are denouncing that there is any thing like Kashmir problem. They want this to be handled now militarily and get a military decision. That is why one also hears of preparedness to cross the cease-fire line to recapture Azad Kashmir etc.

I am sure in your support you won't be ready to support all this. Hence I plead for clarification of this and another statement to the Kashmiris at this junctive would be helpful. Today all political parties (in the country) stand is that Kashmir's accession is complete and by recapturing Azad Kashmir area, this problem will come to and end for ever. It is possible to mobilise again popular will to resist outside onslaught on grounds that when normalcy comes all will work for negotiated settlement. But if this is not coming forth and Kashmir's fate has to be decided by military might, then they feel like being entrapped in two fires - from India and Pak side and this frustrates them and this makes them inactive. In this statement an appeal to the rest of the country to respond to Kashmiri people's secular outlook better be included. However while I write this, Roop Narayanji has gone to Maulana Sahib for getting briefing for conveying to you. So this should be taken in context of what Maulana Sahib tells him.

The war mongers may compel the authorities to take desperate step. I plead for mobilizing strength to support those in authorities who are resisting this approach. We should try hard to get the present situation isolated. Otherwise all will be destroyed without the problem being solved.

Sd/-

(Mridula Sarabhai)

(NMM&L File No. 89, PP 1-2)

Pakistan Forefieted Right on Kashmir After Aggression: JP

(Press statement of JP released on 17 September, 1965, Patna)

I had not thought it necessary to add anything to my initial statement expressing my full support of the government's action in dealing with Pakistan's aggression in Jammu and Kashmir. In this period the country has been most ably led with clarity and firmness, and our armed forces have been fighting valiantly under brilliant leadership, all discontents and agitations have been voluntarily muted, all political parties have forgotten their differences and rallied behind the Prime Minister, the people have been calm, unafraid, united and determined to do their best. There was nothing that needed to be said by a private citizen like me.

But now a moment has come when I feel I must speak out, not to my country and my people but to the people and Government of Pakistan and to the peoples and governments of the world.

I speak as one who believes in peace and conciliation and abhors war. Even outside this subcontinent something is known about my efforts and the efforts of my colleagues in the India-Pakistan conciliation group to bring the two countries nearer in friendship and cooperation to the mutual benefit of both and the benefit of the whole of Southeast Asia. It is known that we persisted in our efforts even at the cost of considerable misunderstanding in our country. I therefore hope my words will not be brushed aside as partisan propaganda.

The conditions set by Pakistan for a cease-fire and withdrawal of forces imply that Pakistan considers it within its right to wage war against India if India does not agree to a plebiscite in Kashmir. This indeed is an extraordinary claim and needs to be looked at closely.

The world takes it for granted that Pakistan has a right to interfere in Kashmir because it is a party to the dispute. This is not so. At any rate it is not so any longer.

Kashmir's Accession

It is necessary to recall that originally neither India nor Pakistan had any right in Kashmir, though both had their undoubted interest in future of the state. But according to law, the future of the state was in the hands of Maharaja Hari Singh and his people. Pakistan however lost its patience and attacked the defenseless state with no other intent than to attach the territory. The Maharaja, with the full support of Sheikh Abdullah and the people of Kashmir, acceded to the Indian Union.

Since that day India became a party to the issue in Kashmir. Pakistan had nothing to do with Kashmir in terms of the settlement between the British Government, the Indian National Congress and the Muslim League. In fact it was India itself which made it a party in the naive hope that the Security Council would name the aggressor and discipline it. But let it be clear that even then the only sense in which Pakistan was made a party was in the capacity of an aggressor, with no other responsibility or hand in the matter than to vacate the aggression.

Not only was the original aggression not vacated for one reason or another but Pakistan has now committed another and still more massive aggression in Kashmir, again with the same intent as before, namely to occupy the state by force. By this deliberate and blatant action Pakistan has forfeited whatever place it had obtained in the Kashmir issue.

Pakistan has feigned deep concern for the wishes of the people of Kashmir. Was its aggression in 1947 and the present one in accordance with the wishes of the people? Does anybody believe that if the Pakistanis had succeeded in annexing the state they would have invited the UN, withdrawn their forces and asked the Secretary-General to ascertain the wishes of the people? It is not known whether they have held a plebiscite in what they call Azad Kashmir. It is clear then that the plebiscite plea is only a smokescreen behind which Pakistan has been making tireless plans to annex the state of Jammu and Kashmir.

Therefore Pakistan and the world should understand now that recent events have established the truth that if there is any issue now in Kashmir, it is between the people of Kashmir and the Government of India. Further, there should be no doubt that the present leaders of India would settle the issue to the satisfaction of the people of Jammu and Kashmir. India is a democracy, and if only Pakistan were to keep its hands off nothing but the wishes of the people would prevail in Kashmir as in the rest of India.

Finally, let me say that I shall continue to believe in India-Pakistan conciliation because both countries must live as friends. But if Pakistan wants war with India because it is denied a hand in the Kashmir issue conciliation must wait until better sense prevails.

(*Nation Building in India: Jayaprakash Narayan* Edited by Brahmanand, P 270, following is an abridged version of it published in the form of a statement circulated by the UNI on 18 September, 1965)

Pakistan's Aggression

(Translated from original draft in Hindi signed by JP)

Patna, 17 September 1965

One possibility that comes to my mind is that Sheikh Sahib should declare that he could not say any thing about the past infiltration (of armed persons from Pakistan in August 1965) as he was in jail which facilitated the infiltration. But if the Government of India comes to an agreement with him (on the basis of full autonomy or something else acceptable to both the parties), he would resist any attempt to create mischief by Pakistan, with full power. But on this question Sheikh Sahib has not opened up. It is for him to take the decision. In this connection he will have to keep in mind the fact that what was possible before 5 August 1965, is now impossible. Any solution which leads to deaccession of Kashmir is not possible now. Perhaps autonomy within India is still possible; though I doubt if it would be possible before next elections. But the matter can be mooted with the Prime Minister.

The above mentioned solution can be possible if Sheikh Sahib is willing to oppose the infiltration and tell Pakistan plainly that by sending infiltrators to Kashmir it has invaded Kashmir and advise it to withdraw them without delay.

If Sheikh Sahib is willing to adopt this type of attitude, his release should be possible.

Lal Bahadur ji takes measured steps and rarely shares with any body what is in his mind. Therefore there should be somebody of his personal confidence who should mediate between him and the Sheikh Sahib.

If a firm basis is established between the go-between and Sheikh Sahib, it can be settled what should be their public statement.

(NMM&L. File No. 88, pp5-7) Sd/-

(Jayaprakash Narayanan)

British Socialists and Kashmir

Jayapraksh Narayan

Vicky has drawn a poignant cartoon in working Gandhi to shame India. He has every right to do so. But does that help? If you throw Gandhi on our face and we invoke Christ against the Christian nations will it lead anywhere? Was it not an English poet laureate who spoke poignantly of the progress made 2000 years of Marx? Had Thomas Hardy lived he would no doubt have talked of even more horrible things than poison gas. If Asia, or India, keeps taunting the Christians about loving their enemy, would that stop America or Britain or France from manufacturing ghastly bombs and God knows what other unspeakable horrors?

My answer to Vicky, not by way rhetoric at all, is that strange as it may sound Mr Shastri is much more conscious of Gandhi than Wilson or Johnson or de Gaulle of Jesus Christ. Many Westerners, who never liked Gandhi anyway or understood him, have persuaded themselves that Gandhi is dead and buried in India. They are utterly mistaken. Gandhi still lives within us. But the path he treads is a difficult one, and it will take much time for us, or for that matter any nation, to follow it with success. The question involved is not of individuals following Gandhi, but of the government. Reinhold Niebuhr has shown how man can be moral, but how difficult it is — he would say it is impossible — for society to be moral.

If British socialists are content to limit their horizons to their national interests, as they seem to be doing, I have nothing to say. It is possible that they find it more profitable to have Pakistan on their side than India. After all Pakistan is an ally in CENTO and SEATO, and the rulers of Pakistan were ranged against the Indian freedom movement and were on the side of the British.

Mischief of 1947

But should British socialists want to apply their socialist principles to their international dealing they might as well begin to think in terms of undoing the mischief of 1947.

The partition of India solved no question at all as the sad history of Indo- Pak relations testifies. Nationality or nationhood has nothing to do with religion, and socialism is the first to affirm that. At the time of partition the Congress Socialist Party as might be recalled was dead opposed to partition and would have opposed it in AICC had not Gandhiji advised us not to "divide the house." Gandhi himself utterly opposed it, but he was reluctant to disown those whom he had raised to the position of national leaders. He might have done that, as he said, if he had been ten years younger. Partition was based on the pernicious principle of religion determining nationality. It was a pity that was done under a socialist government. Mr Atlee might have however found the pressure of the reactionary British administration in

India too powerful to resist. But since that fateful event of partition it should have been the job of the British socialists not to feed religious fires but attempt to bring sanity to the subcontinent and bring the divided parts nearer. But they have done just the opposite.

Pakistan's Claims

Pakistan is considered to have a claim to the valley of Kashmir solely because it is overwhelmingly Muslim. The British Government, with the powerful support of Mr Jinnah, laid down the law that the Indian princes, were free to choose their future after the lapse of British paramountcy. The Indian Congress resisted that view and insisted that the voice of the people of the Indian states rather than the princes should prevail.

Socialism should have come to the support of that democratic principle. But the government stood by the letter of the law, and even though the princes were mere puppets in the hands of the Viceroy and had no real power they were given the role power to determine the future without any reference to their subjects. Mr Jinnah stood wholeheartedly for the rights of the princes, not because he was in love with them but because he had hopes that by intriguing with them (indeed the intrigues were already on) he could further dismember India, or the "rest of India" as the phrase ran at that time.

The British socialists, against all the principles of democracy and socialism, were a party to that conspiracy to essay the dismemberment of India, and thus keep the divided country at their mercy. The colossus of the North had not risen above the horizon yet, though it could not have taken much thought for a well informed government to realize that the position of Generalissimo Chiang kai shek was becoming more and more untenable. To have deliberately effected not only the great partition of the subcontinent but also sown the seeds of numerous other little partitions in the hope of exploiting the divisions for British nationalist interests was, to say the least, not being very faithful to socialism.

Kashmir

The remarkable thing however is that after vesting the princes with unlimited power, except for limitations regarding contiguity and viability, the British socialists, or rather the British Labour Party-except such rare individuals as Nye Bevan who said when he visited India that it had a cast-iron case on Kashmir-from the very beginning started to undo the decision taken by the Maharaja of Kashmir. (It is well known that the Maharaja wanted to opt for independence and was sending feelers to both sides.) So illogical was the position of the British Labour Government that when in 1947 Pakistan lost patience and invaded Kashmir-India was nowhere in the picture yet- that government refused to call it aggression and condemn Pakistan for it.

The Maharaja of Kashmir then decided to accede to India and seek military aid. The accession was accepted and military aid rushed. Mahatma Gandhi was alive and he gave approval to that act of succour. The British Government however turned a blind eye to the accession and picked upon Mr Nehru's high-minded pledge that when the aggressor withdrew and normalcy returned the wishes of the people of Kashmir would be ascertained. Mr Nehru was not bound under the terms of the Independence of India Act passed by the British parliament to give any such assurance, and indeed it has no status in international law. But since then the British Labour Party, along with the Conservatives, have been harping on the promised referendum, which was not required by law, and ignoring the decision of the Maharaja, which has full validity in law. The only reason that they have been doing so is that their thinking is based on communal philosophy rather than on socialist philosophy.

I am not saying that the Kashmiris should be denied the right to decide their future. Indeed I am still trying to tell my government and my people that the issue in Kashmir has to be settled between the leaders and the people of Kashmir and India. But on what ground could Pakistan demand that it be allowed to take a hand in the settlement apart from the fact that it is a Muslim nation? What right has Pakistan not only to press the issue peacefully but also to wage war against India? And how can a socialist government support all that as Mr Wilson appears to be doing? By encouraging political aspirations based on religion the British socialists are sowing the seeds of disaster, and its fruits will be gathered neither by British nor by Pakistan but by China.

Need for Confederation

If British socialists therefore wish to play a constructive role in this part of the world they should set their sights on the far distance and work out the steps leading to the goal. For the stability of this area, for its growth and development, for restoring geopolitical balances in this part of the world, and for democracy and socialism there is no alternative to the willing partnership of the independent, sovereign states of the Indian subcontinent whether you call the partnership a confederation, association, union community, concord or whatever you wish. Will the socialists of Britain have the courage and the wisdom, will they be faithful enough to socialism, to see this and desist from seeking petty advantage through petty intrigue? They will find the Indian socialists more than willing to cooperate. Let them remember that anything that divides the peoples of the world is reactionary, anything that brings them closer is progressive. That is the human task of this atomic age.

(Unpublished and undated, printed in *National Building in India: Jayaprakash Narayan,* Edited by Brahmanand P 275)

Letter from Mridula

(Strictly personal)

Rajdoot Marg,
New Delhi
20 October 1965
My dear J.P.

Naga problem over shadows every thing just now yet if you can spare time for Kashmir. I shall be grateful. If you can do so before you meet Lal Bahadur Ji, I shall be obliged. Pooranchanderji is also here I met him.I told him that from J.J. I learnt that you are very busy. So would it not be proper that we two meet you together? He said he will ask you and let me know.

With best wishes and hoping success in Naga problem.

Sd/-
(Mridula)

No power can transfer Kashmir to Pakistan : JP

MYSORE, Nov 29 (PTI)—Mr J.P. Narayan said here today he could not conceive of "any power on earth being able to transfer Kashmir from India to Pakistan, nor can I see how Pakistan can ever take the valley by force from India."

The Sarvodaya leader, who was delivering the convocation address of the Mysore University, said in the face of Pakistan's aggression, surreptitious at first through armed infiltration, and then open and massive across the international border in Chhamb, the government had no alternative but to take action for the defence of the country.

"No other stand could have been right where Pakistan was demonstrably determined to take by force what it could not have by diplomacy — particularly when it has no legal or moral right to what it wants to grab," Mr Narayan added.

Pakistan by its repeated acts of aggression, had forfeited the right to have any say in regard to Kashmir's future.

He said Kashmir could not exist as an independent state, because Pakistan would not allow it to survive. It would be foolish for any Kashmiri leader to nurse any hope on those lines. No solution had any chance of succeeding which involved de-accession of the state from India.

"Kashmiri and Indian leaders could find a just solution to the problem", if both sides are conscious of the limits set for them by circumstances," he added.

The Sarvodaya leader, looking at the problem of peace as it faced India, referred to India's policy of non-alignment and said though it was conceived as a means by which India could exercise independence in international affairs and also as an instrument of peace, "the way in which it was applied to concrete issues, it turned out to be a shield for a policy of weakness that rather encouraged aggression."

Mr Narayan said Mr Nehru's moral authority and that of India as a country, looked upon to give a lead to the reconstruction of a world without war, stood very high at the United Nations and among the Governments of the world. This was an asset "worth many divisions of armed forces and millions of dollars at aid."

"But at the very start, we gave the world a jolt on account of our Kashmir policy," Mr Narayan said.

President's Reminder

He called upon the people to hearken to the words of President Radhakrishnan, who had been reminding them repeatedly in past months of truths about war and peace, and to "refuse to be carried away by the success euphoria that has overtaken us."

Mr Narayan said "neither the Indo-Pak conflict nor the India-China conflict can ever be solved by war."

"I know, as you know, that even after the most devastating war, peace has to be made," he said adding that war "is not the permanent condition of man: it is peace."

"I know further that war is a pestilence that will destroy my country, as it will destroy Pakistan, as it will destroy China. We all desperately need peace in order to grow and develop, to be able to feed and clothe ourselves, to educate our children, to fight disease and premature death," he said.

To work for peace, Mr Narayan went on, was not cowardice.

Mr Narayan said India's case had been misunderstood. Many nations were under the misapprehension that India had deprived Pakistan "by force or something" what in justice belonged to her. Pakistan, he said, had never laid claim to Kashmir. Her plea was that the future of Kashmir should be decided according to the wishes of the people, hoping that they would opt for Pakistan "which is mere wishful thinking than anything else."

(*Hindustan Times,* 30 November 1965)

Letter from Mridula Sarabhai to JP

C/o Office of Police Commissioner,

Ahmedabad-4.

9 December 1965

My dear Shri J.P.,

From the newspapers I see that you have been constantly on the move during this month and I know how busy and preoccupied you are. So wonder if I should take your time. But I want to let you know the latest about him and hence this.

There had been no government reaction to my reminder about which I wrote to Vinobaji in my letter of 15-11-65. I had written to Shri J.J. Singh also about this so that I do not repeat.

I am sorry to learn about Radhakrishnaji's illness. I have written to Shri J.J. and also Shaffee Shaeb to find out more about him so that I can write to him. I had written a letter meant for him and Narayanbhai at the Varanasi address. I received the postal A/D receipt form and the letter must be waiting for them.

Herewith a copy of the news item being the reply of the Prime Minister to a question asked by a member in the Rajya Sabha. I am reminded of Jawaharlalji's handicap in 1947 and later, how he was kept in the dark by all and the Himalayan efforts he made to find out truth. I have written to Lal Bahadurji for need for caution and make a thorough inquiry. Until I was interned I had been pleading with him to intervene and stop the havoc that the Jan Sanghis were playing. Inquiry through the same agencies will never bring results. I have suggested asking you if he wants further information.

With best wishes to both of you and all other friends,

Yours sincerely,

Sd/-

Mridula Sarabhai

Shri Jayaprakash Narayan

The Future of Tashkent OR The Future of Indo-Pak Relations: JP

Two rays of hope have recently appeared in the darkening Indo-Pakistan skies: One, Mr. Kosygin's statement that he would spare no effect to save the Tashkent accord: the other, the exchange of greetings between the Prime Minister and President Ayub Khan, as her plane flew over West Pakistan. Every effort must be made to see that these rays do not fade out again but that they multiply and spread to light up the entire sub-continental sky. This calls for fresh initiative from either side. It does not seem possible for President Ayub Khan, faced as he is with powerful opposition, to take any helpful step. The initiative clearly is with India: and to fail at this critical moment and remain waiting on events, may destroy all chances of reviving the drooping spirit of Tashkent.

Two possible initiatives occur to me. If Indo-Pak relations, which seem at the moment to have got derailed, are to be put back on the Tashkent track, it is urgent that the Prime Minister and President Ayub Khan meet as soon as possible; and instead of waiting for some one else to arrange the meeting, Mrs Indira Gandhi should herself invite the President to New Delhi. She has now had the advantage of talks with Mr. Kosygin who must have told her all that had been left untold in the Tashkent declaration. She has also had the benefit of talks with Mr. Johnson and Mr. Wilson. These talks should have given her the necessary background for a fruitful down-to-earth talk with the Pakistan President. Until the two leaders meet and review the whole position and reach some broad agreement as to the direction to be given to Indo-Pak relations, meetings of ministers would only aggravate the sense of frustration that is growing on both sides.

There is a view that Pakistan must behave better before there could be any thought of a summit meeting. That to my mind is to put the proverbial cart before the horse. It is precisely in order that the rapid deterioration in Indo-Pak relations may be arrested that I am making the above suggestion.

There is another view that a meeting at that level cannot be conceived of without careful and adequate preparation. As a general preposition that is no doubt true. But in the given situation it is impossible for ministers or officers to "prepare" for any thing. Pakistan representatives would block every effort to discuss any question of common interest by simply insisting that the Kashmir question be first taken up and settled. Once again, it is precisely to resolve that very deadlock that a meeting between the Prime Minister and President Ayub Khan is being suggested.

How can the two leaders resolve the deadlock? They will surely not be able to solve the Kashmir question. No solution of that question is indeed possible at any number of summit meetings as long as the present approach of Pakistan to it continues, namely that Kashmir must be settled before any progress could be possible towards Indo-Pak friendship.

It was this very deadlock that the Tashkent meeting was intended to resolve. That deadlock had lasted for 18 years and had finally led to a war. That war too had failed to settle any thing. Clearly new approach to Indo-Pak relations had to be found if the "welfare of the 600 million people of India and Pakistan" was to be assured. The historic significance of the Tashkent meeting was that it did succeed in finding a new approach. The agreement that was signed there placed in the fore-front not the issue of Kashmir but the need for "understanding and friendly relations" between the two countries, and viewed Kashmir" against that background". Had Pakistan's stand at Tashkent been that without prior settlement of Kashmir, there could be no question of friendship with India, there would have been no agreement at all. But the fact that there was an agreement, even though a Kashmir settlement was not even distantly visible, clearly implies that the view taken there was that as gradually mutual suspicions and distrust were removed and trade, cultural and other kinds of cooperation developed, a psychological transformation would eventually take place on both sides that would render even an intractable problem like Kashmir tractable. The experience of history has repeatedly shown that in an atmosphere of mutual suspicion and hostility even minor disputes become insoluble. On the other hand, it has been found that once mutual understanding had been brought about, even the most complicated disputes become miraculously transformed and simple to settle this is as true of disputes between brothers as between nations.

The above interpretation does not imply that Pakistan had agreed at Tashkent to put the Kashmir issue in cold storage. It was, of course, understood that the question would be raised (even as it was raised at Tashkent), but that Pakistan would not use it to block all efforts towards the agreed goal of Indo-Pak friendship.

New Approach to Kashmir at Tashkent

I am persuaded that President Ayub Khan had unreservedly accepted the new approach at Tashkent: otherwise there would have been no meaning in his signing the agreement. But he seems to have been pushed against his will by the implacable anti-India elements in his country who want neither a Kashmir settlement nor friendship with India. Perhaps they do not themselves know what they want except to see India go down.

In this situation, a meeting between Prime Minister Indira Gandhi and President Ayub Khan might prove to be a turning point, particularly when Mrs. Gandhi has had the benefit of a personal talk with Mr. Kosygin. I am sure the Pakistan President would not want to go back on his word. And an invitation to New Delhi and a frank talk with the Prime Minister might enable him to work in concert with Mrs. Gandhi to save the Tashkent accord in the interest of the 600 million people of the sub-continent to which they are jointly committed. Without such a meeting I cannot imagine how the Government of India can intelligently determine its policy towards Pakistan in the coming crucial months. The result would be that we would be pushed willy nilly into directions which in our considered judgment we would never want to follow.

The other initiative I have in my mind is in regard to the internal affairs of the state of Jammu and Kashmir. Here again we seem to be drifting. Unfortunately, the general public in India have been kept utterly in the dark as to the true state of affairs in that hapless state. The world, however, is not in the dark. And as we have discovered to our sorrow the world counts for a good deal in our internal affairs whether it be our food or our armaments. Let us, therefore, face the fact: no matter what manner of pose we strike in regard to the Kashmir question, the world cannot be impressed as long as we continue by repression to keep the discontent in the valley suppressed. Our case is that Kashmir is a part of India and Kashmiris are Indian citizens. That precisely should be all the more reason why we should do justice to our countrymen of the valley and make them contented and happy. That, however, would be impossible as long as we keep in detention leaders such as Sheikh Abdullah, Mirza Afzal Beg and Maulana Masoodi and hundreds of other Kashmiris.

The above, I believe, would generally be conceded in private in New Delhi. But there is deep fear of Sheikh Abdullah's action after he is released. At the same time, it has to be realized that no self-respecting political leader can be expected as long as he is in confinement to indicate his future course of action, particularly when he knows that his release depended upon promise of good behaviour. Finding itself in this quandary New Delhi, I fear, considers it prudent to wait for a "favourable" opportunity. Unfortunately, this way of thinking leaves the initiative to those in both the countries who hate Tashkent from the bottom of their heart.

Sheikh Against Merger with Pakistan

The quandary, however, is not so difficult as it is made out to be. It has been known these many years that Sheikh Saheb has been resolutely against Kashmir being merged with Pakistan. He did, no doubt, entertain ideas of some kind of an independent Kashmir; but I believe he is realist enough to realize that (a) no solution of the Kashmir question could ever be accepted by India, after the last war with Pakistan, that involved de-accession of the state, or any part of it, from the Union; and (b) an independent state in that part of the world could have little chance of survival in face of Pakistan's consuming hunger for the valley of Kashmir and the emergence of the Chinese power in the region-a power that cannot be expected to exercise self denial in relation to its weak neighbours. Finally, it should be borne in mind that in every major step in war or peace, there is always an element of risk. No one who is unprepared to take risks can hope to be either a great soldier or a great statesman. Therefore, it is my humble advice, to the Prime Minister and her colleagues to set at liberty Sheikh Abdullah and his colleagues and the others imprisoned for political reasons, in Jammu and Kashmir and invite the Sheikh and such others as he may want for talks at Delhi. The talks would be bound to be prolonged and there would be patience required and much ingenuity for compromise.

The consent and cooperation of the Government of Jammu and Kashmir would be necessary for the success of this initiative. I hope that their cooperation would be forthcoming, because I cannot imagine their wanting indefinitely to rule by repression.

The question arises what kind of a settlement would Sheikh Saheb want. Clearly he cannot be expected to agree to the present status of the state and may want to go back to the original position of limited accession. In other words, he may want full internal autonomy for the state with the centre exercising authority and control in defence, external relations and communications. That will need to be considered with an open mind on both sides, particularly in view of the development since 1947. Dr. Karan Singh's imaginative suggestion about reorganization of the state might also be examined in this context. Finally, there is the possibility of Sheikh Saheb's playing a constructive part in preserving and promoting the spirit and aims of the Tashkent declaration. Indo-Pak friendship has been his passion since his release in 1964. Now that both the countries have accepted friendship as their common aim, Sheikh Saheb's services might prove to be invaluable.

These two initiative might break the present deadlock and save the agreement made at Tashkent and help in the realization of its aims. It is not unreasonable to expect that the good wishes of both the U.S.S.R. and U.S.A. would be readily available for both the initiatives.

Sd/-

Jayaprakash Narayan

(NMM&L, File No. 88)

Tashkent Declaration

Following is the joint statement on Tashkent Declaration issued by Shri Jayaprakash Narayan, Chairman A.B. Shanti Sena Mandal and Shri Manmohan Chaudhuri, President, Sarva Seva Sangh, on 28 January 1966, from Varanasi.

Tashkent Day

The two nations of India and Pakistan were born eighteen years ago in the midst of intense mutual bitterness and it was only the martyrdom of Mahatma Gandhi that was able to restore normalcy in their relationship. Subsequently differencs, misunderstandings and disputes went on gathering momentum and the climax was reached in the Indo-Pak clash a few months ago. This was a great misfortune not only for these two countries but also for the world at large. While these two countries had to plan for greater expenditures on war preparation diverting resources from developmental programmes essential for their millions of improverished masses, their mutual hostility was also a threat to world peace. But fortunately the leaders of the two countries had not lost mental equilibrium and there were neighbours deeply interested in bridging the gulf between them and willing to persevere for the cause. The result was the Tashkent declaration, which heralded the beginning of a new, and hopeful chapter in the history of Indo-Pak relations.

Our great leader, the Late Lal Bahadur Shastri sealed the compact with his life and the general acclaim with which declaration was hailed by the peoples of the two countries shows that the latter were sick of hatred and strife and were longing for the fresh air of goodwill and peace. The peoples and publicmen of the world have also by and large welcomed it heartily. The future of the 600 million people of this subcontinent is the magnificent and inspiring thought that moved the leaders of the two countries to end their hostility and bitterness. Now it is the duty of all of us to give concrete shape to the aspirations enshrined in the declartion.

Both countries have common roots in the historical past and a common cultural heritage. The great rivers, the himalayas and the ocean serve them both. Their economies were also interdependent.

If we continue to think and act in terms of "the 600 million", we will be able to discover a hundred ways of cooperation and joint effort in the interest of these millions. Thus the two countries can jointly achieve the welfare of their masses and be a force for peace and progress in the world as well.

So, it is time we pledged ourselves to make a success of the new era presaged by the Tashkent declaration and to never allow hatred and strife to darken our lives again. For this we appeal to the people of India to observe February 11 next as Tashkent day. On that day let us assemble in public meetings and affirm our support for the Tashkent declaration. Let us also express our firm determination to seek peaceful solutions to all disputes with our neighbour and to renounce the use of force for the same. On that day let us appreciate the role of the UNO in the present day world as a forum of world public opinion and resolve to do all we can to strengthen it as an instrument of world peace.

We can also on that day solemnly resolve to give our support to whatever steps the governments take to improve relations between the two countries, to make a serious effort to understand and appreciate the hopes and aspirations, the problems and difficultires and the cultural and spiritual values of our neighbours, and express our readiness to extend our helping hand during natural calamities etc.

The last message of the Late Shastriji was "we fought resolutely to save our country, now we will have to fight still more resolutely for the sake of peace." We must pledge ourselves on the 11th February to carry out this behest with all our strength.

12

Era of Indira Gandhi

J.P's Letter to Indira Gandhi

New Delhi,
January 20, 1966

My Dear Indu,

Please accept my sincere congratulations. You have taken on a tremendous burden and my heart goes out to you in this hour of trial and anxiety. In Bhai you had an unequalled preceptor, and Lal Bahadurji by his success both in war and peace has lightened somewhat your heavy burden. But it will be your own inner resources on which you will have to rely, and I have no doubt that if you seek within they will not fail you.

For myself, I pledge my full support- for what it may be worth- in all that you may do in the pursuit of peace and of happiness for the masses of this country. I am here until the 22nd of this month and would have liked to call on you for a few minutes, but I realize you will be too rushed these days.

Enclosed is copy of a statement being issued by the India-Pakistan Conciliation Group.

The Group's services too, as the statement says, are at your disposal in your work for Indo-Pak amity.

With all good wishes for your successful stewardship of the nation.

Yours sincerely,

Sd/-

Shrimati Indira Gandhi, (Jayaprakash Narayan)
New Delhi.

Letter to Indira Gandhi

The Kashmir Problem

Strictly Confidential

(Not for publication or circulation)

Camp: Sarvodaya Ashram
Sokhodeora (Gaya)
June 23, 1966.

When I was in Delhi recently for a day, I learnt that you had asked Mr Sadiq and some of his colleagues to meet you on the 26th for a review of the Kashmir question. In view of the importance of that meeting, I am venturing to place before you some of my ideas in that connection. I hope I am not being a nuisance, and that you will not think I am trying to pressurise you.

The Kashmir question has plagued this country for 19 years. In has cost us a great deal materially and spiritually. We profess democracy, but rule by force in Kashmir- unless we have auto-suggested ourselves into believing that the 2 general elections under Bakshi Saheb had expressed the will of the people, or that the Sadiq government is based on popular support, except for a small minority of pro- Pakistan traitors. We profess secularism, but let Hindu nationalism stampede us into trying to establish it by repression.

Kashmir had distorted India's image for the world as nothing else has done. There is no nation in the world, not even Russia, which appreciates our Kashmir policy, though some of them might, for their own reasons, give us their support.

No matter how much and how loud and how long we shout that Kashmir is an inalienable part of India and that, therefore, there was no Kashmir problem, the fact remains that a serious and urgent problem faces, and will continue to face, us in that part of the country.

That problem exists not because Pakistan wants to grab Kashmir, but because there is deep and widespread political discontent among the people. The people of India might be kept in the dark about the true state of affairs in the Valley, but every chancellery in New Delhi knows the truth, and almost every foreign correspondent. It would appear that all but our Intelligence know the facts; or, perhaps, we too know the facts but do not wish to face them and hope that someone - may be Sadiq Sahab or Qasim Saheb- might one day perform some miracle that would bring about a psychological revolution in the Valley.

Historical events, some without some within our control, have narrowed down greatly the room for manoeuverability that the government of India may have now. For instance, any manner of de-accession of any part of the state is now impracticable - no matter how just or fair according to the principles of democracy and secularism. Whatever be the solution, it has to be found within the limitations of the accession.

Sheikh's Role

It is here that Sheikh Saheb's role may become decisive. I have been pressing for his release not because he is a friend. Friendship, no doubt, counts in every human situation, but I hope I have enough moral discipline to allow without protest even my nearest and dearest one to be sent to the gallows if that were the demand of justice- I would have added 'and of national interest' had it not been for the fact that many times it is possible to be sure what is in the national interest and different persons, all equally patriotic, may have different interpretations of it in a given situation.

On this count too, let me say, it was not justice to have arrested and detained Sheikh Abdullah without giving him a chance to clear himself of the charges so wildly made against him. On his part, he had established his bonafides sufficiently by deciding to return to his country and answer his detractors.

Nor do I think that he is a traitor. Godse thought that Gandhiji was a traitor. The R.S.S thinks that Jayaprakash is a traitor. Godse was an individual, the R.S.S is a private organization, a democratic government represents the people and has principles and procedures according to which it functions. Nobody can be held to be a traitor by the Government of India unless it has been established in accordance with due process of law. If the Government finds it difficult to do that, it is cowardly to use the D.I.R. and continue to use it indefinitely, even when no palpable danger to the country's defence remains.

It was I think indiscreet of Sheikh Saheb to have met Chou-en-lai. But that is all that can be said about it. No fair minded person would consider that as a treasonous act. When the Chinese had attacked in 1962, had he not written to the Prime Minister ' expressing our deep anguish'? Did he not on May 25,1964 publicly rebuke in Rawalpindi Chaudhari Ghulam Abbas for having sought Chinese intervention? In London did he not say at a press Conference. (*Times*, March19,1965) that China' s claims on Ladakh were inadmissible?

Much has been made of Sheikh's statements abroad. I doubt if on an objective examination, those statements, as published in the foreign press and not their garbled versions in India, would amount to anything more than what he had been saying in India. I agree that it would have been better if Sheikh Saheb had spoken less and more guardedly. But Sheikh Saheb cannot be expected to be anything but himself- he just cannot keep quiet. This is a common failing of us Indians. Have not Union Cabinet members been speaking out of turn not only in India but even abroad even in Jawahar Lalji's life time?

I would like to close this chapter with one more quotation from the Sheikh. Before he had left for his trip abroad this is what he had said at a farewell function at the Constitution Club on February 10, 1965: "We might have difference among ourselves. But after all India is the homeland of us all. If God forbid, India ceases to be India and goes down, how can others be saved? We have to look at problems from that angle."

But I have not been agitating for the Sheikh's release because he is a friend, or just because I am concerned about civil liberties. These considerations may be in the background. My primary concern in this matter has been to seek a solution of the Kashmir problem. As I see it, there is any chance of this matter being settled, it is with the help of Sheikh Abdullah. I am not hundred per cent sure of this- no one can be. But the odds appear to me to be favourable enough to urge Sheikh Abdullah's unconditional release. An element of risk may be there, but there is risk in every big political or military decision, in fact in most human decisions, as even when two persons decide to wed.

Here may I digress a little ? Nandaji seems to have told Shri R.K. Patil that Jayaprakash is completely out of touch with public sentiment on the question of Kashmir and Sheikh

Abdullah. I suspect that more of your colleagues are of that view. I therefore want to offer a few comments to clear the air- incidentally that might help your colleagues to come to right decision.

First of all, some people (mostly crypto-communists, and Hindu Nationalists of all hues) have created a certain image of Jayaprakash Narayan- a silly idealist or a hidden traitor- whatever that man says or does is twisted to fit that image. For instance, I am supposed to have advocated the giving away of Nagaland to the Nagas, Kashmir to the Pakistanis. I have never even remotely made any such suggestion. Even in the case of Aksai Chin, I had suggested a lease (an internationally recognized transaction and one that was agreed to by India in a recent Indo-Nepal deal). That lease too was suggested as a measure of give and take, i.e., if China agreed to India's counter demand, may be in the Chumbi valley or elsewhere along the 2500 miles of border. But having created a false image, it was easy for any one to throw stones at it.

But that did not alienate Jayaprakash from public sentiment. Without appearing to be vain, I make bold to say that except for you personally, there is no one in your Government who is as constantly and widely in touch with the people as I am. Almost daily I address public meetings, and invariably my experience has been that I am heard in pin-drop silence and afterwards people come to assure me that they had been completely misled and if that was I meant, they were all for it. The only two of my meetings that were disturbed were in Delhi at the time of my visit to West Pakistan and the trouble makers were R.S.S boys whose minds were closed. I am not saying that every one who listens is persuaded- but I am saying that the views I propound -with frankness and sincerity- are far from being out of touch with public sentiment.

Leader should Lead

Lastly (in this digressive count), the leaders of this country are not doing justice to the people. It is the job of leaders to lead, but most of them are too timid and weak to speak out the truth, to advocate unpopular policies, and, if the need arose, to face the wrath of the people. For my part, I have faith in our people- they are sound and intelligent. If they are given all the facts, they can take the right decisions. May I say here, without appearing to flatter you, that by your recent bold decisions you have shown that you are attempting to give the people courageous leadership.

Returning to the main theme of this letter, why do I plead for Sheikh Saheb's release? Because that may give us the only chance we may have of solving the Kashmir problem. Why? Because, in the event of the Government of India reaching an agreement with him about the future status of Kashmir, which will have to be within the limits of accession, the Sheikh is the only Kashmiri leader who could swing Muslim opinion in the valley towards his side. I believe it is obvious that the farthest that any status within the Indian Union can go is full internal autonomy, i.e., a return to the original terms of the accession.

Several questions arise at this point. Will Sheikh Saheb agree to any such status? If he did, would he succeed in persuading the Kashmiris to rally round him? Would not autonomous Kashmir, sooner or later, attempt to secede from the Union?

Nandaji tries to cloud the whole issue by asking for proof that the Sheikh's thinking has changed. Earlier, he seemed to think otherwise. Referring to the interview of Shri Radhakrishna and Shri Narayan Desai with Sheikh Saheb, Nandaji had stated in the Rajya Sabha on November 26, 1965, that the Sarvodaya leaders' meeting had produced a 'very positive reaction'.

Be that as it may, all this talk of the Sheikh not having changed appears puerile to me. Keeping people in jail is not the best way of inducing them to be more malleable. Nandaji should have learnt that much from his own experience in British Indian prisons.

Moreover, supposing the Sheikh were released in a fanfare of official propaganda about the Sheikh having changed, would an iota be left of his political utility for India? After that if the Sheikh were to arrive in Srinagar, would the crowds be chanting ' Sher-I- Kashmir zindabad' or 'Bharat Ka Pithu Murdabad'? What chance would he have of persuading the Kashmiris to become good Indian citizens? All this is so obvious that it is amazing that the Home Minister is unable to see it.

On the contrary I am sure that on his release Sheikh Saheb would again reiterate the right of the Kashmiris to decide their future; he would again declare that the accession was not final and that the so-called general elections had not expressed the people's will. We should have maturity enough to understand that and not to denounce him as a Pakistani agent. He can never hope to persuade the Kashmiris to accept an autonomous position within India if he did not make it clear that it was they and not anybody else who is to take that decision. Instead of that, if he came out and declared that the issue had been settled already when he was in prison by the Kashmir Constituent Assembly and the two general elections that followed, his voice would carry no more weight than that of Bakshi Saheb did or of Sadiq Saheb does.

The more important question is, how would Sheikh Abdullah want the Kashmiris to 'decide their future'? I am sure not by a plebiscite. Then how? One way, and the best in the circumstance, would be to let the people decide at the general election in 1967. The Sheikh could do that by fighting the election on the basis of his agreement with the Government of India (as envisaged above). Could the Kashmiri people be enthused over autonomy within the Union? I think they could, by Sheikh Saheb frankly telling them that was the only way they could save themselves form self-destruction as a result of their territory becoming a battle ground for India and Pakistan: that if it could be shown that they had taken that decision freely at an election run by their genuine leaders (like himself) Pakistan would have no ground left to interfere in their affairs, that was the best way to bring about Indo-Pak amity; that they would he rid of the overbearing Indian police and enjoy full freedom to order their lives as they liked. If all that were put across to the people by one in whom they had trust, I have every hope that they would acquiesce willingly.

Autonomy for Kashmir

I may be asked, what ground have I for believing that Sheikh Abdullah would accept autonomy within India. A part of the argument I had given in a press statement, which had received your and your government's notice at the time. I reproduce it below.

'It has been known these many years that Sheikh Saheb had been resolutely against Kashmir being merged with Pakistan. He did, no doubt, entertain ideas of some kind of an independent

Kashmir; but I believe he is a realist enough to realize that (a) no solution of the Kashmir question could ever be accepted by India, after the last war with Pakistan, that involved de-accession of the State, or any part of it, from the Union; and (b) an independent state in that part of the world could have little chance of survival in face of Pakistan's consuming hunger for the valley of Kashmir and the emergence of the Chinese power in the region-a power that cannot be expected to exercise self-denial in relation to its weak neighbours."

In addition to the above argument, I have this to say, Sheikh Saheb had told Narayan and Radhakrishan that he would be prepared even to accept the status of full internal autonomy for Kashmir, provided history were not allowed to repeat itself. By that he meant, provided the autonomy was not gradually whittled down and the Centre did not interfere in the state's internal affairs.

The last evidence I have is the report of Gul Shah, of which J.J. has already apprised you fully.

I grant that my case is not fool-proof. But no case can be. Nandaji's own case is far from it. To hold a general election in Kashmir with Sheikh Abdullah in prison is like the British ordering an election in India while Jawaharlal Nehru was held in prison. No fair minded person would call it a fair election. Nor would that election settle any political issue more than the two earlier ones did. And if we miss the chance of using the next general election to win the consent of the people to their place within the union, I cannot see what other device will be left to India to settle the problem. To think that we will eventually wear down the people and force them to accept the union at least passively is to delude ourselves. That might conceivably have happened had Kashmir not been geographically located where it is. In its present location, and with seething discontent among the people, it would never be left in peace by Pakistan. China is bound sooner or later to take a hand in the sport of fishing in troubled waters. With the issue settled to the satisfaction of the great majority of the people, the external mischief- makers would not find a favourable soil for sowing their mischief.

Internationally, India's prestige would soar. No reasonable government would then be able to point an accusing finger at us.

Another question may be asked: will Sheikh Abdullah negotiate with the Government of India to the exclusion of Pakistan? Well, he told the two Sarvodaya friends that in the light of the Indo- Pak war and its consequences, he was quite prepared to have bilateral talks with India. He called that the 'first stage,' meaning thereby that later on Pakistan would have to be brought into the picture and persuaded to accept the compact made between him and the Government of India. I see nothing offensive in this approach. Sooner or later Pakistan's support to any real settlement in Kashmir will have to be obtained, so that the ceasefire line might be normalized (rationalized?), disengagement of the armed forces of the two countries could be secured and the tension between the two countries with its terrible affect on Kashmir might be eased. Instead of resenting Sheikh Saheb's anxiety to secure Pakistan's acceptance of his compact with India, we should ourselves take the initiative and use his good offices in this behalf in the manner found feasible.

I am sorry to have inflicted on you such a long letter. But I felt it was duty to my country to put these thoughts before you and your colleagues.

With kindest regards,
Yours Sincerely,
Sd/-
(Jayaprakash Narayan)

Smt. Indira Gandhi,
Prime Minister of India,
New Delhi.

(*The Quest and the Goal: Philosophy of Jayaprakash Narayan* JP Commemoration Volume (1978-79) Seventy Sixth Birthday Celebration Committee Madran P 772; 1)

A Fresh Approach

(Text of JP's speech in Delhi on 29 June 1966)

I suggest a fresh approach to Indo-Pak relations. Relations between India and Pakistan are on an entirely different footing from those between other countries. India and Pakistan are two different countries, two different states, but they are the home of one single people. I do not think that this basic truth has been fully appreciated either by Indians or Pakistanis. Let me say at the outset that partition, as the 17 years of post-independence history of India and Pakistan have conclusively proved, has been a complete failure. It has solved no problem but has created many more than existed before. Yet partition is a fact and has to be accepted. But the ill effects of the partition must be removed. They can be removed not by force, not by coercion, not by conquest. They can be removed only by love, by understanding, by cooperation. Happily in the last few months there seem to have been new psychological forces at work both in Pakistan and in India. Only this afternoon I was reading a statement by president Ayub Khan in the National Assembly of Pakistan. Again and again he emphasized the need for a change of heart on both sides. I wish to underline that. I do not think our dispute with Pakistan can ever be settled unless there is really a change of heart on both sides. I am not sure if a change of heart has taken place in Rawalpindi. But Rawalpindi has at least recognized the need for a change of heart, which is something.

I hope Delhi also has realized the need for a change of heart. If such a change tales place all these disputes which have assumed such gigantic proportions would be immediately cut to size, and it would be possible to tackle and solve them. I do not wish to minimize the problems that face us. I am not saying that there is a magic wand which can be waved to solve all of them at once. Much patience and perseverance are required. Progress will be slow. If both sides decide that in their own interest they must find a way to live together in friendship and cooperation, their very economic, historical, geographical, political, social and cultural conditions would begin to operate in favour of those objectives. Of all the outstanding issues between the two countries the issue of Kashmir is the most important and the most difficult. But with a change of heart even Kashmir can be solved.

Need for Positive Approach

So far the dominant approach of both sides has been to concentrate on settling the issues in dispute. At one time there was a theory that a beginning should be made with lesser disputes, and as they were settled one by one the more difficult ones could be taken up. Thus by the time the two countries came to discuss Kashmir, a favourable psychological climate would have been created. This in a sense was a negative approach, and though it yielded some results I doubt whether it would take us much further. If for instance even the summit meeting were to plunge headlong into a discussion of Kashmir and there was no settlement this would prove a disaster for both countries. At present the attitudes on Kashmir in both India and Pakistan have become so ossified that public opinion might not permit sufficient manoeuverability even to the summit. I am therefore suggesting a positive approach, that is an approach that goes behind the disputes. While admitting that Kashmir is the chief irritant I do not think that Indo-Pak relations are what they are on account of Kashmir. Kashmir is only a symptom of the disease. The disease is the deep-seated mutual distrust between the two countries. Each suspects the other of harbouring the blackest designs against the other. The problem in Kashmir cannot be solved unless this distrust were removed. On its part the distrust cannot go by magic or make-believe.

President Ayub Khan called, in one of his recent broadcasts, for a change of heart and said that if there was such a change no dispute would remain unsolved. That was a wise statement, and now it is for both sides to get together to find out how a change of heart, in other words replacement of the distrust with trust, could be brought about. In my humble opinion this could be done not by harping on disputes and differences but by sitting down together to discover if there were any areas of common interest in which the two countries could agree to work together for their mutual benefit. I hold firmly that there are large areas of his kind. And if they are jointly explored and discovered and worked together the present cloud of distrust could be dispelled and a change of heart brought about. When that happens even an issue like Kashmir will not appear as forbidding as it does today.

I might add that it is not necessary to keep separate what I have called the positive and negative approaches. They could indeed be taken up together. But then failure to solve any dispute such as Kashmir should not be allowed to interfere with the search for common interests and fields of activity.

Common Defence

President Ayub Khan has revived his plea for common defence. India should give serious thought to that no matter how bristling with difficulties it might be. It might be pointed out that defence cannot be discussed unless Kashmir is settled. True. But at present each side looks at Kashmir from the point of view of its own defence. The issue would take on a different complexion when looked at from the point of view of common defence.

The question of defence is linked with that of foreign policy. There too, in spite of the apparent wide differences between nonalignment and alignment, I do not think it would be impossible to reach an understanding, particularly when both alignment and nonalignment are changing their substance.

Other areas of interest are obviously industry and commerce and communications and freer movement of peoples from either side. If those areas were explored and agreements reached in regard to them, so that even advisory joint councils were set up, the working of these councils for a couple of years or so might go far in creating mutual trust and understanding. That should help in the settlement of such disputes as might still be outstanding or might arise in the future.

In the last few months I have from time to time spoken about Kashmir and have been roundly abused for when I have said. The press has attacked me. Political leaders have attacked me. Members of Parliament have attacked me. Twenty seven Congress members of Parliament issued a statement attacking me. I have received in this period I do not know how many abusive letters-with the filthiest unimaginable abuse. I have even been threatened.

I do not claim that I am wiser than the rest of my countrymen. I do not claim that I have readymade solution for this problem. But let me emphasise that no problem which involves human beings-the children and the future generations-can be solved in a legalistic manner or by force. It may appear today that the Chinese Communists have solved the problem of Tibet. But I am convinced that the day is not far off-I may not live to see that day-when the people of Tibet will regain their freedom and Tibet will become an independent country and be admitted into the comity of nations.

Dangerous Frame of Mind

I have been abused most of all saying that the problem of Kashmir is a human one. No abuse, no criticism, no argument has convinced me that there was need to change a single word of what I have said. A very dangerous frame of mind is being created in our country. We are beginning to think like a big power. If there is a difficult problem we think the easiest way to solve it is by using force. If there is trouble in Kashmir, if there is difference of opinion in Kashmir, we say we shall rule Kashmir by force. And I have heard responsible people say in Delhi that no Kashmiri has yet been known to die for a cause. They therefore think their policy of force will have easy success

But what about Nagaland? There also the same philosophy of force has caught hold of our minds. At least the Nagas have given proof that they can die for a cause, and yet in the ultimate analysis it is on force that we wish to rely whether in Kashmir or Nagaland. I think this is a self-destructive philosophy and runs wholly counter to all that our own movement for independence stood for.

The Sarvodaya movement has a special responsibility in this matter because if the present trend of thought in the country is not checked it would end up eventually repudiating Mahatma Gandhi and all he lived and died for.

Indira Gandhi's Letter to JP

No. 1160-PMO/66

Prime Minister's House
New Delhi
July 6, 1966

My dear Jayaprakash ji,

Thank you for your letter of June 23. I am sorry I could not reply earlier. I have been touring a great deal.

Thank you for sharing your views on Kashmir and Sheikh Sahib. I wonder if you are likely to come to Delhi some time next month so that we could discuss the matter. I should welcome such an opportunity.

Tomorrow evening I leave for my trip to Cairo, Brioni and Moscow. I hope to be back in Delhi on July 17. The Parliament Session begins on the 25th.

I hope you are both well. Please remember me to Prabhaji.

With kind regards to both of you,

Yours sincerely
Sd/-
Indira Gandhi

Shri Jayaprakash Narayan
Kadam Kuan,
Patna

Indira Gandhi's Letter to JP

CONFIDENTIAL

No. 1236-PMO/66

2 August 1966

My dear Jayaprakashji,

I have received your letter of July 17.

I have no objection to your meeting Sheikh Sahib while you are in Kodaikanal. The Home Ministry are issuing necessary instructions in the matter. I am sure you will agree that it would not be desirable for your talks to find their way into the press or otherwise become public. Any public disclosure at this stage would not be helpful.

I have since also received your other letter of July 24 with which you were good enough to send me a copy of your article for the London Observer. I shall read it with interest.

I look forward to meeting you.

With kind regards,

Yours sincerely

Sd/-

Indira Gandhi

Prime Minister

Shri Jayaprakash Narayan
Kadam Kuan,
Patna - 3.

JP-Sheikh Talks End

Kodaikanal, Aug. 7 (PTI)—The three-day talks between Mr Jayaprakash Narayan Sarvodaya leader, and Sheikh Abdullah now under detention here, concluded this afternoon.

After the talks, Mr Narayan told newsmen at his residence that the talks were over and he was leaving for Madras this evening.

When asked whether he felt the talks had been satisfactory, he declined to say anything except that he did not consider him as unsatisfactory.

Today's talks lasted another two hours and a quarter. Mr Narayan had altogether over nine hours of talks in the course of three days. Mr R.K. Patil, a member of the Executive Committee of the Sarva Seva Sangh, also met Sheikh Abdullah yesterday and had three hours of talks with him separately. Mr and Mrs Narayan and Mr Patil had lunch with the Sheikh today also.

(Hindustan Times, 8 August, 1966)

Talks with Sheikh Narayan not Satisfied

Madras, Aug. 8—Sarvodaya leader, Mr Jayaprakash Narayan told me today it would not be in the national interest for him to divulge anything regarding his talks with Sheikh Abdullah.

Mr Narayan, who returned here this morning from Kodaikanal, appeared to be in a somewhat depressed mood.

Mr Narayan will arrive in Delhi on or about August 21 for a four-day stay, when he will convey to the Prime Minister the gist of his talks with the Kashmir leader.

After his several hours of talks with Sheikh Abdullah between August 5 and 7, all that Mr Narayan told reporters was that the discussions were not "unsatisfactory."

Kohinoor Bungalow, where Sheikh Abdullah lives, was cordoned off by the security men during Mr Narayan's visit.

PTI adds: Mr Narayan today called on Mr C. Rajagapalachari and had an hour long discussion with him. It is understood Mr Narayan conveyed to Mr Rajagopalchari a gist of his talks with Sheikh Abdullah.

(Hindustan Times, 9 August, 1966)

Meeting with JP at Personal Level: PM

New Delhi, Aug. 22—Prime Minister Indira Gandhi told the Lok Sabha today that Mr Jayaprakash Narayan had met Sheikh Abdullah on his own initiative. Their meeting did not represent any move on the part of the government nor had government changed its policy as a result of their meeting, she added.

Mrs Gandhi gave this clarification in an intervention in the course of supplementaries on a statement by Home Minister G.L. Nanda in response to a calling-attention notice by Mr H.C. Mathur (Cong) on newspaper reports that Kashmir Chief Minister G.M. Sadiq had complained on the centre's unilateral decisions which had an "unsettling effect" on Kashmir affairs.

Answering insistent demands from several members that the Prime Minister should make a categorical statement, Mrs Gandhi reiterated Mr. Nanda's statement that "Kashmir is not negotiable and that the accession of the state is final and irrevocable."

Mr Nanda, in his statement, said that the Centre had not consulted the Chief Minister before giving permission to Mr Narayan as no new policy issue was involved, Mr Narayan was meting the Sheikh at his own request as an old friend and the government felt that there could be no harm in the meeting. Moreover, many other people had been permitted to meet the Sheikh, Mr Nanda said.

Nanda's Clarification

Answering adverse comments on the permission granted to Mr Narayan, Mr Nanda said in the beginning the state Chief Minister had some apprehension that a meeting between Mr Narayan and the Sheikh might have some unsettling effect. Mr Sadiq, however, did not consider it so now.

Mr Nanda also pointed out that Mr Narayan's stand on the Kashmir question had undergone a change since the last Indo-Pakistan conflict. The Sarvodya leader had made it clear that Pakistan was no longer a party to the Kashmir dispute and that it was a matter between the people of that state and the rest of India. Mr Narayan had also ruled out the question of an independent Kashmir, Mr. Nanda said.

Mr Mathur referred to a speech of the state Education Minister, Mr D.P. Dhar, that the Centre had yet to accept their request for the application of certain Central Acts to the state.

In reply, Mr Nanda said that Article 356 of the Constitution providing for President's rule over the state had already been applied and certain important laws were being processed for extension over the state. Legislation in this respect had been got ready and the government hoped to introduce it in this session of Parliament, if it was possible.

Earlier, Mr Nanda said their was identity of general approach between the Sadiq Ministry and the central government. It would be taking a wholly unrealistic view of the state of affairs in Kashmir for anyone to suggest that a meeting between the

Sheikh and Mr Narayan was going to unsettle things there. There was no uncertainty whatsoever about the future of the state.

"We have made clear repeatedly that Kashmir is not negotiable and that accession of the state to India is final and irrevocable." Mr Nanda declared.

(Hindustan Times, 23 August 1966)

RK Patil Reports on Kashmir

C/o Gandhi Samarak Nidhi,
Rajgaht, New Delhi
6th September, 1966

My dear Jayaprakash ji,

As you wanted an appreciation of the reactions, that arose in the Kashmir valley, on account of our visit to Sh. Abdullah in Kodaikanal, I decided to visit Kashmir immediately instead of waiting for another meeting with Shri Nandaji. So I left for Srinagar on the 29th.

The general reaction amongst the Kashmiri Pandit class is that the visit should not have been allowed. It is likely to serve no useful purpose. Sh Abdullah is unlikely to change his view-point, and it is useless to pursue him. He is like a dry cloud from which no rain can be expected. This class believes in strong rule, and feels that the Muslim opinion in the valley can never be conciliated. They can understand only strong rule, and the government of India must provide that. I enclose a cutting from *Martand* which represents this view. This is the same class which also feels that even Sh. Abdullah cannot deliver the goods now, such has been the nature of the shift in the Kashmiri Muslim opinion.

This, however, is a minority view confined generally to the Kashmiri Pandit class. The National Conference people (Bakshi Ghulam Mohd's party) have welcomed the visit. They feel that the Sheikh needs to be wooed and brought round. So is the reaction amongst the govt and a very large section of the National Congress which supports it. Like the National Congress they are also for keeping up a dialogue with the Sheikh. They however do not like the publicity that was given to this meeting. Sadiq, the CM of Kashmir, told me quite clearly that his objection was not to JP's visit, to which he said he had already agreed in my various interviews with him, but to the fact that the All-India Radio had the news on three successive days in all its transmissions. And even before JP's visit, papers from Delhi had given advanced publicity to the prospective visit. He said he had not bargained for such publicity, which had an unsettling effect on the situation in the valley. He had also the complaint that the Government of India had not apprised him of the visit before hand. His objection therefore was not to the visit, but the manner in which it was publicised.

Even in Jammu, where the reaction was likely to be adverse, the visit was favourably received. A cutting from the *Ujala* is enclosed. In fact the great majority off enlightened opinion in the whole state has welcomed the visit, and feels that a reconciliation with the Sheikh should be brought about.

Amongst the Plebiscite Front, the visit was not only welcomed, but gave rise to certain expectations. They felt that this was just the beginning of a dialogue which would be continued, and it may lead ultimately to the release of the Sheikh and other leaders at present detained in jail. While this group has welcomed the visit, they could not hide a sense of disappointment and dissatisfaction about the outcome. They feel frustrated at the fact that nothing substantial has come out of it.

Sadiq's tirade against the Centre has generally been commented upon as an unmistakenable sign of his weak position, and in glaring contrast with the Government's claim that the position of the National Congress has been stablisied in the state. An editorial of the *Kashmir Times* represents this general view.

Balraj Puri has written an article in the *Kashmir Times* which tried to depict possible posture which Sh. Abdullah may take. I thought it was rather important, and so I obtained a copy which is enclosed.

In Kashmir election preparations are afoot. A Delimitation Commission has been appointed. The contesting parties which are already in the field are (i) the National Congress (Syed Mir Qasim), (ii) the National Conference (Bakshi Ghulam Mohd), and (iii) the Jana Sangh. This last party has a following only in the predominately Hindu Districts of the Jammu province. It is generally felt that the National Conference will give a tough fight to the Congress but the latter will be able to secure an overall majority. The Plebiscite Front has decided not to contest the elections officially. In some cases, they may support independent candidates. Shri Raghunath Vaishnvi tried to induce the Front to contest the election, but his move has not succeeded.

I met Bakshi Ghulam Mohd this time, and also Sadiq Saheb. The latter interview I consider important, so I am enclosing a verbatim account of it. Bakshi told me that you had arranged for a meeting on Kashmir in the first week of October in Delhi. I am trying to get in touch with J.J. Singh and find out if this is so. This has now been confirmed.

I propose to see Nandaji after the Parliament is over, and then to go to Nagpur for a week. Form the 20th or so, I would be spending a fortnight or so in the Poonch District of the Jammu Province. If you have any communication, it may be addressed to me here.

Yours Sincerely

Sd/-

(R.K. Patil)

(NMM&L. File No. 88, P 36-40)

Annexure: Report on Interview with Sadiq

Report of R.K. Patil on Interview with GM Sadiq

I interviewed Sadiq Saheb on the Ist September 1966. I was looking forward to this interview with some apprehension, in view of Sadiq's statement in the press about JP's meeting Abdullah. But in the sequel all my apprehensions were set at rest. The interview originally fixed for 1/2 an hour dragged to 1½ hours. At the end of the interview, I asked Sadiq Saheb, if he had any message for JP. He asked me to convey his regards to JP. I told him I would also add that Sadiq had said that if Sh. Abdullah accepted the accession, he would have no quarrel with him and Sadiq heartily agreed.

I started the interview by saying that I had come to acquaint him with all the developments that took place after I last saw him on the 14th June. I narrated briefly my visit to Jammu, Doda, Baderwah and Kishtwar, Vinoba, Nandaji and finally JP's and my visit to Sh. Abdullah. I told him that I had told Nandaji that Sadiq Saheb had approved of our visit, and told him that in this context his statement to the Press came as a complete surprise and put me in the wrong. I took up the position that Sadiq had behaved unfairly to me in the whole affair.

Sadiq accepted and reiterated the position that he had agreed to the visit, but he said he objected to the publicity that was given. It was on the AIR for all the three days and even long before the actual visit the Delhi papers had given publicity to it. All this had a some what unsettling effect on the situation in Kashmir. He tried to minimise his statement to the Press by saying that it was not a regular press interview he had given. A press reporter came to him for something else, and he had casually mentioned this to him. I asked him how he explained Shri D.P. Dhar saying that he was 'amused' at the whole episode. Sadiq said he could not answer for him, perhaps he had also the subsequent parliamentary reaction in his mind, when he said so.

He then asked me what transpired in the interview. I told him that the major part of the interview was between JP and Sheikh Saheb, when I was not present. JP visited him in all for 9 hours, when I was not present. And though I had an independent interview with the Sheikh for about two hours, I confined myself to a few questions. I tried to ascertain from him the causes for his change in his attitude towards the accession. He would therefore have to refer to JP for the details of the interview, but I gathered that Sheikh Saheb was not unwilling to consider an arrangement for the future relationship of the state of J&K with India, which maintained the accession, but provided for a greater autonomy.

Sadiq asked me if I knew the Sheikh Saheb well for any length of time. On my replying in the negative, he said I should bear in mind two things about the Sheikh. The first was that he tried to read more into things than what they actually were. For instance, if you saw him even by yourself he would feel that you had been sent by the Government of India. Sadiq gave me an illustration of this during the Quit Kashmir movement of 1946. The slogan had been given and there was nothing left for the Maharaja except to order Sheikh Saheb's arrest. But Sheikh Saheb continued to believe that he would not be arrested on the strength of a report of a barber who used to visit the residency on professional business, and who reported that he had heard the Resident talking to somebody about Sheikh Abdullah. Sheikh Saheb had just put somethings together and the result was that he proved to be wrong. He was arrested shortly.

And secondly Sheikh Abdullah means one thing, while the person he talks to understands another thing. Sadiq gave an interesting account of this during their struggle. It seems a case was going on against Sheikh Abdullah during the Quit-Kashmir phase, and a statement in court on behalf of Sheikh Abdullah had to be prepared. Bakshi saw him, talked to him about the statement, and brought from Sheikh Abdullah in writing a few points on the basis of which the statement was to be prepared. In the draft statement Bakshi added the words 'responsible government under the aegis of the Maharaja'. That is how he interpreted Sheikh Abdullah's attitude as a result of his talks. But Sadiq said this should not be added, as the Quit Kashmir movement involved removal of the Maharaja and his authority. The matter was again referred to Sheikh Abdullah and he said Sadiq was right. Sadiq was obviously suggesting that JP should take Sheikh Abdullah's statements more critically. Sadiq continued that he came across a certain letter from JP to the Prime Minister, in which JP said that Sheikh Abdullah should be released, he should be allowed to adhere to his stand on consulting the people, there should be no restrictions on what he spoke, and then somehow he will bring round the people to the accession (I did not contradict Sadiq, as I was not clear what letter he was referring to). Now Sadiq said all this is mysticism to him. How is all this going to happen. We can never allow an election to be converted into a plebiscite. I can understand, he said, ascertaining the peoples' views in the course of a free and fair election, but never a situation in which the people of Kashmir are asked to elect, between India and Pakistan and Independence. Not only must Sheikh Abdullah's view be for the accession, but he must tell them (as he told the Constituent Assembly - mine) that so far as he was concerned, he felt that they had no other choice which was good for them. The method of ascertaining view of the people - if this was a correct expression - is as important as the fact of ascertainment.

He said if Sheikh Abdullah is prepared to work within the accession he, for one, would have no quarrel with him. And he was also for autonomy for Kashmir. He would oppose deletion of Section 370. Dealing with the reasons advanced by Sheikh Abdullah for undergoing a change of view, he said even now, he was faced to some extent with the same problems as faced Sheikh

Abdullah. The Jana Sangh agitation was there. The communal outlook of the services was there. He was fighting against both. He was aware that these problems had also plagued Sheikh Abdullah. But he had asked him to have them out with Pandit Nehru. Sheikh Abdullah never did so. He allowed things to simmer in his mind, and all this led to an explosion like a festering sore. (Sheikh Abdullah told me that he failed to get redress even after he had brought these things to Nehru's notice orally and in writing - Mine). He hesitated to talk freely to Pandit Nehru.

Finally I asked him if we could start our work (Centre) here. I pointed out that he had already agreed to such a course in my first visit, but I wanted to have it confirmed. He said he had no objection to this. Not only that, he would welcome such a course.

(I have already written to Narayan Desai about opening a Centre in Srinagar, and that he should visit Kashmir for this purpose.)

I finished the interview with an enhanced regard for Sadiq Saheb.

Sd/-

7.9.1966 (R.K. Patil)

JP's Reply to Patil's Report on Kashmir

Patna

September 12, 1966

My dear Patil Sahib,

I thank you for your letter and the report on your last visit to Kashmir. I read the report with great interest. It generally confirms what I had expected you to find, except for the fact that I did not expect, after Mr Sadiq's public outburst, that the Kashmir government reaction would be so positive. Below are a few comments:

1. I hope you did make it clear that whatever publicity my visit to Kodaikanal had received was certainly not due to me. If you remember, I had made no statement either before or after meeting the Sheikh. Mr Sadiq, moreover, should have realised that when a person like me met a detenue like Sheikh Abdullah, it was bound to become big news.

For that neither the government of India nor Jayaprakash Narayan could be blamed. Conceivably the government could have instructed the A.I.R. to keep mum, but I doubt if that would have been in accordance to the canons of freedom.

2. If Mr Sadiq had no objection to my meeting the Sheikh and was opposed only to the publicity, then in fairness to me he should have, as a gentleman, made his position clear. As it happens - and you know this yourself - that Mr Sadiq's statement was used by the Indian press, particularly the language press, to abuse me and paint me as a meddlesome fool who should better be behind prison bars. I suppose the good name and honour of a life-long servant of this country was of no concern to Mr Sadiq.
3. The plea of Mr Sadiq that he had no intention to make a statement and had only casually mentioned it to a newspaperman, bespeaks a rather weak character.
4. Why did the government of India not apprise Mr Sadiq of my visit is not my concern. But the chief minister, I think, should not have given vent to his grievance so publicly.
5. I hope that when you told Mr Sadiq that "Sheikh Saheb was not unwilling to consider an arrangement for the future relationship of the state of J&K with India, which maintained the accession, but provided for greater autonomy" (it was not 'greater' but 'full' autonomy that we had discussed), you also took care to tell him about the vital reservations that the Sheikh had made. This is not clear from your report. In case you did not make this clear, you should take care to do so during your next visit. I have serious doubts about Government of India's ability or willingness to meet the first two objections (as you would remember them) satisfactorily enough to encourage Sheikh Saheb to consider the full autonomy formula.
6. It is surprising to learn from your report that Mr Sadiq also believes in autonomy for Kashmir. He seems to have changed his opinion because some months back when I had raised this question with him, he had tried to explain at some length why he thought that autonomy was not beneficial for Kashmir. Also, it is not known that he ever

opposed the gradual erosion of autonomy that has taken place during his own regime.

7. Mr Sadiq's barber story is too ridiculous for words. It is really surprising that he should have considered it to be of such importance as to mention it to you to prove Sheikh Saheb's credulous nature.

8. Equally ridiculous is his other story, this time intended to prove the Sheikh's unreliability. It is a common experience that when an oral statement is recorded, unintentional discrepancies creep in. As a frequent rapporteur at seminars, you yourself must have had such experience. The difficulty is the greater when the subject is subtle and complicated.

9. Lastly, I have one little complaint against yourself. When Mr Sadiq caricatured to you what I had written in my letter to the Prime Minister, you say in your report that you "did not contradict Sadiq as I was not clear what letter he was referring to." Surely you know that on the issue of Kashmir I have written only one letter to Indiraji of which you have a copy - the same one which I had read out to the Prabandh Samiti at Sitabdiara. In any case, even if you thought that there was another letter, should you not have, on the basis of what you knew already disabused Mr Sadiq's mind? There was no mystery or mysticism in my proposal. I have never wanted an election to be turned into a plebiscite. You know my views well: we have discussed it so often. I regret that you did not explain my position to Mr Sadiq.

You end your report by saying that you came away from your interview with Mr Sadiq "with an enhanced regard for Sadiq saheb". I am sure Mr Sadiq is a very estimable person, but the picture of him that emerges from your interview does not induce in one any great regard for that worthy gentleman.

Yours sincerely

Sd/-

(Jayaprakash Narayan)

Shri R.K Patil,
Civil Lines,
Nagpur.

Free Abdullah for Peace in Kashmir, Says JP

Dhanbad, Sept 7 (PTI)—Sarvodya leader, Mr Jayaprakash Narayan, has reiterated here that unless Sheikh Abdullah was released and allowed to lead Kashmir, there could be no settlement of the Kashmir problem.

Mr Narayan dealt with the Kashmir problem in a three-hour speech at a public meeting here last evening.

While he did not disclose the details of his recent discussions with Sheikh Abdullah, Mr Narayan said that the Sheikh never wanted Kashmir to accede to Pakistan.

According to Mr Narayan, Sheikh Abdullah, in his speech at a conference of Muslim nations at Jeddah, two years ago, had categorically stated that Kashmir did not belong to Pakistan and strongly defended the action of the Indian government against Pakistani calumnies.

Mr Narayan said that Sheikh Abdullah later on had met the Chinese Premier, Mr Chou-En-lai, but in his talks with the latter had not said anything against Indian interests. It would, therefore, be wrong to call Sheikh Abdullah a traitor to India, Mr Narayan added.

Sino-Indian Dispute

Mr Narayan said what Sheikh Abdullah wanted was full autonomy for Kashmir within the Indian union.

Mr Narayan also referred to his discussions with President Ayub Khan and said that when he told the latter that no Indian government could part with Kashmir Valley and remain in power, President Ayub Khan also told him (Mr Narayan) categorically that no government in Pakistan could remain in power if it did not promise to get possession of Kashmir.

Mr Narayan said this would result in eternal tension between India and Pakistan and occasional wars between the two countries.

On the Sino-Indian border dispute, Mr Narayan said: "Here also, we should take the initiative to settle our differences through the good offices of an arbitrator."

Mr Narayan: "It is no use referring to the Colombo proposals for a settlement of the Sino-Indian differences as the External Affairs Minister, Mr Swaran Singh, has been doing repeatedly."

Mr Narayan suggested that India should approach China for a settlement and offer to her on lease the road which she had built across Aksai Chin.

(Hindustan Times, 8, September 1966)

13

Delhi Seminar on Kashmir

JJ Singh's Letter to JP

101, Friends Colony,
New Delhi - 14,
September 4th 1966

Dear J.P.,

Quite a few of us feel that all is not well in Kashmir. The resent tremors that went through the present Kashmir leadership just because Shri Jayaprakash Narayan met Sheikh Mohammad Abdullah indicate the precarious nature of stability in the state. It is true that Kashmir is part of India and its territory is not negotiable. The accession is "final and irrevocable". But should we be content with the accession of the real estate only? Should we not make effort for mental and emotional integration of the people of Kashmir with the rest of India.. What steps can be taken at the governmental and the non-governmental level to achieve this end? Can any useful role be played by Sheikh Mohammad Abdullah in this vital task. Can steps be taken to ensure free and fair elections in 1967, in the state of Jammu and Kashmir.

These and many other question arise in the search for peace and understanding between the people of Kashmir and the people in the rest of the country.

To exchange ideas and to reach, if possible, some solutions, it has been decided to hold a seminar in New Delhi.

The seminar will be held at the India International Centre, New Delhi, on October 4th, 5th and 6th.

An early reply will be greatly appreciated.

Yours sincerely
Sd/-
(J.J. Singh)

Organising Secretary.
Mr. Jayaprakash Narayan
Kadam Khan
Patna, Bihar.

(NMM&L. File No. 90)

Presidential Address

J.P. Narayan

JP presided over a seminar on Kashmir at India International Centre in New Delhi on 4 to 6 October 1966. The participants included, besides JP, M/s CD Deshmukh, Col B.H. Zaidi, PN Sapru, JJ Singh, Mohan Singh Mehta, S. Mulgaokar and Balraj Puri.

I do not think there is need for me to say very much because in this group here perhaps I am the one who has been speaking the most about this question. But as Chairman, I believe, I am expected again to say something so that my views could be brought to your notice. Now first of all I would like to point out that my views on this question have been changing as the situation has changed from time to time. I do not wish to apologise for it, because after all we have to take into account all aspects of the situation as these may be at a certain time. However, I think that in the course of these changes in my views I have not given up what I considered to be the underlying principle in this dispute regarding Kashmir. Without trying to go into the history of this dispute which, as you know, is rather long and complicated, I would begin with the situation as it is today.

I think it is of primary importance for us and for others concerned to decide whether the question of Kashmir is a settled question. As far as I have been able to understand, the Government of India's position is that the question has already been settled and there is noting more to be done about it. The arguments they advance to support this position is that the accession of the state to India in law is final, complete and irrevocable. Well, I do not know about the irrevocability, because nothing in history is really not a legal or constitutional question but a political question. As I see it the dispute has four parties to it: The government of India, the people of the state, the government of Pakistan and the United Nations. Yet, while there are these four parties, I do think that basically this dispute is between the government of India and the people of the state and if it was solved to the satisfaction of these two parties in an honest, creditable manner, in a manner which could be demonstrated to impartial observers throughout the world as having no deceit about it, and if a mutually satisfactory relationship is evolved between the government of India and the people of Kashmir, then it seems to me very clear that both the government of Pakistan and the United Nations will have to fall in line. They will have no option but to reconcile themselves to whatever the people of Kashmir and the Government of India mutually agree upon.

As I read the situation, the real desire of the Government of Pakistan is to seize the valley. Twice they tried to capture it by force, but they failed. But they have been saying openly, except in the very early days, that it is for the people of Kashmir to decide. Now if the people of the state really do so and the most popular leaders of the state like Sheikh Abdullah, Mirza Afzal Beg, etc. are party to it then I think Pakistan will have to agree that the people of the state have given their verdict. I think some way could be found to demonstrate to the world that this agreement between the Government of India and the leaders of Kashmir has the backing of the people of the state. I personally do not think that a plebiscite is at all possible, or, would be agreed to by India. I also do not think that plebiscite would be a good way of deciding this question. I think it would be very wrong. But I think plebiscite is not the only way in which the wishes of the people can be ascertained. Even the world community is coming to recognise other ways of doing so, such as in Saba, when Malaysia and Indonesia together agreed that the Secretary General of the United Nations should find out what the people wanted, whether they wanted to be a part of Indonesia or a part of Malayasia. May be, other ways could be found. I think even a general election, provided it is an honest general election, where the issues on which the people are supposed to express themselves are clearly placed before them and in which all the leaders of the people are allowed to take part, could convince the world. It may not convince the Government of Pakistan to begin with, though in their own hearts they would see that this solution was based on the verdict of the people. But it would certainly convince the world.

Dispute Basically Between Govt. of India and Kashmir

I would, therefore, repeat that the dispute basically is between the Government of India and the people of Kashmir. Of course, as I said earlier, the Government of India thinks that the issue is settled. I have read lots of press comments, particularly in the editorials of the language papers, to the effect that a man like me is unnecessarily and foolishly stirring up trouble, that there is quiet on the Kashmir front, that the people have reconciled themselves to whatever arrangements have been made for them and so on. I do not know whether the Government of India really believe all this, but I shall not be surprised to learn that they really do so. They have their intelligence working there, but they may think that the present leaders of the Congress in Kashmir would work some miracle in the next few years and win the majority of the people of the valley of the state, to the side of India. I do not think that the situation is like that at all. I have not been to Kashmir since January 1947. That was the one and the only time that I visited Kashmir or any part of Kashmir, when Maharaja Hari Singh was still ruling and Mr. Kak was the Prime Minister and there was every danger of my being arrested. But I was not. I stayed there for half a day and a night, made a speech, met some of the leaders who were still out and came away. Since then I have not been there. But I have tried to remain in touch with the situation through friends and others. Whatever information I have leads me to the conclusion that perhaps there is more discontent today amongst the Muslims of the state than at any earlier time. There is more anti-India feeling among them than before. This may not be all the time on the surface, but it is certainly below the surface and not very far below the surface. I do not think it would be possible for the Government of India, or the Government of Kashmir, the Congress Government of Kashmir, to win over the people, no matter what plans of development or what other plans of emotional integration they might have. I do not also think it is possible for them to solve the question by force. I hear a lot about a Kashmiri never having been known to have died for a cause throughout history. It may be so, but history changes and we would be shutting our eyes to the situation as it is growing or developing throughout the world. I think nationalism may be very stupid, but now it is there, it is the most important force today in the world against which no ideology, no religion, nothing else, seems to be an effective barrier. Nationalism is the most important force today in human society and there cannot be such a thing as the Kashmir government being able to suppress that nationalism. I do not even know if Indians could ever behave like that, for it would be like India's soul committing suicide. Yes, it will be a suicide of the soul of India, if India tried to suppress the Kashmiri people by force. But suppose we undertake to do it, can we ever succeed? My clear answer is that we will never succeed and deep discontent will remain the state. And this with two hostile nations, one of them a very powerful nation, a world power, on the borders. Possibly, if Kashmir were within the heart of India, somewhere in the middle of India and if we were ready to deny our whole history, and all our traditions, our culture and civilisation, may be some Indian government could have settled the question by force, disperse the population and colonise the area by Hindus and others. But I do not think any of these things is possible in Kashmir. If any large scale colonisation was to take place, even the Sadiq government would turn against it. I am absolutely certain, therefore, that any policy based on force cannot succeed. This view was shared by no less a person than Pandit Jawahar Lal Nehru. For eleven years a policy based on force was pursued. Sheikh Abdullah was in jail and Bakshi Ghulam Mohammed, who is much more efficient than Mr Sadiq, was in power and he used every means to put down the opposition. But he failed. Panditji had finally to release Sheikh Abdullah and the cases against him were dropped. I think the situation now is much worse than at that time and I think again we will be faced with the same result, no matter how long we keep the Sheikh and his colleagues in jail and whatever else we do there. Therefore I think it is in the interest of the Indian people, it is in the interest of the people of Kashmir, the people of the whole state of Jammu and Kashmir, in the interest of this sub-continent and in the interest of the world that this question is settled between the two primary parties to the dispute.

Sheikh Alone can Sway People of Kashmir

How can this be settled? I do not think this question can be settled by leaving Sheikh Abdullah out of it. He will have to be brought into the picture and, as many of you know, this was the Government of India's view at one time and the view of the Kashmir government too. I do not know what happened since then. During these last six months or so that whole policy has changed. But I think Sheikh Abdulah is one person who is still in a position to sway the people of the valley, the Muslims of the whole state, or, to be precise, that part of the state that is with India. He can influence the people of Kashmir to take whatever course of action he thinks best for them under the circumstances, in their own interest. Now, the question arises, what would Sheikh Abdulah want? Could there be any possibility of an agreement between him and the Government of India? Well, my answer is that if the Government of India is realistic, it should try to reach an agreement with him. If it fails, it will not then be blamed by the world. The world will than be convinced that we have made a serious attempt, gone to the farthest limit to which we could under the circumstances. We would then have more friends in the world. The world public opinion cannot be treated with contempt as some people here in New Delhi pretend to assert. On the contrary, it is of the greatest importance that we pay some head to that opinion. However, if serious attempts were made, not some kind of political trick to be played with Sheikh Abdullah but really sincerely, efforts to arrive at a settlement with him, my own feeling, based upon my talk with him and the earlier talks of my friends Mr Narayan Desai and Mr Radha Krishna, both of whom are here, is that there is a possibility, I would not say with certainty, of agreement being reached with Sheikh Sahib.

Reasonable Solution of Kashmiri

The third point that I wish to make in course of these preliminary remarks is to explain that I consider to be a reasonable solution of the problem as we are facing it today. I am not saying that Pakistan has no place in this dispute. It certainly has. The cease fire line is there, its army is there on the other side and we have ourselves made Pakistan a party to the dispute in the Security Council. It was open to us to eliminate Pakistan when the dispute began, because Pakistan itself at one time denied any hand in the aggression of 1947 when Zaffarallah Khan made a statement to that effect before the Security Council. Any how that is past history. The fact is that even after we settle with the people of Kashmir, we will have to, with the help of the Kashmir government, may be, settle this question of the Cease Fire Line and Azad Kashmir; some kind of political settlement with the Pakistan government will have to be reached. Again I am saying Pakistan government, because about the people of Pakistan I do not know how strongly they feel about it: in East Pakistan the feeling about Kashmir is certainly not strong. I think in South India, feeling at one time was not so strong but after the last war with Pakistan, in which many Southern officers and men laid down their lives, emotionally South India has also got involved. However, I have said on an earlier occasion that after this war Pakistan has no locus standii in this dispute. While on the face of it, it seems to be nonsense because after all the dispute in the Security Council is there. The Cease Fire Line is there, Azad Kashmir is there - occupied Kashmir we call it and they call our portion of Kashmir as occupied Kashmir. Even then what I meant was, and I still stand by it, that when there are two parties to a dispute and they agree to talk it over, each party has a place in the talks. But then if one party draws its sword out and says, "all right you accept my version of it or otherwise I will chop your head Off", the only answer from the other party will be, "all right chop my head off, but then you can have no place in negotiations." It is in that sense that I had said that after the war, Pakistan had no locus standii in the Kashmir dispute. There was the Kutch Agreement and hopes were held out by both sides that this agreement would lead to the easing of tension and lo and behold the infiltration started. May be, at the very time when the signatures were put down on that parchment this was being done by Pakistan. I really could not understand this at all. The constitutional amendment in respect of Article 370 had been made before Kutch. Since Kutch there had been no provocation from the side of India, so far as I remember.

From all the information that foreign sources have given us, it seems to us that President Ayub Khan had been persuaded - he was not in favour of it in the beginning - to go along with the hawks there on the assumption that India would not attack through the Punjab border and if India decided to fight it out in Jammu and Kashmir area then it would not be difficult to cut Jammu and Kashmir off from India; and in that way the whole of Kashmir state could be occupied and then the question would be settled for all times, as they think the Azad Kashmir issue had been settled. But our government decided that this could not be allowed to take place, and what was not expected to happen by Pakistan did happen. Whatever that might be, the Pakistan govt did embark on a military gamble. They had done this for the second time and it was particularly reprehensible since it had happened so soon after the Kutch Agreement. It was in that context that I had said that they had no locus standii in Kashmir. But I am not shutting my eyes to the fact that the Cease Fire Line is there, Azad Kashmir is there and the dispute is before the international community. In that sense Pakistan is certainly a party to it. However, as I said earlier, if there is a real settlement with the people of the state to which all sections including those represented by Sheikh Abdullah are a party, then I think the grounds from under Pakistan's feet would be knocked out and their leaders will have to accept it sooner or later. They may raise a sort of hoo ha there about it and even start denouncing Sheikh Abdullah as a traitor, but ultimately they will have to accept it.

Deaccession Not Possible

I was proceeding to say what I think is the best solution in the present circumstances. I had earlier thought, as some of your know, that perhaps is the fairest solution of this problem could be that India agreed to Pakistan's keeping 'Azad Kashmir', the Cease Fire Line was rationalised, Jammu and Ladakh remained in India and the valley was made into an autonomous state, demilitarised and neutralised, neither a part of India nor a part of Pakistan. Now I do not think that after the last war such a solution is any longer practicable. Even if any of us here, having the most friendly feelings for Pakistan and for the people of Kashmir and wanting a settlement and keen to be as generous about it as possible, were the Prime Minister of India, it would not be possible for him to place before the people of this country a solution which involved some kind of deaccession from India of any part of Kashmir. I do not think it is practicable politics. Besides, any autonomous or independent state of the valley, even if neutralised and demilitarised, is not likely to be allowed to remain autonomous or independent very long and there would always be present the danger of war between India and Pakistan, or between India and China, and also the danger of internal subversion, and the people of Kashmir would be most unhappy. Before the emergence of China as a great and aggressive power, perhaps such a settlement might have been arrived at with Pakistan being a party to it. But I do not know whether even this can be said now, after the last military adventure by Pakistan. Frankly I have to admit that I did not expect this from President Ayub Khan. I know him. I have had several talks with him. Some other friends also went with me last time (1964) when I went there on my second visit. I have been very much impressed by President Ayub's personality, by his sincerity about friendship with India and so on. Therefore, it was a shock to me that so soon after the Kutch Agreement he should have allowed a large scale secret invasion, which infiltration really meant. I am now not prepared to accept the bona fides of the Pakistan Government, any Pakistan government, regarding an independent or autonomous state of the valley. Therefore, I think that whatever solution is possible between the government of India and the people of Kashmir it has to be within the framework of the accession. The utmost that the Government of India can do is to go back to the 1947-53 days, that is, go back to the time when the state had acceded to India only in three subjects. This will mean providing for the fullest possible autonomy. The centre may look after Defence, External Affairs and Communications, may be also Currency, but the rest should be the concern of the people of the state, the undivided state as today, a part of India. I am not saying that this should be done on the basis of partition. The state must remain as it is in the context of a settlement with leaders, genuine leaders or more popular leaders. I am not saying Mr. Ghulam Mohammed Sadiq is not a leader, he certainly is a leader, but the more popular leaders like Sheikh Abdullah and Mirza Afzal Beg will also have to be associated with any settlement which we wish to be lasting. Any such settlement might have quite a sizeable portion of the Muslim population in the valley dissatisfied, and if there is any one who could make this palatable to such people, I think it is only Sheikh Abdullah, provided of course, that such a settlement is acceptable to him.

There are all kinds of difficulties about this formula based on full internal autonomy. On difficulty may be in regard to the partition of the state, as I have already spoken just now. The other difficulty might be relating to security. The state was autonomous to begin with but its autonomy gradually eroded and some sort of constitutional and other arrangements will have to be made to see that this sort of thing is not repeated again. There may be other difficulties. I do not know. But I honestly do not see that it is possible for any government of India to go beyond this at the present time. I have some hope. I would not say I am certain that Sheikh Abdulah might be in a position to accept such a settlement. It is only for him to say. But I have a feeling that after consulting his colleagues, may be some soundings in the valley, he might be prepared to accept this. If that were to happen then I think a treaty could be signed with Pakistan, may be after two to three years when Pakistan realised that this really had the backing of the people of Kashmir. For, in the changed context, the slogan, 'Let the people decide', would sound hollow and would be laughted at. If Pakistan continues to sing that song, Pakistan would be placed in more or less the same position as perhaps India is in the world today on this issue. I do not think any body in the world will be with Pakistan in the new situation, and some kind of treaty, some arrangement about Cease Fire Line etc., could be reached. In brief this is my thinking at present on this subject.

I feel that a settlement must be acceptable both politically and morally. Politically, of course, I have said that nothing else seems practicable. Even over a small matter like the release of Sheikh Abdullah, all who are in power have been saying, and every body else is singing in unison with them, that Sheikh Abdullah cannot be released, it is too dangerous, and so on. But even supposing there was some hope there, the utmost that could be hoped cannot go beyond what I have outlined above. This is also politically sound, a right thing to do. Morally also this does seem to be to be right. I have already told you that I think about independence for the valley, in the changed situation. If I were a Kashmiri Muslim, I do not think I would be happy about it. I think by and large on account of Sheikh Abdullah's leadership the Muslims of the valley have democratic and secular ideas and also believe in some sort of progressive economic ideas, which may perhaps be described as socialism. They are poor people, most of them, they are wedded to radical socio-economic programmes and ideas and I do not think they would get any of those things in Pakistan. They know that East Pakistan has lost its identity and its personality. The Pathans have lost it, as West Pakistan is dominated more or less by Punjabi Muslims. I think Kashmiris will find such dominating even less palatable than perhaps East Pakistanis are finding it. So I would say an autonomous status for Kashmir within the Indian union would be in the best interest of the people of the valley also. Therefore I say that it is morally also right, provided the people were to accept this.

If they do not accept it, then it is a different matter. We should not try to force it down their throats. That would be morally wrong. It may be considered to be politically expedient, but I have already told you that this kind of expediency in that geographical situation would not succeed. It would be a disaster. I would be happy if Mr Sadiq and Mr Qasim were to succeed in winning over the Kashmiri Muslims to India's side. But I am absolutely sure that they will not succeed in doing so.

Morally not Politically Obnoxious to Rule by Force

In that case if we continue to rule by force and suppress these people and crush them or change the racial or religious character of their state by colonisation, or by any other means, then I think that means politically a most obnoxious thing and morally also a most obnoxious thing to do. Kashmir has cost us a great deal and it is time that every one who is a patriot in this country thought seriously about a really good solution. I have already told you what I think is a really good solution.

JP's remarks: Mr Bazaz's statement has made a sensation. Mr Mohammad Shah was telling me that he did not agree with Mr Bazaz's statement that there were one thousand or more people in jail under Sheikh Abdullah's rule in those early days. I put it to Mr Bazaz and he said that in the jail in which he was himself imprisioned there were about two hundred people belonging to his own party, the Kissan Mazdoor Party. I said why should Sheikh Abdullah put so many people in prison. He said that those who were insisting on the right of plebiscite to be exercised, they were the people whom he put out of harm by putting them in prison. This is a question of fact. Mohammad Shah says that only a dozen or so were in jail, whereas Mr Bazaz says there were thousands. I leave it to Mr Bazaz to clarify this point further.

Now I would like first to invite those friends who have not taken the trouble of writing papers to speak.

(At the end of the seminar, JP made the following concluding observations)

(NMM&L, File No. 90)

JP's Observations

We must be conscious of one thing: the views that so far have been expressed here are very different from the views held by the Government of India and the Congress party. You know what those views are and they have been recently talking about them and very recently the Prime Minister was talking about them when she went to Kashmir.

The other point is that facts that seem to us to be incontestable are not accepted by the Government. Their facts are different. In talking to them we are at cross purposes. When we say there is discontentment, they say it is all nonsense; I think they feed the people of the country also, those who read newspapers or listen to radio or look at the newsreel, with this interpretation of the situation. Everywhere I hear things which are quite at variance with what the government says. Now who is to be believed? They say that every thing is quite normal and only if we remain firm every thing is going to turn out well. If any other sets of facts are placed before the people, we are accused of being unpatriotic.

The third point is about Sheikh Abdullah's statement regarding accession. I hear a good deal about it in political circles. There are three categories of statements made by Sheikh Abdullah. In the first category are the speeches made by him in the Assembly in Kashmir or in the Security Council in New York. The second category consists of those speeches which he made before the National Conference, Press Conferences, etc. The third category of speeches or statements attributed to him are the public speeches. My view is that no credence is to be placed on the reports of the public speeches. Very often when I read a report of a speech I had made, I hardly recognise myself. Pandit Jawaharlal jee also often complained that he was not correctly reported. When I took up certain things with Shri Lal Bahadur Shastri, saying why he said this or that, he said, "I never said that". So when Prime Ministers are misrepresented in the press, we can easily imagine what can happen to others. The fact is when one is speaking in public, it is a long speech, an impassioned speech, the leader is being carried away and the speeches are in turn carried away by the reporters. So I will not give any serious consideration to the last category of speeches.

I have personally examined some of Sheikh Abdullah's statements and his position until 1953 had been that there was accession to India and it had his full support, but it had also been agreed upon that accession shall be ratified in some manner by the people. When the question of Constituent Assembly came up I myself heard that Sheikh Abdullah had suggested that the decision of the Constituent Assembly might be treated as representing the verdict of the people, but Mr. Nehru said, "No, how can that be?". Shri B.N. Rao and Shri Gopalswamy Ayanger said in the Security Council that nobody could stop the Constituent Assembly from committing itself to any policy regarding accession, but the decision of the Constituent Assembly would not commit the Government of India, because the latter were concerned with the people's verdict. Thus until 1953, the Sheikh's position was that the accession had been accepted by him, but it was understood that it would have to be ratified in some way or the other by the people. He was prepared to have the ratification by the Constituent Assembly, but India herself said no. So the political question of ratification comes. This is very important. It is very clear from Sheikh Abdullah's statements that he never went back on this: the need for ratification in some manner or the other. Not necessarily plebiscite, because in that case he would not have said, 'let the Constituent Assembly decide.' He of course said that whenever this question was placed before the people of Kashmir his recommendation to them would be to ratify the accession. His latest position is that he is not committed to accept whatever has happened after his arrest. He does not, therefore, accept the Constituent Assembly's decision after his arrest as the verdict of the people or even a verdict of the party of which he himself was the leader till the day of his arrest. So he is not concerned with what has been said or done under the rule of Mr Bakshi Ghulam Mohammad. Hence it is no use quoting from his past speeches. At no time have I seen Sheikh Abdullah saying that accession was complete, final and irrevocable. Every time he had said this has been done with his support, he had advised it in the circumstances, as there was no other alternative, but this was to be subject to rectification by the people of Kashmir in some way or other. I wanted to clarify these points, as they are bound to come up again and again.

Elections Don't Represent Popular Verdict

We, of course, have been saying that there have been three general elections in Kashmir and their verdict has clearly been in favour of India. But the Security Council is not convinced that there was an election held in Kashmir which really represented the will of the people. And the same position is likely to remain after the fourth general election. With Sheikh Abdullah and Mirza Afzal Beg in jail, no matter how much we are going to shout about free and fair election, it is not going to convince any body in the world. On the other hand, if Sheikh Abdullah were in a position to say that he had the full freedom to campaign and his people had complete freedom and there was no coercion, I think the situation today is such that the Security Council will have to accept the result of such an election as the verdict of the people. Sheikh Abdullah is not going to say all this to please India, or to save India's face; he will say it only if he is convinced of this. That is why I have been pleading that we should convince Sheikh Abdullah that the solution outlined above is the best and also give him enough time to accept our position and to persuade the Muslims of Kashmir and, later on, the Pakistan government. The Pakistan government may not be in the picture in the first place, but it might come in later on. So this is what I feel. I do hope my own position is properly understood. This is rather a complex position, but whatever it is I think there should be no misunderstanding.

I think all the friends and the participants have had their say. After listening to the speeches this morning I felt that I should not repeat what I said at the beginning. I may read out to you a letter which I wrote to the Prime Minister suggesting the release of Sheikh Abdulah. It created quite a bit of a stir in the newspapers, but it has not been possible so far to publish it.

Do you think it is possible for us to issue a statement or is there any need for us to issue any statement. Please think over it. I personally think that probably this kind of statement, statement which was drawn up, does take us further and also at the same time does express a consensus that at least appeared until last evening. Of course two very strong and able statements were made today which many not come within the range of this statement. So let me just need it out.

"In the belief that the situation in Kashmir is developing in a manner detrimental to the real interest of India and Kashmir and that the issue called for wider public debate, a seminar met in New Delhi at the India International Centre from 4th October to 6th October 1967 under the Chairmanship of Shri Jayaprakash Narayan. There was a free and frank discussion and diverse views were expressed on the short term and the long term aspects of the problem of Kashmir. The consensus emerged that a solution in Kashmir could only be sought within the framework of accession to India." This is important. Mark you. Mark the words 'could only be'. I am only talking of possibilities, not that each one of us subscribes to it. But the objective analysis is that a solution could only be sought within the framework of accession to India. Further, the relations between the state and the Centre should be decided according to the wishes of the people determined through an election which should be fair and free. For initiating such process the seminar suggests the release of Sheikh Mohammad Abdullah and his colleagues from detention as the first essential step. The seminar accepted their key role in bringing stability in Kashmir and was of the view that Sheikh Abdullah was not opposed to Kashmir's accession to India in all circumstances."

October 7, 1966

(NMM&L File No. 90)

Plea for Removal of Curbs on Sheikh Abdullah

A seminar on Kashmir held in New Delhi felt that relations between the centre and the state of Jammu and Kashmir within the framework of the constitution should be "determined through a free and fair election" in the state.

The seminar was held under the chairmanship of Mr Jayaprakash Narayan, Sarvodaya leader, from Oct 4 to 6 to enable a free and frank discussion of the issue which "called for a wider public debate".

In initiating the process to find out the wishes of the people of the state, the seminar appealed to the Union government to remove restrictions on the free movement of Sheikh Abdullah and Mirza Afzal Beg. Another appeal was made to the Government of Jammu and Kashmir to release all political prisoners.

The seminar felt that such a course was necessary for "restoring normalcy" in Kashmir and minimising "international misconceptions" in regard to the question of Kashmir.

Those who participated in the seminar were Dr. C.D. Deshmukh, Syed Mubarak Shah Naqashbandi, Mr P.N. Sapru, Col. B.H. Zaidi MP, Mr Mulgaokar, Mr. S.P. Godrej, Dr. P.S. Loknathan, Mr. Shiva Rao,Mr. Khushwant Singh, Mr D.L. Mazumdar, Mr. S.L. Popalai, Mr. Chanchal Sarkar, Mr Radhakrishna, Mr Sugata Dasgupta, Mr Rajeshwar Patel, MP, Mr R.K. Patil, Mr Prem Nath Bazaz, Mr A.C Sen, Dr. Bimla Prasad, Mr. C.C. Desai, Mr. Balraj Puri, Mr. Narayan Desai and Mr. J.J. Singh. — UNI

(*Times of India,* 8 October 1966)

Protest Letter to T.O.I., H.T., I.E.

101, Friends Colony
New Delhi - 14.

October 16, 1966

The Editor,
Times of India, Hindustan Times, Indian Express,
New Delhi.

Sir,

I write to protest against the unfair manner in which an important public issue like Kashmir has been treated in your columns. As you may be aware a seminar on Kashmir was held in New Delhi under my chairmanship from October 4 to 6. There were 24 participants each one of whom occupies an important position in the public life of this country. And yet even the short statement, embodying the seminar's consensus that was sent to your esteemed journal for publication, along with the list of the participants was found to be undeserving of publication in full. The brief report published in your paper did justice neither to the seminar nor to your readers who were entitled to know what the participants have to say. A healthy public debate is impossible under such conditions of one-sided publicity. And where healthy debate is denied, democracy is weakened and the decisions taken are more likely than not to go wrong.

Yours etc.

Sd/-

(Jayaprakash Narayan)

(NMM&L, File No. 90)

J.P.'s Meddling

Shri Dhanraj Bargotra, Chairman Jammu and Kashmir PSP, has accused Shri Jayaprakash Narayan of confusing the Kashmir issue. JP's suggestion of conducting an opinion poll is meaningless and is an attempt to bolster the morale of those advocating secession, Shri Bargotra feels.

Shri Bargotra says he fails to understand what JP exactly means by opinion poll. The suggestion is vague and will only complicate the issue further. JP's oft-repeated vague suggestions are doing more harm than good to the settlement of the issue. Whenever the people begin to reconcile, JP shows them a way that "Kashmir is not a settled issue." This is an invasion on the peace of the state by JP", he says.

Shri Bargotra strongly criticises JP for comparing Jammu and Kashmir state with the country under the British rule. He asserts that "we of the Jammu and Kashmir state are as much free as JP himself. To term us as slaves is utter nonsense and JP has thereby insulted every resident of the state of Jammu and Kashmir."

(*Janata*, February 5, 1967, Page No. 11)

Free Sheikh, End Kashmir Problem: JP

Hyderabad, April 26 (UNI) — "To think there is no Kashmir problem is to behave like ostriches," Mr Jayaprakash Narayan, Sarvodaya leader, told a news conference here today.

The Sarvodaya leader strongly advocated the release of Sheikh Abdullah and said he could play a part under favourable conditions in solving the Kashmir problem.

Mr Narayan, however, said that "any solution has to be with Kashmir as part of the Indian Union."

As to what the political status of Kashmir vis-à-vis the Indian Union should be, he said it was "an open question." The people of Kashmir had a right of expression as in the case of Nagaland.

Mr Narayan said there was political discontent in Kashmir. With the existing state of affairs the people were not satisfied with political arrangement. Elections were "fairly fair" in the rest of India but unfortunately not in Kashmir.

Mr Narayan said that a section of the press and politicians did not present Sheikh Abdullah objectively. The role of the Sheikh during his last foreign tour was to his credit. He pointed out that at the Islamic Conference held at Jeddah, the Sheikh's speech was a discomfiture to the Pakistan representative. Unfortunately these were not reported in the Indian Press.

It was very unfair to keep a person in detention. If there was any charge against the Sheikh Saheb, "by all means try him," he said.

Narayan said there were several ways of ascertaining the wishes of the people in the state other than plebiscite.

He would not rule out the international community finding out the wishes of the people in Kashmir. There was no question of Pakistan not accepting it for it had all along been saying that it only wanted the right expression of the people of Kashmir.

(*Hindustan Times*, 27 April 1967)

JP Welcomes Sheikh Release

Patna, Jan 3 (PTI): Mr Jayaprakash Narayan, the Sarvodaya leader, has welcomed Sheikh Abdullah to freedom and also congratulated the Union government for having done the right at last.

Mr Narayan in a statement today said: "I do hope that the Government of India, opposition party leaders as well as the Sheikh Saheb, his colleagues and other leaders of Jammu and Kashmir, would not let the present opportunity go waste again.

"While the Sheikh Saheb's release is a vindication, though belated, of India's democratic way of life, that is the less important aspect of it. What is more important is utilization of this opportunity constructively and imaginatively for satisfying the aspirations of the people of Kashmir for a status that would give them self-respect and self-government as part of the larger Indian community.

Once that aim is achieved, it should not be difficult to settle the dispute with Pakistan on the Kashmir question."

(Hindustan Times, 4 January 1968)

JP Explains Stand on Kashmir to New Yorkers

NEW YORK, March 30 (PTI) -Mr Jaya Parkash Narayan, the Sarvodaya leader, arrived here yesterday from Washington.

He is on a tour of America as guest of the Quakers Organization.

In New York among others, Mr Narayan is due to meet UN Secretary-Generalu Thant.

In Washington, Mr Narayan met Secretary of State Dean Rusk and Pakistan's Ambassador to Washington Agha Hilali.

Besides these official meetings, he has also been meeting a number of private groups and addressing seminars.

Within Statute

In a series of meetings with American private groups and journalists in Washington, Mr Narayan emphasized that after the 1965 Indo-Pakistan conflict, the Kashmir question could be settled only within the framework of the Indian Constitution and Kashmir being part of the Indian Union.

However, within this framework, Mr Narayan advocated radical solutions including greater autonomy for Jammu and Kashmir State within the Union and within Kashmir itself, autonomy for Jammu.

Mr Narayan also emphasized that India would have to settle with Sheikh Abdullah for any Kashmir solution.

While he was not sure whether the course he advocated would be acceptable to the Sheikh, Mr Narayan argued, however, that if the Sheikh reached a settlement with India, Pakistan would have to accept it.

Mr Narayan in essence also suggested that India should forget the territory under Pakistani occupation and the territory under Chinese occupation whether seized from India by China or obtained as gift from President Ayub Khan.

(Hindustan Times 31.3.1968)

14

J&K People's Convention

Abdullah Invitation to JP

Sher-e-Kashmir Manzil,
Soura, Srinagar
31st July, 1968

My dear JP,

No one is more conscious of the tragic consequences of the stalemate over Kashmir than yourself. Each day's delay in resolving it aggravates the situation, deepening further the political instability and economic distress of the people of the state. Far from enjoying the fruits of freedom, our people, during the past two decades, have faced incalculable hardships, in every walk of life; their social and political life has been paralysed and economically they have been crippled. What a life of misery and dishonour they are going through is revealed to some extent in the report of Ms Vimla Thakar, who was deputed for on the spot enquiry by Sarva Seva Sangh, which must have come to your notice also. This report gives only a glimpse of the total picture. Recently reports of similar tragic incidents came to my notice in Gool Gulab Garh (Reasi) where I was on tour. In the valley also instances of such nature are not uncommon.

My own view of the matter is that the main cause for the stalemate and the resultant agony is the failure to recognise that the problem is solely that of the people of the state, and that it is not a dispute between the two of its neighbours, as it has been treated for the last 21 years at every level. This basically wrong approach has eluded a just and equitable solution.

No doubt that this political stalemate has not only nearly destroyed good neighbourly relations between India and Pakistan but is inflicting tremendous economic hardships on the people of the sub-continent; nevertheless, the real sufferers are the people of the state themselves, who are becoming increasingly restive and are understandably anxious to finally settle their political future and end their agony. To that end their desire is to wrest the initiative and make an earnest effort to bring about an equitable settlement of the dispute.

Accordingly, I propose to hold a Convention of the liberal minded and intellectual citizens of the state by the middle of September, 1968, with a view to arrive at such conclusions as may bring about a lasting and honourable solution. Letter is attached herewith for your perusal. In view of your close association with this question as also your deep interest in the well being of the people, it is our desire to request you to inaugurate the Convention in Srinagar and we earnestly hope that you will kindly accept the request. I am anxiously awaiting your intimation of acceptance.

I hope you are doing well. Kindly give my regards to Prabhaji.

Yours sincerely

Sd/-

(Sheikh Mohd Abdullah)

Shri J.P. Narayan

Patna.

(NMM&L. File No. 93)

Balraj Puri's Letter to JP

Dated 6th Sept., 1968

My dear J.P

I am enclosing a letter which I have written to Sheikh Abdullah on the question of our participation in the State People's Convention that he has convened. In view of the fact that no other significant party from Jammu is likely to attend the convention, I was keen we do get an opportunity to do so. In fact I had suggested that somebody from Jammu be associated with the convention at the sponsoring stage and that the problem of regional relations is included in the agenda. I am still hoping for a favourable response from Sheikh Sahib but as you are reported to have agreed to inaugurate the convention I thought it proper that you should know our position.

May I suggest that on your return you spare a day for Jammu in particular to participate in our celebrations of Gandhi Jayanti apart from other activities that we are planning for the occasion. A large number of Jammu citizens would take a pledge to maintain communal harmony. If you could kindly spare time and agree to administer the oath, its moral, emotional and political value would obviously become tremendous.

With kind regards,

Yours sincerely,

Shri J.P. Narayan, Sd/-

Kadam Kuan, Patna. Balraj Puri

** Sheikh Abdullah agreed to include it in the agenda and I agreed to join the Steering Committee of the Convention and participate in its delibrations.(Ed.)*

GM Sadiq to JP

Chief Minister

Srinagar

No. CMS (Genl)/14/68

Sept 25, 1968

My dear Shri Jayaprakash Ji,

Thank you very much for your letter dated the 14th September. It was indeed such a disappointment not to have been able to meet you. I shall now be looking forward to meeting you when you visit Srinagar next month.

Incidentally, since you will be coming to Kashmir after a very long time you might like to go round and see a bit of the development that has taken place in the valley. If you agree I shall have necessary arrangements made for your visit to some places.

If you like us to make any arrangements in connection with your stay etc. here we shall be only too glad to do so.

With kindest regards,

Yours sincerely

Shri Jayaprakash Narayan, Sd/-

Kadam Kuan, Patna - 3. (G.M. Sadiq)

(NMM&L, File No. 93)

Abdullah's Letter to JP

Mujahid Manzil,
Srinagar,
No. 85 A,
26th Sept 1968

My dear JP,

I and members of the Steering Committee are grateful to you for having accepted our invitation to inaugurate J&K State People's Convention on the 10th instant. I shall feel delighted if Prabha ji could also accompany you. If you want to bring somebody else along with you as your assistant, he, too is most welcome.

Your Board and Lodge has been fixed in the Nedou's Hotel as advised by JJ. You will be received by us at the airport, expecting you by the first flight on the 10th Oct. From the Airport you will be taken to Nedou's where you will have lunch and a little rest. You will start from the Nedou's at 3 pm for Mujahid Manzil to inaugurate the convention.

On the 11th of Oct, the delegates will meet in the Ist Session from 9 am to 1 pm. You are welcome to attend this session if you so choose. The same day you will address a public meeting in the city at 8 PM. On the 12th October, the Convention will meet again from 9 to 12 noon. I and the Members of the Steering Committee will see you off that afternoon.

In between the Sessions of the Convention you will of course have an opportunity to meet the delegates. I trust this program will suit your convenience.

I hope you are doing well.

With kindest regards to both of you,

Yours sincerely
Sd/-
(Sheikh Mohd Abdullah)

Shri Jai Prakash Narain,
Kadam Kuan,
Patna - 3, Bihar.

(NMM&L. File No. 93)

Sheikh Abdullah's Welcome Address at People's Convention

Dated 10 Oct, 1968

It is a matter of great privilege and pleasure for me to welcome you all here today on this historic occasion when we are meeting at a crucial period of our long and chequered history, marked by many vicissitudes, and ups and downs but also by a fair modicum of successes, which God in His great wisdom and bounty had bestowed upon some of our labours. I see before me today a distinguished gathering belonging to the various segments of our society and representing diverse thoughts and opinions in our body politic. That indeed is a measure of the value which this meet carries and earnest of our efforts to explore the situation to the best of our ability.

This is no occasion to dig the past for its own sake, to indulge in recriminations or rancour, as we bear ill-well to none. If we in this convention seek to do any post-mortem of the past events we are solely motivated by our desire to find a way out of our present impasse. In doing so, I hope and pray that we shall not be guided by any narrow or parochial considerations but by the larger interests of our people; and we may therefore bring to bear on our task that catholicity and urbanity of outlook, a dispassionate consideration of our problems and an objectivity which is both informed and constructive and is free from any taint of malice, ill-will or disaffection in our attempt to get down to the heart of our problem. Where there is no place to apportion praise or blame for our present malaise.

The task that I have indicated above is, therefore, one of stocktaking, of heart searching of turning to God for His gracious guidance, so that no words that may fall from our lips may wittingly or unwittingly wound any susceptibilities or arouse any passions; but in a clam, cool and calculated manner. We may proceed to our task not deflected from our course by the provocations that have been hurled at us or still may be hurled at us, even questioning our very bonafides and our credentials.

Nehru's Commitments

We, who have laboured so long in this great adventure for our people's freedom and emancipation from tyranny, have not a clean slate to right upon. To quote the words of the great departed leader, Mr. Nehru, who had stated as far back as June 26th, 1952:

"We have not got a clean slate to write upon; we are limited, inhibited by our commitments to the United Nations, by this, by that. But nevertheless, the basic fact remains that we have declared- and even it we had not declared the fact would remain- that it is the people of Kashmir who must decide. And I say with all respect to our Constitution that it just does not matter what your Constitution says, if the people of Kashmir do not want it, it will not go there..... Let us suppose there was proper plebiscite there - and the people of Kashmir said, "We do not want to be with India." Well, we are committed to it, we would accept it. It might pain us but we would not send an army against them; we might accept it, however much hurt we might feel about it, and we should change our Constitution about it."

In another speech in the same vein on August 7, 1952 he had stated:-

"It is an international problem. It would be an international problem anyhow if it concerned any other nation besides Indian, and it does. It became further an international problem because a large number of other countries also took an interest and gave advice.... So while the accession was complete in law and fact, the other fact which has nothing to do with the law also remains, namely, our pledge to the people of Kashmir -if you like, to the people of the world-that this matter can be reaffirmed or cancelled or cut out by the people of Kashmir if they so wish. We do not want to win people against their will and with the help of armed force, and if the people of Jammu and Kashmir State so wish it, to part company from us, they can go their way and we shall go our way. We want no forced marriages, no forced unions like this.....

So, we accept this basic proposition that this question is going to be decided finally by the good will and pleasure of the people of Kashmir, not, I say, by the good will and pleasure of even this Parliament if it so chooses, not because this Parliament may not have the strength to decide it- I do not deny that- but because this Parliament has not only laid down in this particular matter that a certain policy will be pursued in regard to Jammu and Kashmir State but it has been our policy.....

But whether it is a pain and a torment, if the people of Kashmir want to go out, let them go because we will not keep them against their will however painful it may be to us. That is the policy that India will pursue and because India will pursue that policy, people will not leave her. People will cling to her come to her. Because the strongest bonds that bind will not be the bonds of your armies or even of your constitution to which so much reference has been made, but bonds which are stronger than the constitution and laws and armies-bonds that bind through love and affection and understanding of various peoples. Therefore, we must be clear in our minds, that this question in regard to the future of Jammu and Kashmir State can ultimately only be decided by the people of Jammu and Kashmir State. Having come to that conclusion then, let us fashion our other policies accordingly, then let us not find fault with something here and there because it does not fit in with our wishes."

Gandhi's Observations

Gandhi ji made the following observations on August 5th, 1947 which are as relevant today as when they were made.

He had no hesitation in saying that the will of the Kashmiris was supreme law in Kashmir and Jammu... "The common sense dictated that the will of Kashmiris should decide the fate of Kashmir and Jammu. The sooner it was done, the better."

India will he free on 15th August, what of Kashmir? A deputation of workers asked him that question at Jammu. " That will depend on the people of Kashmir," Gandhi ji replied: They all wanted to know whether Kashmir would join the Union or Pakistan. "That again" answered Gandhi Ji: "should be decided by the will of the Kashmiris."

On the conclusion of his visit to Kashmir he wrote to Pt. Nehru:

"that both (Maharaja and Maharani) admitted that with the lapse of British Paramountcy, the true Paramountcy of the people of Kashmir will commence. However; much thay might wish to join with the Union, they would have to make the choice in accordance with the wishes of the people."

May, I say in all humility that Gandhi and Nehru, the twin stars that have shone on the firmament of India and who dominated the scene for over half a century are synonymous with India and that not only their honour is bound up with their word but the honour of India is likewise bound up with their word, and any attempt made to wriggle out of any solemn pledges given by them would tend to sully the image of India and tarnish it as nothing else would do.

Gentlemen, I am circulating a copy of an Article that I contributed to the " *Foreign Affairs* Journal" of America at their request which deals briefly with the genesis of the Kashmir question. It is, therefore, not necessary for me to refer in this address to any of these matters in details. Suffice if to say that it embodies some suggestions which had been canvassed to settle this much vexed question of the State, which I commend to your consideration. While I have no desire to prejudice your consideration thereof, I wish to say that the Dixon Plan referred to therein suffers from the obvious defect that it denies to the areas other than the "Valley and adjoining areas" what it concedes in the case of the Valley and its adjoining areas.

International Aspects of the Problem

It is, however, noteworthy to add that there is the international aspect of the problem, the guarantees given to the International community and more particularly to the people of Jammu and Kashmir; guarantees and pledges which were rooted in their hoary past and were sanctified by the blood and sweat and the tears that went with them. These tears continue to be shed: and though about a quarter of a century has passed, when freedom dawned on the sub-continent the people of Jammu and Kashmir continue to toil and labour under unmitigated suffering patiently borne for the vindication of their just rights and fair play and justice as God's great dispensation to them. While we pay lip service to these great principles and ideals, we do precious little to further the realization of these objective, but relentlessly pursue courses leading to the opposite direction and to the denial to them of the fruits of their portion of freedom. I do not think I have over drawn the picture. The State of Jammu and Kashmir continues to be divided and to remain mutilated and truncated and large sections of its people have been separated over the years, driven from their homes, with no immediate prospects of being re-united or settled in their own hearths and homes or those of their near and dear ones. The movement across the two separated parts of the State is so meager as to be non-existent. When some of us talk glibly of the economic regeneration of the state and consider that it is the only question to be tackled, they tend to lose the sight of the trees for the wood. I had been away from the scene for 13 years, enjoying only an occasional spell of freedom, and during these long years those who have been at the helm of affairs or continue to be at the helm, had a unique opportunity to translate their past pledges into a reality. I blame no one for the present state of affairs; but with all the power of the State, the vast funds that had come into their possession, have they been able to ameliorate materially the condition of the masses? Have they succeeded in rehabilitating their uprooted brothers, in ushering in an era of comparative prosperity and happiness? Is it not a fact that the people of the State, particularly the people in the Valley, when it is snow bound, are denied the very elementary necessities of life? Had not unemployment both among the educated classes of the people and otherwise, increased? Is not discontent mounting up everyday and the burdens of life instead of showing any signs of demunition tend to multiply? We have to find an answer to the questions that I have posed; and that needs a certain amount of clear thinking and a great deal of honesty of purpose. Is not all this symptomatic of a deeper malady which afflicts the body politic, the uncertainty, the suspense that has crept into and is eating the very vitals of the community, the uncertainty resulting from an uncertain future-a future which holds no promise of stable peace and security, particularly in the sub-continent as recent events had woefully shown. If I have cried myself hoarse in the days after I regained my freedom since my last incarceration, I have been moved largely by the consideration that we may do our little bit to see that the events of the recent past are not repeated and that we are spared the horrors of another holocaust with all its hazards and perils to the safety of the teeming millions in the sub-continent, a possibility heightened by the addition of stock-piling that is proceeding apace and the arms race that is going on around us. With the confrontation of rival armies on our borders, and their presence amidst us, can we, the people of the State, afford to be complacent and shut our eyes to the lurking dangers inherent in such a situation, which may well spell our doom and of the generations yet unborn and seal our fate irrevocably. If we counsel the resolution of the disputes amongst the neighbours as the best way of preserving our own existence, is the labour and time spent on such confabulations wasted in any manner? I repeat, we the people of the State, have had an agonizing time. There have been eruptions of violence. Our men, women and children and particularly our boys and girls have had to face great suffering and tribulations. We must seek to end this unhappy state of affairs, and if we meet here today to consider this basic problem as to how best to alleviate the suffering of our people, what way there is out of the present imbroglio which would free them from their present shackles of poverty, ignorance and disease, and also from the crippling and corroding influences which are at work, so that they are able to face their future with confidence, I think the attempt is well worth being made; for it is their welfare, their happiness which should in the ultimate analysis count; and the world community and particularly the two great countries, India and Pakistan, should see our plight and lend a helping hand, so that we may fashion our destiny according to our wishes and the genius of our people, in a free atmosphere not vitiated by force or coercion but assisted by the mutual goodwill of the two great neighbours and others in whose interest also it is that all irritants between them should be eliminated quickly to enable them not only to better the lot of their people, but to be able to pull their weight in the comity of nations to which they are fully entitled by the compulsions of history and geography.

Human Cause

Gentlemen, I have permitted myself a few reminiscences in the hope and belief that God in his infinite mercy may guide our labours here so that it may never he said that we failed ourselves and our people at this supreme hour of our destiny. May the people of the State of Jammu and Kashmir, the people of the sub-continent, and the people of the world at large, be able to live a life free from fear and exploitation, and may all nations, big or small, be able to fashion their lives according to their own needs without let or hindrance by others. May we here in this Convention be influenced not by pettifogging, but by a sense of high purpose and the vision of larger human causes which transcend and cut across all barriers of caste, creed, colour, race, language and the like and underline the universality of human brotherhood and the oneness of the family of man of God's earth.

Before I conclude, I must express my profound gratitude to Shri Jayaprakash Narayan for his having inaugurated this

Convention. This I know he did at a great personal inconvenience to himself and in spite of a great deal of pressure on his time and also some uncharitable view taken of his action in certain quarters. His presence amidst us will, I venture to think, fortify and sustain us in our work. I must also thank you all, the participants in the Convention and observers, for having taken the trouble of attending this Convention, particularly those of you who have come from long distances. My thanks are also due to the gentlemen of the press for the unstinted co-operation extended to us by them in our present task.

I can not close this address without expressing my deep sense of grief that the powers that be did not see the wisdom of providing the requisite facilities to the nationals of the state from across the Ceasefire Line and others to attend this Convention. I have no doubt that their presence here would have been of invaluable assistance in furthering the cause that I had set out earlier. Thank You.

(N.M.M&L, File No 91)

Inaugural Speech of Jayaprakash Narayan at J&K State People's Convention

10 October 1968

I am thankful to Sheikh Mohammad Abdullah for asking me to inaugurate this important convention. As you perhaps know, I have come after some hesitation, indeed, after an initially negative decision. Two main considerations finally persuaded me to come. One, my affection and regard for Sheikh Sahib's and, two, the hope that my plain words spoken from the heart, might on the one hand, help you to reach a practical decision, and, on the other, influence Indian public opinion also to take a realistic and constructive view of the situation.

Only once before have I had the pleasure of visiting your state. That was in January 1947, when Mr. Ram Chandra Kak was Prime Minister and Sheikh Saheb was in prison with some of his colleagues. Bakshi Ghulam Mohammed was then working underground in Delhi, so as to keep in touch with the national leaders and help the Kashmir movement from there. It was he who had planned that first visit of ours — then too my wife was with me; and he had accompanied us as far as Rawalpindi, from where we travelled in the company of the late Munshi Ahmed Din and some workers of the National Conference.

That was a very brief visit, as unfortunately the present one is going to be. On that occasion all that I was able to do was to have discussions with some of the workers who were conducting the movement in the absence of their leaders, and to make a public speech in my very inadequate Urdu, it was, I believe, at Mujahid Manzil.

I visit the State again after an interval of 21 years and 9 months — a long period full of fateful events. But during this period, even without visiting the state, I have tried to keep in touch with the changing situation here. I have also tried during all this time to look at the Kashmir problem - as indeed at all other problems — from the point of view of certain basic political principles and values that I hold dear. At this Convention too I shall try to do the same. Perhaps I should add that in the past 21 years, though my mode of political action has undergone change and development, those principles and values have remained for me unaltered. In fact, it was in order to pursue those basic convictions more effectively that I altered my mode of political functioning.

Kashmir and India

This Convention of the people of Jammu and Kashmir state is of the most critical significance. It is, I believe, the first time in history of Jammu and Kashmir that such a move has been made. Its success might well mean the dawn of a new and brighter day not only for the people of this state but also of the whole country. Its failure on the other hand might dash, if not for all time at least for the foreseeable future, all hopes of easing the political and psychological tensions, the uncertainties and fears that have plagued this state for the past many years, particularly since 1953. I therefore hope that the participants in this convention will be mindful of the very serious responsibility they have accepted. Their task calls for a constructive approach and a determination not to permit their deliberations to end in indecision or failure. I hope you will face this crucial task with humility of spirit, a preparedness to understand one another, and a realistic appreciation of the limitations the circumstances have imposed on all those seeking a satisfactory answer to this vexed question.

In view of the exceptional importance of this Convention it is a matter of deep disappointment that the state Congress and the Jana Sangh have refused to take part in it. No doubt they have reasons for their refusal-and I do not wish to minimize them- but it is never constructive and certainly not in keeping with the spirit of democracy to refuse to talk to those with whom one is in disagreement, even complete disagreement. I have faith in human reason, and I believe that given the democratic spirit of give and take there is no tangle that human reason cannot straighten out.

The problems of the state are in such a state of confusion and complexity, and most of the leaders in the rest of the country are so casual in dealing with them and so self-satisfied with mouthing shibboleths, that a Convention of leaders representing different points of view in the state to hammer out a general consensus among themselves on the future of the state is manifestly a step in the right direction. The views that have been expressed in public statement by the state Congress and Jana Sangh leaders -and they are no doubt important views- could have been expressed at this Convention to facilitate the emergence of such a consensus.

It seems to me therefore that a great opportunity for political understanding in the state has been thrown away. But as the London Economist said in a recent issue " what matters about congresses and conferences is not only who goes into them but what comes out of them." So let me hope that what will come out of this Convention will really mark the beginning of a new development which brings peace and happiness where uncertainty and trouble have reigned for many years.

Need for Settlement

Before dealing with some of the vital issues before this Convention I should like to speak briefly to those in this state and the rest of the country who claim that there is nothing left to settle in Kashmir, that the state is as irrevocably a part of India as, let us say, Uttar Pradesh. All those who give expression to this view are not really of one mind on the question. There are for instance the Bharatiya Jana Sangh and elements in the Congress and the Government of India who hold that Article 370 of the Constitution of India should be abrogated and the state fully " integrated" with the union of India, and further that Indian citizens should be able freely to buy land and settle down in the state. There are others like Chief Minister G.M Sadiq, who assert that the state is truly integral part of India though they concede that the quantum of autonomy the state should enjoy is a negotiable matter. There are also several variations on this general theme such as that Jammu should be separated from the state or that the area should be given a measure of regional autonomy within the state. There are also intermediate views between these proposals.

On the other hand, Sheikh Abdullah and many people associated with him do not agree that the state's accession is final and irrevocable. Had Sheikh Saheb been just an individual of little consequence surrounded by a handful of other similar individuals his opinion could have been ignored. But if one does not want to indulge in wishful thinking it has to be recognized, however unpleasant and inconvenient this might be to some, that Sheikh Abdullah continues to be a key figure in the state because he still commands impressive mass support in the valley as well as in certain other parts of the state. That being so, for a large number of people the question of Kashmir cannot be deemed to have been settled unless the Sheikh is a party to the settlement.

Abdullah's Leadership

It is not necessary to remind you that it there was one man more responsible than anybody else for the accession of the state to the Indian Union in 1947 it was Sheikh Mohammed Abdullah. Another historical event deserves mention in this context : at the time of independence, when overwhelming number of Muslims throughout undivided India had rallied under the banner of Mr Jinnah and subscribed to his two-nation theory, two shining exceptions stood out in bold dissent: the Northwest Frontier Province and the state of Jammu and Kashmir. The Muslim masses in these two regions refused to be swept off their feet by the cry of a separate Muslim nation. That was due, let it be remembered, to the leadership of two deeply religious and towering, charismatic Muslims: Khan Abdul Ghaffar Khan and Sheikh Abdullah.

After partition and the creation of Pakistan it was Sheikh Abdullah again who led, in the face of Pakistani aggression, the people of his state to throw in their lot with India. It was his consistently courageous, non-communal and enlightened leadership which gives the opportunity today to every Indian to hold up Kashmir as a noble example of Indian secularism. Even over the recent incidents at the Srinagar Engineering College, Sheikh demonstrated once again his uncompromising opposition to communalism.

These events, to mention only a few of many similar ones, place the leadership of Sheikh Abdullah and his views in true perspective.

Discontent in the Valley

There is another salient fact about this state to which I should like to draw the attention to these who assert that there is nothing left to settle in regard to Kashmir. That is the fact of widespread and persistent discontent in the valley. Part of the discontent is undoubtedly of the same nature that one finds, in some measure or other, all over the country. But there is also no doubt that the greater part of it is peculiar to the state and stems from the political situation: in particular, from the lack of agreement with Sheikh Abdullah and the absence of genuine democracy and good government in the state. Some of the recent judgments on the election petitions in the state provide a significant commentary on the working of democracy here.

It seems to me that all those who loudly proclaim that Kashmir is an inalienable part of India should feel deeply concerned over this persistent discontent. But regrettably one does not find such concern in these quarters. The majority of them believe in a policy of drift and pathetically trust to time to settle all problems. It does not occur to them that time has not settled this particular problem in 21 years. Another 21 years are hardly likely to settle it along the path of indecision and opportunism. Indeed, if the situation is allowed to drift further and Sheikh Abdullah continues to be ignored, extremism would keep on growing apace and the consequences might well be incalculable.

Use of Force

There are of course those for whom the solution of every problem lies in force. To them it is little significance how popular Sheikh Abdullah is and how disaffected are his followers. Force in their reckoning will take care of all that. Such a naive and reactionary view appeals naturally to a certain type of mind.

But the large-scale use of force, especially in such a sensitive spot of the world as Kashmir carries with it immense risks. There is also a real danger that the continued reliance on force in Kashmir may erode democracy in other parts of India, create and feed communal conflict, and become a running sore in the body politic and economy of the country.

Need for a Positive Decision

I have dealt at some length and with complete frankness with the basis principles which govern my views on the problem of Kashmir. With equal frankness let me turn now to those who are assembled here for this Convention. Over the years a variety of solutions have been offered by different people with their own interpretations of the right of the people to self-determination. The point I should like to emphasise is that it is high time that a definite and realistic decision were taken now.

Time and circumstances move fast in a revolutionary age like the one in which we live. Statesmanship demands quick decisions in keeping with such changes. The question of Kashmir is not an academic one which can be debated indefinitely and in the abstract while the economic and social needs of her people suffer sad neglect. It is very much a political question, but the choices in politics are always limited by a combination of circumstances which cannot be ignored.

There is frequent reference in a discussion of the Kashmir problem to the right of self-determination. That claim rests on an assurance first given on behalf of the government of India by Lord Mountbatten in his letter to Maharaja Sir Hari Singh in these words: " As soon as law and order have been restored and the soil is cleared of the invader, the question of the state's accession should be settled by a reference to the people." It is but fair to point out that even now a large part of the state continues to be in alien hands. As a further complication there was the tragic conflict of 1965, and a recurrence of such conflict cannot be ruled out so long as Pakistan declines to accept a no-war pact.

Right of Self-Determination

Let me also remind you that the world of 1968 is far removed in outlook and mood from the world of 1947. In these intervening years new factors have emerged which have radically altered the essential nature of the issues involved in a solution of the problem of Kashmir. The right to self-determination, viewed against such a changed background, needs to be interpreted afresh in keeping with today's needs of the people of Kashmir.

There is of course a broader implication in the right to self-determination, namely the inherent right of every people to determine their way of life and the form and character of their institutions. But this is an extremely complicated matter, and in the context of the modern nation-state the complications are further compounded. Now I am not an admirer of the nation-state and in fact regard it as an already outmoded and outdated concept. But it exists, and seems to arouse the strongest sentiment that moves and unites men today. It cuts across the boundaries of religion, race, language, culture and ideology, including the ideology of communism.

In the context of the nation-state it is extremely difficult to define and geographically demarcate "a people." Are the Kashmiris a people? Then what about the Dogras and the Ladakhis? Where will you drew the line? You can look around the world and see for yourselves how doggedly the existing nation-states, no matter how haphazardly created, fight against any of their "peoples" wanting to break away or to exercise their right to self-determination.

This is a hard fact of which due notice must be taken. Whether one likes it or not, the Indian nation-state, also a haphazard creation owing to the tragedy of partition, has its geographical boundaries demarcated. India is no more prepared than Pakistan, or for that matter any other nation-state, willingly and peacefully to let any part of the country break away on any plea whatever. Let this fact be duly appreciated. No doubt military means, can be used to enforce the right to self-determination, but a breakaway part of a nation-state is never likely to achieve its end or maintain it for long by such means, unless it is helped by other powerful nation-states for their own selfish ends. Such a possibility is however entirely irrelevant to the discussion here, because I am not aware that there is anybody present who advocates a military or violent solution.

Other factors too, must be taken into account. The fate of the people of this region-Jammu, Kashmir and Ladakh-was determined over a hundred years ago, not primarily in their own interests but by the consideration that the state lay wedged between three empires: Czarist Russia, China and Britain. The old rivals of the last century have no doubt disappeared, but the clash of interests continues in a different garb in today's world and despite the noble aims and principles of the UN Charter, continue to become helpless pawns in the game of power politics of big states.

No Solution Outside India

These are unpleasant but inescapable realities and as your friend and well- wisher I am bound to speak the truth as I see it. This Convention must understand clearly that after the 1965 conflict no Government of India can accept a solution which places Kashmir outside the Union of India. Or to put it positively, a solution has to be found within the framework of the Union. This statement should not surprise any of you because this is not the first time that I am making it publicly. As some of you at least must know, this also happens to be the view of many others in the country who have been trying over the past several years to create public opinion in favour of an agreed settlement in Kashmir.

These then are the limitations imposed by circumstances to which I have referred in my opening remarks. Statesmanship on your side requires that you should adapt your policy and programme to suit the facts of the situation. To ignore them will only mean further tension, resulting so far as your people are concerned in frustration, uncertainty and misery.

These observations obviously raise a number of questions. Let me deal with some of them. I know that Sheikh Saheb and his colleagues have been emphasizing the right of the people to decide their future. I have indicated the considerations which much qualify this right. It may, of course, be argued that the people have the right to decide whether they accept or not such qualifying considerations, and if they do, what kind of political settlement they would have within those limitations.

The main issue I would place before you today is how can the people decide these complicated and grave issues without clear and umabigious advice from their leaders? I feel strongly , and wish to say to you with all the emphasis I can command, that this is the occasion when you owe it to yourself and to the people to make up your minds and advise them unambiguously on these vital issues. I do not think it will be difficult for the leaders gathered here to go to the people and convince them that the decisions reached here are the best possible solutions in the circumstances and would guarantee them peace, happiness and honour. If this Convention is not to be a mere exercise in political debate but represents an earnest and constructive effort to find a practical way out of the present impasse I am convinced that this is the wisest course open to it.

Role of Pakistan

Another large question that my suggestion raises is how Pakistan will react to a settlement within the limits pointed out by me. It is often urged that unless Pakistan is at least tacitly reconciled to the situation here there can be no guarantee of peace and security in the state. This is true. So let us see what possible Pakistani reaction there could be. Pakistan's public stand has always been that the people of this state should themselves decide their fate. If you therefore take a decision here and persuade the people to endorse it, as I have no doubt you will be able to, Pakistan will have no valid grievances or cause for complaint. World opinion too would acclaim a settlement acceptable to the people of Kashmir and restrain Pakistan from the pursuit of any policy but that of acceptance or acquiescence. Should that happen it may prove the beginning of a new and happy chapter in the history of India-Pakistan relations.

The last question, and the most important, is about the possible reaction of the Government of India. I have no doubt that your acceptance of this would clear the ground for a meaningful dialogue between your leaders and the Government of India. In that event even other leaders of the state who have stayed away from this Convention may join forces with you. It seems to me that a new day would have truly dawned then.

Such questions as the constitutional status of the state within the Indian union, a guarantee that status would not be unilaterally altered, etc, will remain to be discussed. But the proper place for such discussions is not here but at a later stage with the government of India's representatives at the conference table. I am aware that in some quarters there is a view which is opposed to any state being given a special position. But I doubt whether such a view can be maintained in the changing circumstances of India. For historical reasons modifications will have to be made in the general pattern.

Larger Autonomy

Such modifications in fact exist even today. There is also pressure from the states for a larger measure of autonomy. It would be wrong to consider such trends disruptive of national unity. On the other hand any attempt to impose rigid uniformity from above is bound to create tensions which may produce seeds of disruption. With the situation undergoing a great change as a result of the general elections of 1967 there is urgent need to review centre-state relations from an entirely new angle.

In a vast country like ours national unity can only be fostered in an atmosphere of wise understanding of regional sentiments and interests and a spirit of mutual tolerance. So long as political authority was the monopoly of a single party ruling at the centre and in virtually all the states the problem of centre-state relations did not appear of major significance. The general election in February 1967 has resulted in jockeying for power among political groups in a number of states. This is not the place nor the occasion for a detailed discussion of the theme. But it is relevant here to remark that Kashmir is not alone in its efforts to secure maximum autonomy.

Let me once again assure you that these words have been spoken from the heart and are intended to help you arrive at a wise and practical decision. All eyes in the country are turned towards you, and everybody expects your decisions will prove a turning-point towards a happier future.

Since this is the commencement of the Gandhi centenary year it is appropriate that we should turn our thoughts in homage to the man who led us in the freedom struggle. Partition caused him deep anguish; but when he found that it was inevitable because most of his lieutenants were willing to pay that price for freedom, he continued to live in the hope that the separation would be as between friends and their relations could be defined in a treaty to ensure a smooth and harmonious transition. Tragically he did not live long enough after partition to see the fulfillment of such a hope.

It is my earnest prayer that this Convention will so guide its proceedings as to make a renewal of that effort not only possible but also fruitful. There are all over the world today many spots of trouble and explosive danger. If through your decisions the prospects of peace and goodwill can be brightened in the entire region, described as the subcontinent south of the Himalayas, it will be a big step forward towards the world of Mahatma Gandhi's conception.

"Freedom will be Snatched," Abdullah's Reply to J.P.

Reacting to J.P's plea for solution of Kashmir problem within framework of the Indian constitution, Sheikh Abdullah said freedom is never given as a gift, it has to be snatched. The question is not whether what government of India is willing to give us but what people of Kashmir want to achieve. They will get it with force. The only other alternative for us is that we are wiped out in the process. Freedom will not fall from the sky. Hundreds of youngmen will be prepared to be hanged. We are not concerned whether the government of India fulfils its promises. It we have power, we will get it. Or we will destroy ourselves."

Abdullah had hoped that JP would support the cause of the people of Kashmir. For if Indira Gandhi did it, she might be afraid of losing her power. But JP had nothing to lose. He expected JP to openly say that unless India and Pakistan participate in negotiations on Kashmir, the problem would never be solved.

Accusing followers of Gandhi of closing the doors of negotiations, he said, " they forfeited my passport. Their intention was to keep me out of India like Phizo. They were disappointed when I returned. But they detained me."

Referring to Pakistan's attack, he said, "what else could Pakistan do when the doors of negotiations were closed on it."

(Chand Weekly, Jammu, 15 October 1968)

PSP Supports JP's Srinagar Speech

October 11, 1968

Shri Prem Bhasin, PSP General Secretary, hailed in a statement issued here today Shri Jayaprakash Narayan's call for recognition of the reality that a settlement of the Kashmir problem could only be had "within the framework of the (Indian) Union". Shri Bhasin was commenting on the inaugural address of Shri Jayaprakash Narayan delivered at the Kashmir Convention currently in session at Srinagar.

Shri Bhasin added, "Democratic and secular India has always stood for the full implementation of democratic rights in Kashmir as in other parts of India. It has never failed to protest against repression directed against political opponents and arbitrary actions in the course of elections in the state. It has often stressed that Kashmir will have to be provided with special safeguards in the constitution. By accepting Shri Jayaprakash Narayan's advice and working for a solution within the Indian union, Sheikh Abdullah and his colleagues would not only strengthen the hands of these progressive forces in India but help themselves in bridging the present gap between their legitimate aspirations and the inescapable demands of Indian Nationalism, Democracy and Secularism."

Sd/-

(NMM&L. File No. 92) (Prem Bhasin)
General Secretary

Comments of Jammu & Kashmir Youngmen's League (Students Federation) on the Statement of Mr. J. Prakash Narayan in People's Convention, Srinagar

11 October 1968

The Jammu and Kashmir Young Men's League (Students Federation) expresses its grave concern over the statement made by Shri J.P. Narain in the State People's Convention, Srinagar, in which he, among other things, said that after 1965 Indo-Pak war Pakistan has ceased to be a party to Kashmir dispute. We are at a loss to understand as to how and on what grounds Mr

Narain has made this statement which is absolutely incorrect and far from reality. The disturbance which took place in 1965 were the direct result of India's shameful and imperialistic measures to further integrate and Indianise Kashmir. In fact the 1965 disturbances were the demonstration of extreme resentment of the people of Jammu & Kashmir against India's colonial policy with regard to Kashmir. That was an attempt to liberate Kashmir from Indian domination. To divert the disturbance in Kashmir, India fanned atmosphere of 1965 Indo-Pak war. After the War, India signed Tashkent Declaration which was followed by Indo-Pak Agreements. Under those agreements India ceded Haji Peer area of Kashmir to Pakistan and in return got Chhamb area of Kashmir. Then the Commanders-in-Chief of India and Pakistan agreed to minimise the number of their Army in J&K state.

The UN Military observers are still posted in this state after 1965 as they were from 1948 cease-fire agreement. The Kashmir problem is as usual on UN agenda. One third of J&K territory is as usual under the control of Pakistan. Inspite of this Mr. J.P. Narain is saying that Pakistan is not a party to Kashmir dispute. It seems that he believes in Nazi Germany tactics of saying lies in the hope that repeated telling of lies will be accepted by people as truth.

The Pakistan's being a party to Kashmir dispute is as clear and true as the sun rises from the east. We have a great respect for Mr. J.P. Narain. We are sorry to say that by his such a statement he strengthens the doubts of the people of Kashmir that Mr J.P. Narain has come to Kashmir as a political broker sent by crafty and unscrupulous leaders of Indian government. Mr J.P. Narain must understand that Kashmir is a human and international problem having three parties India, Pakistan, Kashmir. The trump card of deciding this issue lies in the hands of people of the state living on both sides of Cease-Fire Line. Any compromise or settlement without the cooperation of Pakistan is meaningless and can never be accepted by the people of Kashmir. Nor can there by any lasting peace in Kashmir unless the Kashmir problem is settled on the basis of right of self-determination in consultation and agreement with Pakistan.

The Indian leaders must realise that the patience of the people of Jammu and Kashmir in general and the students and young generation in particular has exhausted. If sense of justice and humanity does not prevail upon the Government of India, the people of Kashmir living on both sides of Cease-Fire Line will be left with no alternative but to rise like Algerians and liquidate Indian colonialism or be perished with it. The whole sub-continent of India and Pakistan shall have to face the horrors of a decisive war starting from Kashmir.

It is high time for India to utilise the precious services of Sher-e-Kashmir, and settle this international problem of Kashmir honourably and equitably with the cooperation of Pakistan also.

The Young Men's League (Students Federation) of Jammu and Kashmir expects Mr J.P. Narain to understand the realities impartially and use his high influence for settling the Kashmir problem with the cooperation of Pakistan so that the reign of peace and prosperity may dawn on the sub-continent permanently.

Sd/-

(Abdul Rashid Dar)

Chief Organiser,

J&K Youngmen's League (Students Federation),

Sringar.

(NMM&L. File No. 92)

JP Surprised by Sheikh's Speech

Bid to Appease Extremists

Mr Jayaprakash Narayan said on Saturday that Sheikh Abdullah's speech at the Kashmir State People's Convention was largely meant to appease the extremists in the valley who were getting disillusioned with his leadership.

Mr Narayan said at Palam airport on his arrival from Srinagar that the last, however, had not yet been heard from the Sheikh. The Kashmir leader had not rejected his plea that the state leaders should convince the people and start a dialogue with the government of India for a "special position" for Jammu and Kashmir within the framework of the union.

He said he was a little surprised by the tone of Sheikh Abdullah's speech. Asked if the Sheikh had gone back a couple of years in demanding a round table conference between India, Pakistan and Kashmir after hopes held out recently that the

Kashmir leader might be brought round to a solution of the problem within the Indian union, Mr Narayan said: "He is right that unless Pakistan agrees there can be no lasting solution to the problem but, first thing ought to be thrashed out between Delhi and Srinagar."

Asked if the Sheikh's strong utterances were born out of some kind of frustration with the Government of India. Mr Narayan said: He is a little piqued with the Government of India.

Earlier before leaving Srinagar, Mr Narayan attended a reception given to him by the Kashmir Press Club, says the *Statesman* staff correspondent. Mr Narayan said Sheikh Abdullah had not completely brushed aside his (Mr Narayan's) view that a solution of the Kashmir question could be found within the framework of the Indian union Sheikh Abdullah was present by special invitation.

Dialogue

Mr Narayan said he had understood Sheikh Abdullah speech in a "somewhat different manner" and though it did appear that he (Sheikh) had "more or less repudiated what I had said," the main theme of the speech was to assure the people that nothing would be done behind their back.

"I should have been very happy if Sheikh Sahib had made his observations in a somewhat different way", he added.

Mr Narayan, however said he was not going back disappointed.

The Sarvodaya leader said he would continue his efforts to have a dialogue between Sheikh Abdullah and Central leaders. The Sheikh had not refused to talk to Central leaders nor had the Central leaders closed the door for talks with him and his colleagues.

Mr Narayan said the Indian constitution had allowed "a fair amount of autonomy" to the states. That had become clear following formation of non-Congress government in some states after the last general election.

Talking to reporters informally Sheikh Abdullah said as the Convention was trying to find an agreed formula, it would not be proper for him to say whether the solution should be within a particular framework.

(Statesmen, 13 October 1968)

Dange's Letter to JP

S.A. Dange
Member of Parliament
24, Canning Lane,
New Delhi.
16 Oct 1968

My dear JP,

The Kashmir Conference reports in the press tempted me to write to you.

Your stand on Kashmir is realistic and politically correct. If Kashmir is not to be made a cockpit of imperialist cold war manoeuvers ripening into hot war once again, things there must be resolved quickly.

Your two points, that is, solution within Indian Union and special status should satisfy the Sheikh. But unfortunately, he is too embittered by the long wait in detentions. Moreover, he feels and talks like a "King of Kashmir", trying to preserve "his people" and kingdom from two "giant grabbers" India and Pakistan. At the same time, he is a little soft to Pakistan, that being, perhaps, due to a slight tinge of religious affinity though it is to his credit that he is not communal minded at all. And he also thinks that by "physical affinity", the trade of Kashmir has to flow towards Pakistan, as it is more difficult or almost impossible to flow via India by the nature of the terrain on India's side.

But one can not leave things at that. The newspapers are no help. In fact, their reports tried to make it appear as if both of you are now swords drawn: your negation of that attitude was good. So the next move has to be taken. The Indian ruling circles must be made to move in the direction of defining concretely the "special status" and conferring it on Kashmir. Secondly, the regime must be made more democratic and subject to the will of the people, that of course, being a point which is common to all parts of India - not only Kashmir.

I just thought of writing a few lines after reading press reports about your address to the Conference.

I had once talked to the Sheikh on those lines. I bluntly asked him why he does not call himself an Indian and acknowledge

Indian nationality. He said he did it as a reaction to those who wanted to force things on him and misrepresent him. Otherwise, had he not been at the UNO as an Indian in the Indian delegation? And so on.

Anyway, we all should move in the matter before another flare comes up.

If the Assam thing settles down as it promises to and the Nagas come to realism, we should not forget to tackle Kashmir quickly for a proper settlement.

This letter is personal to you.

I am sending you a few booklets (separately) you may like to read.

With greetings,
Yours sincerely
Sd/-
(S.A. Dange)

Shri Jayaprakash Narayan,
Patna.

(NMM&L. File No. 93)

JP's Letter to Abdullah

New Delhi
October 27, 1968

My dear Sheikh Saheb,

I returned from Kabul on the 20th and have been here since. The Gandhi Centenary Seminar, which was inaugurated by Prime Minister Etmadi, was a fine success. Badshah Khan was one of the distinguished speakers. When I went to see him at Jalalabad days later he enquired about you and the Convention.

In the past week I have been meeting quite a number of people, including ministers, journalists, political leaders etc. all in connection with Kashmir. It is too early to give you my impressions of these talks, which I shall continue. I am of course discussing the question within the framework of my inaugural speech.

I have also met here Beg Saheb, Premnathji Bazaz, Karra Saheb, Bakshi Saheb and Sadiq Saheb. What I learn from them about the speeches at the Convention, the resolution that were adopted and, above all, about the wonderful way in which you conducted the proceedings and your concluding speech, made me extremely happy I congratulate you most warmly on your great success.

There is appreciation in the appropriate circles here of what you have done, but perhaps it is premature to expect any positive steps yet.

I do not know what your own plans are for the next few months. If I may make a suggestion, I would say that you should function now in all public matters as the President of the Convention and confine your statements and speeches within the four corners of the Convention resolutions.

In the end, I should like to thank you most warmly for the wonderful welcome you and the people of Srinagar gave me. I know that I did not come up to their expectations, but I hope they will find in time that I spoke as a true friend.

Yours sincerely,

Sd/-
(Jayaprakash Narayan)

Sheikh Mohammed Abdullah
Mujahid Manzil,
Srinagar, Kashmir.
(NMM&L. File No. 93)

JP's Letter to Dange

Gopeshwar
October 30, 1968

My dear Shri Dange,

I was very happy to read your letter of the 16th October. You and your party can play a very important role in this matter. I think the Prime Minister, left to herself, would like to move on the lines that we are proposing. The greatest difficulty is her own party. The Deputy Prime Minister, as you know, is dead against such a status being given to Kashmir on the plea that the same status would be demanded by every other state in India. Indeed, he is said to be pressing for the abrogation of Article 370. However, I hope I shall have your cooperation in persuading enough members of the Parliament to take the realistic and reasonable line so that the Government might make some constructive response. I do not know if you have seen the resolution of the Convention. It is quite promising as far as it goes. Sheikh Sahib's concluding speech was also in a very realistic and conciliatory tone. I wish as a first step there could be some verbal response from the Prime Minister to the effect that in spite of her initial misgiving, she is happy to find the Convention trying earnestly to evolve a realistic solution.

I shall be in Delhi when Parliament opens and I hope we shall be able to meet.

With kind regards,

Yours sincerely

Shri S.A. Dange

Sd/-

(Jayaprakash Narayan)

(NMM&L. File No. 93)

Abdullah's Letter to JP

Mujahid Manzir,
Srinagar.
No. 105/A
31st Oct 1968

My dear JP,

I thank you for your letter of Oct 27th, 68, which Mr G.M. Karra, personally handed over to me. I have noted the contents.

My plans for the next few months are just to look after my work in Kashmir. The Ramdan fasts begin somewhere in the 3rd week of November and will end by the middle of December. I would very much like to tour some parts of Jammu province in the month of January. Presently, I have no plans to go beyond Jammu.

I hope you are doing well.

With kindest regards to Prabha ji and to yourself.

Yours sincerely

Sd/-

(Sheikh Mohd Abdullah)

Shri Jayaprakash Narayayan,
Kadam Kuan,
Patna - 3, Bihar.

(NMM&L. File No. 93)

JP's Views Annoy Sheikh Abdullah

Srinagar, Dec 8—Sheikh Abdullah is understood to ha., turned against Mr Jayaprakash Narain and others for expecting him to accept the Indian framework without suggesting any solution of the Kashmir problem itself.

He is reported to have expressed his annoyance at a meeting of the steering committee of the People's Convention which, though expected to continue for two days, adjourned till the end of next month after a brief session yesterday.

Both the pro-India and pro-Pakistan elements here have started asserting that the Convention should be considered dead for all practical purposes. They point out that it was impossible to evolve a solution acceptable to all members of the steering committee. Still the 12-member steering committee continues to exist as nobody wants to be the first to leave it unless the Sheikh makes his final choice.

Meanwhile, significance is being attached to Plebiscite Front Chief Mohammed Afzal Beg's speech here last Thursday on the Sheikh's 63rd birthday on 5 December

He exhorted the people to persuade the government of India to secure the right to a plebiscite. Those who say that the People's Convention has weakened the Plebiscite Front's voice should know it has endorsed our view point that the Kashmir problem exists and has to be solved with the consent of all people in all region, including Azad Kashmir and Gilgit (now under Pakistan)", he added.

At the steering committee of the convention, 58 papers were read on the state's "political status", adds PTI.

After the members give their comments on the papers, a three man subcommittee consisting of Mirza Afzal beg, the Plebiscite Front President. Mr Prem Nath Bazaz, convenor of the steering committee, and Mr Balraj Puri will make a summary of various proposals and suggestions made by the delegates for consideration of the next Convention next year.

(*Hindustan Times,* 9 December 1968)

Abdullah's Letter on JP's Speech in Srinagar

Mujahid Manzil,
Srinagar
No. 237/A
March 6, 1969

My dear JP,

I thank you for your letter of 23rd February, 1969, which I received the other day through Moulvi Farooq. I have given my anxious thought to its contents. In fairness, I feel I should frankly tell you about the reasons of the reactions to your inaugural address at the last convention and your subsequent public speech delivered in Srinagar.

We all know Gandhiji's dedication to the cause of truth. In fact this was the bacon-light by virtue of which he transformed the very basic approach of the public life in the sub-continent. When time came he laid down his precious life to fight against tyranny and untruth. This noble-trait in him knew no compromise, nor did it yield to expediencies; and he fought battles for upholding the cause of truth, unmindful of the fact whether his action would be against his friends or his opponents. After Gandhiji's passing away, many living here and in India consider you amongst the very few persons who in their life symbolise the ideals that he stood for. You are no doubt taken as his heir. Naturally, therefore, people's expectation that you will always stand by the cause of truth is unquestionable.

What is the truth about the Kashmir question? "The drum driven cattle" of the State have been struggling for their right of self-determination ever since 1931. Gandhiji and Panditji stood by them in this struggle. Many a time they had to resolutely defy considerations of expediency etc. however unpalatable that might have been even to some of their colleagues. At the crucial time of the partition of the sub-continent, when the question of State's accession arose, Pakistan wished to annex it with the force of sword. Gandhiji raised his voice, and rightly characterised the Pakistan action as aggression on our people's right of self-determination. He agreed with Panditji's decision to send the Indian troops to help the State in defending our human right that people are the arbiters of their own fate. After a bloody war, Pakistan also subscribed to this objective.

Subsequently, unfortunately, India resiled from her stand and did not hesitate to say that people of the State had forfeited their basic right - the most amusing reasons for this volte-face being that Pakistan had mis-behaved. Thus the Indian government's stand after breaking their pledged word, amounts to punishing Peter for the sins of Paul. No canons of justice can countenance this. In such a situation what would have been Gandhi's stand. Instances in his life provide the answer, which even today is recalled all over the world with pride. When, for example, he learnt that his dearest and closest colleagues in the Government of India were denying Pakistan payment of its dues, and thereby breaking their plighted word, he staked his own life and made his colleagues realise the moral obligation of honouring their pledge.

"People Shocked Over Statement of Gandhi's Heir"

I have said that you are Gandhi's heir in so far you symbolise in yourself adherence to the cause of truth, however unpalatable it might be. Permit me to say that it did surprise, and even shock, many many of your admirers to hear from your lips that Indian government would not keep their pledge by the people of Kashmir as Pakistan had made war on India in 1965. The shock was all the greater when you revealed that even you could not honour the pledge if you were the Prime Minister of India. Could the political climate in the country or the mere apprehension of loss of office have pursuaded Gandhiji to bye-pass his solemn pledge? Such a course would be understandable in the case of men of common clay, but not certainly from those who cherish Gandhi's ideals, and emulate his example. I often feel grieved to see India going down because it is departing from the noble ideals enshrined in the life of the father of the nation. There is darkness all around mainly because we have given go-by to those objective though with all pomp and show we may be celebrating his centenary. Our hope only lies in keeping those ideals alive. As long as we endorse actions of those who, for petty and temporary advantages throw over-board their pledges and commitments and, thereby, betray a people, forgive me to say that, we are aiding and abetting the process of moral degradation. I shudder to think where it will lead us to.

Sd/-

(SM Abdullah)

(NMM&L File No. 93)

Mridula Sarabhai's Letter to JP

31, Rajdoot Marg,
Chanayapuri, New Delhi - 11.
March 13, 1969

My dear Shri JP,

Months have passes since I have had an opportunity to talk to you. Often I had tried to get an appointment with you but this did not materialise. While in Delhi you have been keeping very busy. Then again, you have been unwell and hence I did not 'gate-crash' on you. I had an impression that you would be in Delhi by the end of this month but Shri Sen tells me that you are not likely to be here till April. Hence this letter on an urgent and important matter.

Herewith a note "The Presidential Order of 1954 Curtailing Powers of the Supreme Court", in Kashmir. Under Article 370 it is not necessary for the subject matter of the Presidential order to be discussed by the State Legislature or the Parliament. On Government's recommendation the President is authorised to issue orders as has been done in the case under consideration.

There is lot of bitterness in Kashmir towards the Supreme Court decisions in connection with detention appeals. The general impression is that the Supreme Court is behaving in a "communal and prejudicial" way. Little was known that the Supreme Court had no powers. This has just come out in a ruling that the Supreme Court gave in the case of Sampat Prakash vs. the State of Jammu and Kashmir. The newspaper report of this ruling is incorporated in the note.

It is being said that the term of the Presidential Order will be over this April and if efforts are not made against its extension, it is possible that it may be allowed to lapse. All efforts have to be made to create public opinion and pressure on the government to see that section 35 C is not extended. I, therefore, bring this to your notice and to the notice of other friends with a request to please intervene and use your good offices to stop this order being further extended. In Kashmir debarring the courts from intervening in detention cases, and specially under the Preventive Detention Act, has led to gross misuse of these powers by the government. People have been detained under the Preventive Detention and other Local Acts and then subjected to third degree tortures in the interrogation centres and have been kept in solitary confinement. There are persons in jails since more then 5 years. Nobody can do anything for them unless the executive wants it to be done. It is an inhuman procedure, violating all fundamental and human codes of conduct.

I am sending a copy of this letter to Shri J.J. Singh also and hope to meet him within two or three days, with a request to do the needful. A statement from you and letters to Indiraji, Chavan Saheb and the President will go a long way in strengthening our other efforts. I am also going to meet leaders amongst the MPs and see if they can do any thing and make a representation to the President.

With lots of best wishes to you and Prabhaji,

Yours

Sd/-

(Mridula)

Shri J.P. Narayan,
C/o Sarva Seva Sangh,
Rajghat, Varanasi - 1,
UP
CC: JJ Singh, New Delhi.

(NMM&L File No. 92)

JP's Reply to Abdullah's Letter

Jayaprakash Nagar,
Sitabdiara, Saran
Bihar
March 20, 1969

My dear Sheikh Saheb,

Many thanks for your letter of March 6. While I feel happy at the return of your usual warm personal tone in this letter, I must say I am disappointed that it is not an answer to my letter. All that you have written I had gathered from your speech at the public meeting which we had addressed together at Srinagar. But what I had attempted to say in the last letter was (a) that the opinions that I had expressed in my two speeches in srinagar were not new because they had been expressed publicly and privately on many occasions after the events of 1965; (b) that, therefore, they should have caused no disillusionment or annoyance, and finally (c) that if my known views were to be considered unhelpful, I should not have been invited at all. As a proof of the fact that my letter to the Prime Minister of June 1966, a copy of which I had given you at Kodaikanal. I am sending you again a copy of my speeches at a seminar on Kashmir that some of us had organised at the India International Centre in 1967 in which Mr. Nakshabandi had also participated.

May I very respectfully add that to bring in Gandhiji's name does justice neither to Gandhiji nor to me. No one can tell what Gandhiji would have done if he had been faced with the situation that I and other Gandhians in India faced after the Indo-Pak war. Secondly, I do not think there was, or is, any one who can be called Gandhi's heir. Gandhiji himself was, no doubt, in the habit of naming his heirs. But you know how his chosen heir, Jawaharlal Nehru, was himself responsible, in part at least, for the complications which the question of Kashmir has got entangled. Of all the living Gandhians perhaps Vinobaji is the only one who with some justice can be regarded as being the most creative interpreter of Gandhijis principles and methods. It may, however, surprise you to know that Vinobaji found nothing to disagree with in my inaugural speech. I do not mind being regarded as a fallen Gandhian, but whatever be the truth about my apostasy, you surely had known of it as early as our meeting at Kodaikanal. But I had not gathered the impression there that I had become a Gandhian apostate in your eyes.

Plebiscite No More Practical Solution

Coming to the substance of the matter, I do not think any responsible person, either in Pakistan on in India, has thought for many years now that plebiscite in Jammu & Kashmir was a practical solution of the problem any more. Even President Ayub Khan in 1964 had told me that, though plebiscite was the first priority solution as far as Pakistan was concerned, if India thought it was impractical, he was prepared to discuss any other solution which could be negotiated mutually between the parties concerned. For many years there have been only two alternatives open: a negotiated settlement or a forcible settlement. No doubt, India continues to demand that Pakistan should 'vacate' her aggression, but India knows very well that short of a war which she never seriously contemplates, it is impossible to win back the Pakistan occupied territories. Pakistan also knows equally well that, short of a successful war, she cannot win any of the territories which are part of India today. I am not quite sure if Pakistani leaders have now forsworn war with India, but, if they have, the only alternative left is a negotiated settlement. Therefore, the very word 'plebiscite' is irrelevant to the present situation, and no amount of harping back on the original commitments made by the Government of India can avail.

In my inaugural address I had tried to point the way to a negotiated settlement in two stages: first, a settlement between the Government of India and the leaders of Kashmir, endorsement of which by the people of the State could be obtained at a general election or in some other agreed manner; second, a negotiated settlement subsequently with Pakistan. The second stage may not immediately follow upon the first, but once the people of the state had, in a credible manner, endorsed a settlement made by their leaders with the Government of India, a settlement with Pakistan must follow sooner or later. These, however, are my views, and it is open to the Convention to accept, reject or modify them.

With very warm regards,

Yours sincerely

Sd/-

(Jayaprakash Narayan)

Mr. Sheikh Mohammad Abdullah
Mujahid Manzil,
Srinagar (Kashmir).

(NMM&L File No. 93)

Abdullah's Letter to JP

Srinagar
No. 283/A
April 30,1969

My dear J.P.,

I am sorry there has been some delay in replying your letter of 20th March, which was forwarded to me by J.J., with his letter dated the 27th March.

I think I made it fully clear in my last letter to you that though your views on the solution on Kashmir question were known earlier, but what shocked the people of Kashmir was your expression that even you could not honour the pledges given to them if you were the Prime Minister of India. Naturally, the shock was understandable, because, as I have said, "after Gandhi ji passing away many living here and in India consider you amongst the very few persons who in their life symbolize the ideals that he stood for." It was in this context that I made a reference to what Gandhi ji would have done in the situation that is confronting Indian leaders in Kashmir at present. It is my considered opinion that no canons of justice, morality or law can justify by- passing the pledges solemnly given to the people of Kashmir in regard to their right of self-determination. In my opinion it negates all our professions of adherence to Gandhian ideals to say, or to support, that Kashmiris have forfeited the right because of what Pakistan did or did not do. It was in this context that I sought to seek guidance form Gandhi ji's life when I said, " could the political climate in the country or mere apprehension of loss of office persuade Gandhi ji to by- pass his solemn pledge. Such a course would be understandable in the case of men of common clay, but not certainly from those who cherish Gandhi ji's ideals and emulate his example." I regret to have to say that you seem to have taken my reference to Gandhi ji;'s name amiss. You say, "to bring in Gandhi Ji 's name does justice neither to Gandhi Ji nor to me. No one can tell what Gandhi ji would have done if he had been faced with the situation that I and other Gandhians in India faced after the Indo- Pak war." This is exactly where I beg to differ from you. The departed leader's life provides solid and concrete examples to give a guide line to the Gandhians.

What Gandhi would have done?

In my last letter I referred to the incident in which he offered to stake his life rather than brook to bypass a solmn-pledge given by his dearest colleagues in Govt. of India when Indo- Pak war of 1947 broke-out. It is my unshaken belief that he would never have compromised with " the extraneous situation", when the principle of truth was involved. To my mind it is absolutely clear what Gandhi Ji would have done in this situation, and therefore I respectfully beg to differ form you that reference to him is inappropriate. On the contrary we must try to seek guidance from his life in every crisis.

You have said, in passing, that "Jawahar Lal Nehru was himself responsible, in part at least, for the complications in which the question of Kashmir has got entangled". Be that as it may, Pandit Ji did in 1964 fully realize the necessity of taking a fresh look on his Kashmir policy, when he sent me on a mission to Pakistan to bring about a Conference in which the Kashmir tangle could be amicably resolved. We should not, therefore, in fairness to him, forget that he could and did rise above extraneous considerations when real facts were placed before him.

You have referred to your latter to the Prime Minister of (June 23,1966), of which you sent me a copy. In that letter it has been mentioned that I "would be prepared even to accept the status of full internal autonomy for Kashmir, provided history were not allowed to repeat itself." The whole truth is that when the question of internal autonomy was posed, I referred to some formidable factors in the situation, that had been allowed to grow, even fostered, in Kashmir since 1953. These, for example, are that calculated action has been taken in Kashmir, which has created a psychological base for Pakistan. On the other hand a strong pro-merger sentiment with India has been created in the Jammu plains. It is needless to discuss that govt. action was largely responsible for bringing into being these forces. In the face of these facts, what will be left of the offer of "autonomy" for Kashmir? Besides, the deep rooted feeling that the coup of 1953, may be repeated is there to be contended with, more particularly so in the face of the fate of solmn-pledges so for given.

Your suggestion is that a dialogue should be opened between the leaders of Kashmir and the Govt. of India and then the resultant settlement formula got endorsed by the people of the state and later put to Pakistan. It is a procedural question, in which I would point out a lacuna: Pakistan, naturally will feel that it is being faced with a fait-accompli, and this may lead to the break-down of talks and to fresh agonizing stalemate. The proper course, therefore, is that endorsement by the people of the state should follow rather than precede negotiations with Pakistan.

The main point, however, is that if leaders of India are of opinion that the promise of plebiscite is not practicable now, the onus is on them to suggest a reasonable alternative, which should, in the circumstances, be, by and large, fair and equitable to the all the concerned parties and also appear so to the general world opinion. If we adopt such an attitude of mind and purse it earnestly and honestly, I do hope there is still a chance of finding out a lasting and honourable solution to this vexed problem.

May God give us courage and faith in pursuing the right course.

I hope you are doing well.

With kindest regards,

Yours sincerely,

Sd/-
(Sheikh Mohd Abdullah)

Shri Jai Prakash Narayan,
Kadam Kuan,
Patna-3

(NMM&L File No. 93)

Abdullah's Letter to JP, Contradicting Allegations

Jan 8, 1971
3, Kotla Lane
New Delhi.

My dear JP,

I have gone through the editorial published in today's "*Express*". The Editor has only repeated what has often appeared in this paper against me and the PF. Despite our denials to the charges levelled it has made no difference in his attitude. It appears to me that the man writing these editorials has deliberately and purposely closed his eyes and ears to truth and honesty. Mr Beg has repeatedly declared that there was no intention on the part of the P.F. to wreck the Constitution from within and that his nominees if elected will work within the framework of the Constitution. This too has not made any dent in the most vicious and malicious propaganda that has been let loose against the PF by the deeply entrenched vested interest both in the state and here in India.

The Editor has based all his tirade against me on a telegram which he alleges has been sent by me to the Secretary - General of the Islamic Secretariat on the eve of the Karachi Conference. The Editor could have easily got this fact verified from the

Telegraph office but that would not serve his purpose. There is absolutely no basis in this allegation.

Yours sincerely

(NMM&L File No. 89)

Sd/-

(Sheikh Mohammad Abdullah)

15

Abdullah's Externment

Action Against the Sheikh Foolish, Says JP

10, January 1971

Mr. Jayaprakash Narayan on Saturday urged the Prime Minister and her colleagues to reconsider their action in barring the entry of Sheikh Abdullah and his colleagues into Jammu and Kashmir and arresting a large number of workers of the Plebiscite Front, reports PTI.

In a statement here, Mr. Narayan said even at this late hour Mrs Gandhi and her colleagues could repair the "damage" that had been caused already and prevent further damage that was sure to ensue.

Sheikh Abdullah meanwhile called on Mr Narayan and is understood to have apprised him of the developments leading to the serving of the externment orders.

This was the Sheikh's second meeting with Mr. Narayan, who arrived in Delhi two days ago.

After his first meeting with the Sheikh, Mr Narayan had called on the Prime Minister.

A senior official of the Prime Minister's Secretariat met Mr Narayan on Friday possibly to apprise him of the facts which led to the externment of the Sheikh and the two Plebiscite Front leaders.

Mr. Narayan in his statement said: This mornings news of externment orders served on Sheikh Abdullah, Mirza Afzal Beg and Mr Ghulam Mohamad Shah and of the arrest of hundreds of workers of the Plebiscite Front makes one despair of this country being ever able to tackle the Kashmir problem with intelligence and vision.

From every point of view- national, international, India-Pakistan relations, democratic values and the decencies of life- the action taken by the State Government of Jammu and Kashmir, with the apparent concurrence of the government of India, seems both foolish and cowardly: foolish because it throws away the first chance that had occurred since 1953 of drawing Sheikh Abdullah and his colleagues into the mainstream of Indian public life and of letting the healing capacities of participation in the democratic process produce their beneficent results; cowardly because the patent intention seems to be to save from ignominious defeat those who had been claiming all these years of being the true representative of the people of Kashmir instead of Sheikh Abdullah and his followers who according to them had been steadily falling in the eyes of the people.

Reasons Advanced

The reasons advanced in the order of externment are most unconvincing to say the least. First, the order makes the bland statement that "government is satisfied that the activities of Shri Sheikh Abdullah have for some time past been and continue to be prejudicial to the security of the state" but it "declares that it would be against the public interest to communicate to him (Sheikh Abdullah) the grounds and the particulars on which this restriction order is made."

Finally, it says that the order "shall remain operative for a period of three months." This is too ridiculous for words. It passed one's comprehension why anyone's activities should be considered prejudicial to the security of the forthcoming Parliamentary elections. The obvious interpretation is that the state and Union Governments are determined at all costs to prevent Sheikh Abdullah and his colleagues from contesting the elections to the Lok Sabha.

Nor are the reasons that a section of the press has set forth more convincing. It has been said that the Sheikh and his friends were preaching secession but no proof has been adduced to establish that. It has been said again that the leader of the Plebiscite Front had declared that pledging of loyalty to the Constitution was only a technical affair and that their real intention was to wreck the Constitution from within.

Mirza Afzal Beg has flatly denied having ever said so. Moreover, can there be anything more fantastic than to imagine that just three Members of parliament from the valley of Kashmir could ever wreck a Constitution supported by an entire nation? And even if they were foolish enough to try to do that they would only be alienating thereby every section of opinion in this country. To what purpose one fails to understand.

Furthermore, it may be asked what has the Government done about other parties and persons who have been stating from time to time that only intention in working through the constitutional institutions was to wreck them in the end and who in token of their avowed aims have not hesitated even to burn publicly copies of the Indian Constitution.

No Telegram

An alleged telegram sent by Sheikh Abdullah to the Islamic Secretariat in Karachi has been used as an excuse for a vitreous attack on him. On a personal enquiry this is what the Sheikh wrote to me in a letter yesterday (Friday): "The Editor has based all his tirade against me in a telegram which he alleges has been sent by me to the Secretary General of the Islamic Secretariat on the eve of the Karachi Conference. The Editor could have easily got this fact verified form the Telegraph office but that would not serve his purpose.

There is absolutely no basis in this allegation."

So much for the reasons trotted out. Coming to the international consequences of this unfortunate step. It requires no great imagination to see, that they are likely to be universally adverse. We know quite well that in all these years we have not been able to convert many nations to our side on the Kashmir issue. Even Russia, an erstwhile staunch supporter, has recently turned neutral on the question. This latest act will being us further down in the estimation of the world and cause incalculable damage to the democratic image we have been trying assiduously to project.

Indo-Pak Ties

A last word about India- Pakistan relations. It is universally agreed that the recent General Elections in Pakistan have created a revolutionary situation in consequence of which India-

Pakistan relations stand poised at a turning point which if handled with imagination and deftness might set both countries on a road of growing understanding, co-operation and friendship.

It is sad to reflect that the Prime Minister and her advisers have failed to take into account the damaging effect that their latest action in Kashmir might produce in a situation of such delicacy and historical significance.

In the light of these considerations, the petty gains that might accrue to Mr Sadiq and his party shrink to nothingness when compared to the great losses suffered in every other respect.

I should like, therefore, humbly and respectfully to plead with the Prime Minister and her colleagues to reconsider their action, and even at this late hour repair the damage that has been caused already and prevent further damage that is sure to ensue.

Reactions to Sheikh's Arrest

In Jammu the State Jana Sangh leader, Mr Premnath Dogra, described the Government action as "an election stunt", adds our correspondent. If the Government really wanted to deal with secessionist elements, action would have been taken long ago when the situation in the valley was much worse than today, be said.

Mr O.P. Modi the National Integration front Chief, however, welcomed the Government action and said it vindicated the stand taken by the Integration Front. But his organization considered the action "far from adequate" he said.

The National Conference Chairman, Mr Sham Lal Saraf, said that the "unrealistic attitude adopted by Sheikh Abdullah and Mr Beg had resulted in the retardation of progress in Jammu and Kashmir.

He said, "If Sheikh Abdullah and his other followers had been realistic" his sympathies would have been with them.

Congress(R) Comment

In Jammu the state Congress(R) today called upon the Plebiscite Front leaders to stop questioning the finality of Jammu and Kashmir's accession to India and join the mainstream of national life.

Mr Mohammed Ayub, vice-president of the Pradesh Congress said today that he was voicing the unanimous opinion of his party while urging the Plebiscite Front leadership to dissolve their party and accept the reality of the state's accession to India.

In a rejoinder to the Plebiscite Front president Mirza Mohammed Afzal Beg, the Congress(R) leader said: "No one subscribing to secessionist policies could be allowed to use the elections as a cover to wreck the Constitution from within the legislature."

He added: "Mr Beg's statement that the Front planned to take part in the election within the framework of the Constitution was tantamount to a 'belated realization on the part of the Front leaders about the futility of their political stand.

Mr Ayub said: If me Beg is honest about his latest assertions he should renounce his stand and desist from drawing support and inspiration from hostile forces who are busy hatching conspiracies against the security of India.

Mirwaiz Farooq, president of the pro-Pakistan Awami Action Committee, and Mr Shamim Ahmad Shamim an Independent member of State Assembly described the externment of the Sheikh and Mr Beg as an "act of political gangsterism intended to clear the decks for the mid-term poll for the Lok Sabha."

Mr Mirwaiz in a statement said the action against the Front and its workers "will add to the dissatisfaction and harm the peace in the state."

(*Statesman*, 15 Jan 1971)

Letter of Radhakrishnan to J.P. on Kashmir

Gandhi Peace Foundation,
New Delhi, 110002
January, 15, 1971

My dear JP,

I returned from Sevagram and Calicut on the 11th and learnt from Amresh regarding your discussions here. I had heard over the Radio your statement regards the latest developments in J&K and was glad that you were available for an intervention.

JJ returned here yesterday. We have been discussing the question of our going up to Srinagar. JJ felt that we should go even if it be for 3 or 4 days. We had discussions with Sheikh Saheb and others. The flights have not taken off till today and so there was no way of going. We hope Sen and I will be able to go today. We shall be back on 18th. I should reach Banaras on 19th to start our meeting of the society in the day at 11 a.m. if not after lunch.

The probe in Srinagar is also to find out possibilities of putting up independent candidates. It has been suggested to Mridula that she should stand form srinagar where Bakshi is contesting. One has to understand if the situation will enable her to engage in a fair fight. There are other constituencies too.

As far as Mridula is concerned she would decide only after she knows that she has your full support. Both I and Sheikh Saheb have indeed urged her to stand. We shall only sound the situation and report back. So please advise.

We had a meeting of the Coordinating Committee on Voters Education. We are greatly strengthened by S.S.S.'s decision. There is a good deal of enthusiasm. The Radical Humanists came along to the last meeting. I wish we had the capacity and organization to make this an effective short programme.

With pranams,

Yours,
Sd/-
Radhakrishan
Secy GPF

Blowing up of IA Plane too Shocking for Words: JP

Patna, Feb 4—The Sarvodya leader, Mr Jayaprakash Narayan today warned the government of Pakistan and its nationals that they would be making a costly mistake if they thought that hatred and violence could ever help them to achieve their ends.

In a press statement, issued from the Mushahari block in Muzaffarpur district where he is camping at present, Mr Narayan said "the news about the hijackers finally succeeding in carrying out the threat to destroy the Indian plane is too shocking for words."

In his opinion the most deplorable part of the whole affair was that these incidents should have happened at a time when "the impending establishment of Parliamentary democracy in Pakistan has given rise to a genuine hope about a new chapter is being opened in Indo-Pak relations."

(Indian Express, New Delhi, February 6, 1971)

Mridula Sarabhai's Letter to JP

31, Rajdoot Marg,
Chankayapuri, New Delhi - 11
February 7, 1971

My dear Shri JP,

Greetings.

Radhakrishanji desired that I send you a situation report on Kashmir which would give an idea of the existing undercurrents. We were trying to send this on the 5th but unfortunately I could not get it ready. I learn that now it will reach you only on the 12th February unless a messenger carries it to you to Muzaffarpur.

The typed press reports that have been sent till now are far from satisfactory. Better arrangements have been made to give a clear picture of what appears in the press. I hope a definite change will be found in the handouts that are sent next week.

Sheikh Saheb's silence is also bothering the authorities. The reasons for his silence are mentioned in the report sent. It was really very beneficial to have you here when the externment order on Sheikh Saheb came. He has been going through the same type of psychological conflicts that he faced on 9th August 1953 on his detention.

Sheikh Saheb had suggested that he should go to you during your visit to Patna but then this was postponed on the ground that it will draw lot of attention and unnecessary speculations.

Sheikh Saheb desires me to send you two letters that we have received from Maulana Saheb. I would have sent English or Hindi translation but Sheikh Saheb was against it. He said that JP will get someone to read the letters in original. Only then he will be able to understand the problems that face Maulana Saheb and other friends in Kashmir. We have informed Maulana Saheb that (1) for the present it appears that Indira ji has choosen to throw her lot with those elements in Kashmir which have been conspirators in the past and is likely to give them a long rope; she has written off Sheikh Saheb and feels that by punitive actions she will succeed. (2) The manner in which Indo-Pak tensions are being built up on both sides, there is little hope of working for conciliation. (3) For the government the Kashmir problem is settled and they will not agree to talk on anything in this connection.

Your invitation to the marriage of Fatmi Saheb's daughter has been received. Sheikh Saheb's invitation has not yet been received, but as it has been received by Beg Saheb and others, it might be on way. Would it be a good thing for Sheikh Saheb to take this opportunity to go to Patna and meet you?

With Pranams to you and Prabhavatiji,

Yours

Sd/-

(Mridula)

Shri Jayaprakash Narayan,
Kadam Kuan,
Patna - 3

(NMM&L File No. 95)

Abdullah's Letter to JP on Kashmir Elections

3, Kotla Lane,
New Delhi - 1
9th Feb, 1971

My dear J.P.,

After your departure from Delhi and externment orders served upon Beg, Shah and myself, things have moved very fast and Kashmir Government, in collusion with the Centre, is sparing no effort to re-enact the sordid drama of 9th Aug, 1953. The characters and the plot of the drama bear strong resemblance to what had happened in 1953 and onwards.

Indo-Pak friendship is, undoubtedly, a very desirable objective to be pursued and achieved for the progress and prosperity of both the countries, but it is most vital for the very survival of the people of Kashmir. Therefore, any attempt or action which may adversely affect Indo-Pak relations can never be approved by anybody, who believes in this objective. The recent unfortunate events in the sub-continent have further exaggerated the already strained relation between the two neighbours. The story, however, does not end with the hijacking and blowing up of the plane. The important question is on whom to fix the responsibility? The revelations, made since the incident, by the responsible quarters, have raised grave doubts in my mind and perhaps in the minds of many others, as to the veracity of the stories put out in regard to the agencies responsible for this act. Nevertheless, it has become abundantly clear that the chief hijacker was an employee of the Border Security Force. He had crossed over to Pakistan and reportedly got training in hijacking there; after re-crossing to this side of the ceasefire line, he was reemployed by the Security Force, and stationed on duty at the airport, ostensibly to keep watch on possible hijacking, as reported by the press. The hijacker had told his employers the possibility of skyjacking, which information was communicated to Kashmir government by the agency under whose employ the hijacker was. The Kashmir police wanted to interrogate the person, but according to the Chief Minister, Mr Sadiq, the agency refused to identify him or surrender him to the Kashmir police for interrogation. Finally the man with one of his accomplice, boards the plane with the full knowledge of the Border Security Force, and carries out his mission, forcing the plane to land at Lahore. His first act there was to contact a person who is reported to be the leader of the Kashmir Liberation Front named Mohd Maqbool Butt. Now this Maqbool Butt was involved in some murder case in Kashmir and was tried and sentenced to death (This happened in 1967 when I was in Kodaikanal and Shri DP Dhar currently Indian Ambassador in Moscow was incharge of Home Affairs in Kashmir). But before the execution of the sentence, he mysteriously escaped from jail and crossed the border to Pakistan. How he managed to escape the jail has uptill now remained a mystery. Regarding his enlisting the official assistance in the dramatic escape from the jail, it is being said that he was deliberately allowed to escape and cross over to Pakistan in order to use his services there for furtherance of the plan. The information about the possible hijacking of Indian plane, had been with the Kashmir govt and Central agencies since July, 1969, as reported. But the plan, meaningfully, unfolds itself only after our externment and banning of the Plebiscite Front.

Sinister Conspiracies of Centre and State Governments

Not only hijacking of the plane but many other sinister types of conspiracies are jumping out suddenly of the Pandora box of the Central and Kashmir governments' agencies, and all propaganda media-newspapers, radio and TV - are let loose in full blast to tag these conspiracies upon us in an attempt to justify their arbitrary and wrong action taken against us and cover the real motive behind them. This is exactly what followed my arrest in 1953. I have my information that vigorous efforts are going on both in India and Srinagar, to create and fabricate material, like finding arms dumps and so-called documents, in order to manufacture evidence and create a vicious atmosphere against us and further damage our image in the public eye, as the self-same conspirators had done after 1953.

I have, however, no doubt in my mind that just as their nefarious attempts completely failed in 1953, despite their wasting crores of tax payers' money and earning a very bad name for India, they will surely meet the same end even now. We, who have faith in God and believe in the ultimate triumph of Truth (Satyam Jayate), remain unshakable in our conviction that the ultimate destiny of India and Pakistan lies in their friendship, and therein lies the salvation of people of Kashmir too.

Trial of Plebiscite Front

The Govt of India has appointed Chief Justice of J&K state as the one-man Tribunal under the Unlawful Activities (Prevention) Act, in regard to banning of the Plebiscite Front. Mr. Beg, therefore, will have to appear and argue his case before him, when he is served with the notice.

I am confident that you share my view that actually it is not the Plebiscite Front or a few other individuals who will stand trial before the tribunals or courts, but it is much bigger cause of basic values, human decency and morality, democracy and also Indo-Pak friendship, which are on trial. Therefore, I am sure that we shall continue to have the active sympathies of yourself and other likeminded friends in promoting these ideals.

Since many friends want to know my assessment of the situation, I am taking the liberty of circulating this letter to them.

How is Prabhaji? Kindly convey my greetings and that of Begum Sahiba to her. I hope both of you are doing well.

With kindest regards,

Yours sincerely

Sd/-

(Sheikh Mohd Abdullah)

(NMM&L. File No. 93)

Statement of Observers' on Election in Kashmir

9 March 1971

Statement issued by the team of Observers sent to Kashmir by the Sub-Committee of the National Coordination Committee for Voters Education, to observe 1971 Kashmir election. (Members of Sub-committee: Mr Jayaprakash Narayan, Dr. C.D. Deshmukh, Mr J.J. Singh, Mr V.M. Tarkunde and Mr Radhakrishna). The team spent 7 days in Kashmir watched the polling in all the three Lok Sabha constituencies in Kashmir valley i.e. Srinagar, Baramulla and Anantnag.

In a sense this is the first time during the last 25 years that general election took place in Kashmir. Till 1967, the State Assembly was to elect 4 Rajya Sabha members and 6 Lok Sabha members. Hence whatever elections took place before that were only for the Assembly seats.

In 1951 all except 2 were elected uncontested in the whole of Jammu & Kashmir, while in 1957 election took place in 4 and in 1962 only in 5 Assembly constituencies in the Valley.

In 1967, out of 3 Lok Sabha constituencies one was uncontested and election took place in 2 and in the Assembly constituencies 21 out of 43. Moreover in 1967 most of the major Opposition political groups having boycotted the election - there was hardly any serious contest except a semblance of it.

Govt. and People had No Experience of Elections

In this background, it was but natural that neither the Government machinery in Jammu & Kashmir was at all equipped or trained for conducting such elections nor the people of Kashmir had any experience or education in respect of exercising their franchise.

This is the first and foremost handicap that has been witnessed during 1971 elections in Kashmir.

2. The externment order served on Sheikh Mohd Abdullah and Mirza Mohd Afzal Beg and subsequent large-scale arrests of important and active workers of the Plebiscite Front just after the dissolution of Lok Sabha and decision of holding of mid-term election hardly left any serious opposition to the ruling party's candidates.

Most of the Opposition candidates were further handicapped due to the arrest of their active workers. Mr Shamim Ahmad

Shamim who contested against the ruling party candidate Mr Bakshi Ghulam Mohd, in Srinagar, Lok Sabha constituency alleged that about 85 of his active workers were arrested from the period of filing the nomination and the day of polling. Jamait-e-Islami, whose candidates contested both the Anantnag and Baramullah Lok Sabha seats, have complained arrest of about 250 of their active workers in both these constituencies.

3. The Jamait-e-Islami on the other hand, having entered into the election for the first time and having little experience in election, was greatly handicapped due to these arrests. Jamaiti candidates however conducted their election campaign with the limited number of workers left out and that too in constant apprehension that those workers may also be arrested any moment.

A general complaint of all the Opposition candidates has been about the difficulties they had to experience with regard to obtaining the permission for the use of loud speakers for their meetings. In some cases after a few days of their submitting the application such permission seems to have been refused.

4. As stated earlier there having been no state-wide election in Kashmir during the last 25 years the state government machinery naturally was not at all equipped or experienced for such election. Consequently there was also little training or experience amongst Presiding and Polling officers. In such circumstances, many of the Presiding Officers might have felt that it was their duty to help the ruling party candidates. This was evident in many areas including the military controlled areas of Baramulla Lok Sabha constituency.

Election Irregularation

Jamait-e-Islami feels that irregularities were committed in about 70 polling booths in the Baramulla constituency and in larger number of booths in Anantnag constituency. There was also complaint of stealing of ballot boxes in one of the booths of Anantnag constituency. By 1 O'clock on the day of polling (6.3.1971) in Anantnag constituency, the Jamait boycotted the election in protest against the alleged favouritism of the Presiding Officers and observed hartal and took out procession in Baramullah and Sopore (Baramullah constituency) on 5th and 6th March 1971.

There were allegations that some ballot boxes were brought in Baramullah Treasury without seal or with broken seal and without any cloth cover on them. It was also alleged that some ballot boxes were kept in the houses of local Congress leaders on the night of 4th (the day of polling in Baramullah constituency) before they were brought to the Baramullah Treasury on the 5th.

5. Some of the above allegations appear to be of serious and grave nature. It is felt that the Election Commission should immediately arrange a thorough enquiry into the matter in Anantnag and Baramullah constituencies and if these are found correct must arrange repolling atleast for such polling booths where these irregularities took place.

Observers:
Sd/-
Shri A.K. Karan
Shri Dharampal
Shri Govind Rao Deshpande
Shri A.C. Sen

Gandhi Peace Foundation,
221-223 Deen Dayal Upadhaya Marg,
New Delhi - 110 002.

JP's Letter to Indira on Externment of Abdullah

Sitabdiara
March 26, 1971

Dear Indiraji,

I hope I am not too late already in writing this to you — one reason for the delay was that I wanted to give you enough time to get settled and finish the immediate business of setting up your Council of Ministers and formulation of policies to be set forth in the Presidential address.

This letter is about extension of the externment of Sheikh Mohammad Abdullah, Mirza Afzal Beg and Mr. Gul Md. Shah. It was a great pity that Sheikh Saheb and his friends were not allowed to participate in the Parliamentary elections. Had that been allowed, it would have contributed greatly to the easing of tensions in the valley and strengthened the hopes of its people that their democratic aspirations would find fulfillment within the present constitution. At the same time, Sheikh Abdullah's presence in the Lok Sabha and his participation in the broader political life of the country would have gone far in establishing mutual understanding between him and his colleagues and the rest of the Indian leadership. As it is, Mr Shamim Ahmad Shamim's victory has resulted in a valuable political catharsis in the valley.

There would have been no point in writing about these lost opportunities, had it not been for the reason that they are immediately relevant to the question this letter is about. I do not know what your long-term policy in Kashmir is, but if it is anything like conciliation and winning the hearts and minds of the people, the externment order should be allowed to lapse after its term is over on the 6th or 7th of April and Sheikh Saheb and his friends should be made to feel that in this free and democratic country they were free to go wherever they liked. Now that your position in your party and in the Lok Sabha is so overwhelmingly strong, there should be no inhibition in your acting according to your own judgement.

With best wishes,

Sd/-

(NMM&L. File No. 93) (Jayaprakash Narayan)

Smt Indira Gandhi
Prime Minister of India,
New Delhi.

JP Condemns Externment of Abdullah

Press Statement

I wish I did not have to raise a critical voice at this juncture, but the same reasons which have prompted me in the past weeks to speak out about Bangla Desh impel me to do so now. It is with deep regret that I have learnt about the renewal of the externment order on Sheikh Abdullah and two other leaders of Kahsmir for another three months. Like other universal values, democracy too is indivisible and we cannot be democratic abroad and anti-democratic at home. From all accounts it was clear that the last parliamentary elections, in which the people of Kashmir had a limited opportunity of participating freely, had strengthened the hope in them of being able to run their affairs according to their wishes and thus strengthen the bonds between them and India. That healthy effect has unfortunately been greatly nullified by the fresh orders of externment. Looking ahead into the future, I do sincerely hope that this is not the first step towards thwarting the democratic rights of the people of Kashmir at the elections to the state assembly in 1972. If the government of India have any evidence of unlawful activity on the part of Sheikh Abdullah or the other externed leaders, the more straightforward step is to bring them to trial. The longer and the oftener the rule of law is evaded, the more adverse would the result for this country be.

Sd/-

(NMM&L. File No. 93)

(Jayaprakash Narayan)
Patna
7.4.1971

16

Election in Kashmir

JP: Let Kashmir Decide its Future

New Delhi, Jan. 10—Sarvodya leader Jayaprakash Narayan today suggested that the general election could be used as an occasion for knowing the Kashmir people's views on their relations with India through a method that was short of a plebiscite and was within the constitutional framework.

Asserting that the Kashmir question could be solved only through the initiative of India, he said it seemed to him that Pakistan was firmly opposed to any process of improving relations with India through agreement on lesser issues. It had been insisting on "meaningful talks" which he considered unlikely in the immediate future.

Therefore, Mr Narayan said, India should turn its attention towards the Kashmiri people, allow them to decide on a solution and accept their verdict. It would then be impossible for Pakistan to question such a solution.

He said the Election Commission's schedule for polling had been announced and Kashmir was supposed to go to the polls in February when the valley would be snow-bound. He did not know whether it was too late for an opinion poll in Kashmir. But the timing of holding elections was not material.

Mr Narayan made it clear that the opinion of Kashmiris could not be known as long as leaders like Sheikh Abdullah, Mirza Afzal Beg and Maulana Massoodi were in prison. An election with Indian leaders in jail was not acceptable to the country under British rule. Conforming to the "peculiarities of nation-states" they might feel the elections were fair "but the world will not believe us."

He said he was often misunderstood and despaired at popular reaction to his suggestions for a solution of the Kashmir question. However, he was happy to note that the two super powers (the United States and the Soviet Union) were agreed that India and Pakistan should be friends and "therein lies hopes for its realization."

(Published on 11 Jaunary, 1972)

Can there be Democracy without Fair and Free Elections?

Jayaprakash Narayan

(Contributed specially to the Hindustan Times)

Since I read your perspective and perspicacious editorial on the forthcoming elections in Jammu & Kashmir, in your issue of 13.1.1972, I had been wanting to write to congratulate you with all my heart. I agree with every word that you have said in that editorial. In fact, when rumours were thick in Delhi in the first week of January 1971 that some action was imminent against Sheikh Abdullah and some of his colleagues aimed to deny them the opportunity of participating in the (last) elections to the Lok Sabha, I had raised my voice of protest and also pleaded personally with the Prime Minister and Mr. P.N. Haskar. But to no effect. As a result, India's image as a democracy grievously suffered in the eyes of the world and the people in the Valley were further alienated from the rest of us. Referring to the externment order served on the Kashmiri leaders, I had deplored *inter alia* that we had foolishly thrown away "the first chance that had occurred since 1953 of drawing Sheikh Abdullah and his colleagues into the *mainstream of Indian public life* and of letting the healing capacities of participation in the democratic process produce their beneficent results." I am glad that those words find such a powerful echo in your editorial in the present context.

The context again is that of elections - this time to the Jammu & Kashmir State Assembly. And once again the new Chief Minister, Mr Mir Qasim, with the concurrence, I am sure, of Delhi has announced that the externment orders will remain in force because the condition that obtained before have remained unchanged. That surely is an amazing statement to be made by a responsible political leader. One should have thought that the independence of Bangla Desh and the defeat of the Pakistan army have completely changed the situation in the sub-continent. If no change has occurred in the minds of the Muslims of Jammu and Kashmir, it is an admission of the complete bankruptcy of Mr Qasim's party and his leadership. Personally I do not accept his assessment of the situation. He seems to be motivated more by personal power considerations than reconciliation in the valley and the good of its people. I hope I am wrong, but I can find no other reasonable explanation for his action.

But let me go back to the question of democracy. For the past ten months we have been presenting ourselves to the world as ardent champions of democracy and the rights of man in Bangladesh. What are we going to tell the world when we deny the same rights to our own citizens in one of our States? Whatever Government spokesman might have said before or may say now, there has never been a free and fair election in the State of Jammu and Kashmir. As you have so rightly pointed out in your editorial, freedom and democracy are indivisible. But if Sheikh Abdullah and his externed colleagues are not allowed to return to their State sufficiently before the elections, and the political prisoners, barring those guilty of proven acts of violence, continue to be held in prison - I know some have been released but many are still behind the prison bars - how can our loud professions of democracy be squared with our acts and the world convinced that we do not follow a double standard: one at home and another abroad?

Sheikh would be Agreeable to Solution within India

Let me at that point make my position clear on one important relevant point. There was a time when I used to plead persistently for negotiations with Sheikh Abdullah so as to reach an agreement with him and satisfy his amour propre. That was because I had felt convinced after my prolonged talks with him at Kodaikanal that he would be agreeable to his state remaining within the Indian union, irrespective of Pakistan's wishes, provided we made some face-saving concessions to him. But, unaccountably, talks with him were never seriously held except in fits and starts. I believe the most serious series of talks held were between him and Shri G. Parthasarathi some time after the Sheikh's release from Kodaikanal and his return to Delhi from his state where he had made some rather ambiguous and unfortunate statements. Yet, I believe the nearest point ever reached between the Indian and the Sheikh's views was reached then. But for some inexplicable reason, when the issues were about to be clinched and Shri Parthasarathi was scheduled to meet the Sheikh again in a day or two, Shri Parthasarthi was hastened out to New York without a word of explanation to the Sheikh. Since then there has never been a serious effort made to the possibilities of a political accommodation with the Kashmiri leader.

Question of Quantum of Autonomy

My purpose in relating this past bit of history is not to suggest that the Government of India should once again enter into any negotiations with the Sheikh so as to create the requisite conditions for a credible democratic election in the valley. I have to confess with a heavy heart that Sheikh Saheb's attitude towards the freedom struggle of Bangladesh and his attempt to draw a parallel between the Kashmir and Bangladesh issues have sorely disappointed and disillusioned me. After all that has happened since 1947, it is futile for any Kashmiri leader to keep on harping on Jawaharlal Nehru's assurance to hold a plebiscite in the state when normalcy was restored there. The plebiscite issue is dead for ever. Even the Sheikh cannot put back the clock of history. No question can be raised now about the accession of Jammu & Kashmir to India. Anyone who thinks otherwise is living in a fool's paradise and has failed to grow with the time and grasp the historic significance of the tremendous changes that have taken place in the Indian sub-continent. In fact, I doubt if there are many left in the Valley itself who are any more concerned about it. The only question that may still be considered to be relevant is that of the quantum of autonomy that Jammu & Kashmir should enjoy within the Union of India, and Jammu and Ladakh regions, in their turn, should enjoy within the constitutional framework of that state. But this is not a question in any way peculiar to Jammu & Kashmir. There are several states in this country which have been demanding larger measure of autonomy. There is, for instance, the Rajmannar Committee's report in regard to Tamilnadu. But at the same time it must be recalled with pride the ringing words of Chief Minister Shri Karunanidhi which he is recently reported to have spoken at a public meeting at Thanjavur: "The demand for greater autonomy to the State," he declared, "was never meant to divide the country but only to promote the welfare of the people.... The Prime Minister, Mrs Indira Gandhi, herself could examine the demand for more powers to the States for advancing the people's interest without in any way affecting unity and integrity of the country."

There is enough flexibility in our Constitution and our central and state leaders have been wise enough to appreciate the limits within which the demand for autonomy may be pressed. I myself have been a consistent advocate of a much larger measure of autonomy to the States in view of the vastness of our population and the diversity of our problems. I have also felt that smaller states would make for better government and bring democracy nearer to the people and give them a better sense of participation and, further, that smaller States would also help in removing regional disparities with far less tension and at a faster pace. At the same time I have also been consistently emphasising that the strength and authority of the Union government should not be impaired in any way, nor should the territorial integrity of the country be allowed to be weakened. I believe that within these limits there is enough scope for mutual adjustment, accommodation and give and take.

Hindu and Muslim Communalism Nailed

For these reasons I have never doubted that there was any danger whatever to the integrity of our nation. I am sure India would continue to remain united and keep growing from strength to strength. We have colossal problems, but I am confident that we shall conquer them. Happily, the independence of Bangladesh, the second largest Muslim nation in the world and the role of so-called "Hindu" India in the liberation of the new nation has driven the last nail into the coffin of both Hindu and Muslim communalism in this country. Habits die slowly, but I am sure, even the most bigoted will not fail to get the message of he recent historic events. Incidentally, may I suggest to the government of India to take a leaf out of the book of Bangladesh and ban at least those political parties in this country who still flaunt unabashed their communal character by their very name and action, such as the Hindu Mahasabha and the Muslim League. Casteism, of course, will continue as a terrible blight, but it is more a product of socio-economic backwardness than anything else. Caste as a basis of social organisation has lost whatever validity it might have possessed before, and I am sure that as the country marches forward, casteism will die a natural death. This is not to suggest that there is no need to carry on a ceaseless and enlightened war against this outdated relic of the past, which politics more than anything else is keeping alive.

It is because of this faith in India's future that I am pleading for a free and fair election in the State of Jammu & Kashmir, and am trying to convince all concerned that no election in that State can ever be considered by impartial observers as free and fair unless its externed leaders are allowed to go back in time to participate in it if they so desire. I must admit, however, I am not so sure about lifting the ban on the Plebiscite Front. The very word 'plebiscite' has become meaningless and even treasonous in the present context. I do hope that Mirza Afzal Beg and his colleagues would have courage enough to face the present realities as even Mr Bhutto seems to be doing, though reluctantly and slowly, and would reconsider the situation and transform themselves into a real Indian party. In this connection, I find myself in complete agreement with you, Mr Editor, when you ask the question: after all what are we afraid of? The existing laws are enough to deal effectively with any treasonous or anti-national activity. I am also sure that the people of the Kashmir valley have gone through a sincere heart-searching, and whatever affinity they might have felt before with Pakistan on grounds of religion must have been shattered by the events in Bangladesh. The people of Jammu & Kashmir, particularly its Muslim citizens, are in a position to make a valuable contribution to the establishment of harmonious relations between India and what is left of the old Pakistan. As the Prime Minister and many others, including myself, have been repeatedly saying in the past months, India bears no illwill towards the people of Pakistan and has no wish to see it break up and disintegrate. Disintegration of the residuary Pakistan will make for endless trouble, not only for themselves, but also for India and the entire sub-continent; allowing great power politics to continue to fish in the troubled waters.

Refusal to Concede Autonomy Led to Bangladesh Separation

As I had said in my very first statement on Bangladesh when Sheikh Mujibur Rehman had launched his remarkable non-cooperation movement on the 7th of March, 1971, the territorial integrity of the erstwhile Pakistan depended not on the Bangabandu, whose demand was only for autonomy, but on Yahya Khan and his Government. I should like to quote the relevant words because they are so pertinent to the present crisis in Pakistan.

"Let me make it clear that just as I believe in the territorial integrity of my country, I do not wish to see the breakup of Pakistan. Sheikh Mujibur Rehman himself has been asking for nothing more than full autonomy for his State and in spite of acts of genocide on the part of the West Pakistan military rule, he has desisted from taking the last irrevocable step of secession. That is a measure of his statesmanship. The responsibility of pushing him beyond his self-imposed limit would be entirely upon the civil and military powers in West Pakistan. Let us hope that they would be wise enough not to push him that far."

Alas, as events have shown, they did not possess that wisdom, and tried instead along with such of their perverse friends as Mr. Nixon and Mr. Kissinger to make India the villian of the piece. The integrity of residuary Pakistan depends in the same manner, not on India, which has repeatedly made its position clear, nor on Khan Abdul Wali Khan or Abdus Samad Khan, the Baluch Gandhi, but on President Bhutto himself. He is faced with an identical question: will he have the wisdom to respect the democratic aspirations of the different peoples of Pakistan? Pakistan is not a homogenous country and the cry of Islam alone cannot keep it united. By refusing to agree to President Yahya Khan's order for the execution of Sheikh Mujibur Rehman, Mr Zulfikar Ali Bhutto, who by then had become the Foreign Minister of his Government, has given proof of his political resilience and farsightedness. I hope he will show the same qualities in dealing with the autonomy demand not only of Baluchistan and N.W.F.P., but also of his own state, Sind. His reported refusal to hand over power in the N.W.F.P. and Baluchistan to the National Awami Party, which in alliance with the Jamiat-ul-Ulema-e-Islam has a clear majority in the provincial Assemblies in those States sounds ominous and pregnant with great deal of mischief. He seems to be repeating the blunder committed by Yahya Khan.

Kashmir Should Accept New Realities

If in this situation the Muslims of Jammu & Kashmir finally make up their mind and accept the realities of the situation, and decide sincerely to live as loyal citizens of India, they will not only be contributing to their own rapid progress, development and welfare, but also to the integrity of Pakistan itself by scotching the likely mischief-makers there and denying them the opportunity to divert their people's mind from the urgent tasks of national reconstruction, establishment of sub-continental (not excluding Bangla Desh) peace, goodwill and cooperation so essential for all concerned.

Be that as it may, the Government of India would be making a great contribution to national integration and our cherished ideals of secularism and democracy, if it took courage in both its hands and allowed he externed Kashmiri leaders to return home and play their rightful role as equal citizens of this country in the forthcoming elections. Any other course at this moment would be short-sighted, petty-minded and fraught with future dangers.

As you said in your editorial, the Naga rebels who had been waging an armed struggle against India, were brought to Delhi and the Prime Minister herself had held negotiations with them, and in spite of continued disturbed conditions in that state, free and fair elections were held which have borne such rich fruit. I apprehend no trouble in Sheikh Abdullah and his friends returning home before the elections. And India would then be able to hold its head high and prove to the world that when it supported the cause of democracy in Bangladesh at such great cost and risk, it did not hesitate to uphold the same ideals in one of its own states.

Cease Fire Line be Made International Border

One last point, though not strictly relevant to the elections in Jammu & Kashmir, yet of vital importance in the context of the vexatious dispute regarding Kashmir, deliberately nurtured over the years by Pakistan and some of the great powers. The point is about the "ceasefire" line. After so many years and at least three Pakistani overt and covert aggressions across the line; and particularly after the recent Indo-Pak war, the old ceasefire has no reality or relevance left at all. This is a point on which I find there is general agreement in the country, including its official circles. No body, I think, barring some on the lunatic fringes, is wanting to take back by force the whole Pakistan-occupied part of the original state of Jammu & Kashmir. But there is general agreement that the old ceasefire line and the presence of the UN observers, whose contribution to assuring peace along that line has been nil, have become anachronisms now. It follows, therefore - and on this point too a *national consensus has emerged - that the so-called ceasefire line should be rationalised and re-drawn and converted into a well-defined permanent international border* (emphasis added) so as to guarantee India's security in that region and make it difficult, if not impossible, for Pakistani adventurers to create any further mischief. If that were done, any UN presence in that area would become unnecessary and contrary to international law. I believe, outside India also it is now recognised that the original ceasefire line was irrational and hasitily drawn up without any regard to geography and the requirements of stability and security and the wishes of the people of the area, particularly those of the Maharaja and the then Prime Minister of the state, Sheikh Mohammad Abdullah.

This is a matter on which some amount of give and take may be necessary. One hopes that President Bhutoo is sincerely concerned about establishing firm and friendly relations with India, which is so obviously essential in the interests of both the nations, besides eliminating at the same time the possibility of international intrigues which have wrought so much mischief in the past. I am sure that if Mr Bhutoo rises to the occasion, refuses to be anybody's tool, accepts the facts of history and desires lasting peace with India and mutual cooperation between the two countries, he will not find the Government of India to be unresponsive.

(Published on 1 February 1972)

J.P. Criticises Arrests in Kashmir

12 February, 1972

Patna, Feb 12—Mr. Jayaprakash Narayan, Sarvodaya leader said today that the action taken in Kashmir recently was most unfortunate both in its manner and timing.

In a statement released to the press, Mr. Narayan said that "the leadership has neither shown political maturity nor finesse in its present handling of the Kashmir situation" Mr Narayan said.

Since I last expressed my views on the forthcoming Assembly election in Kashmir, I have seen both favourable and unfavourable comments in the Indian press. Anything said further about the matter at this stage had only an academic value, because events there have already taken an irreversible course. However, it is still important to make the issue clearer and separate it from the question of dealing with anti-national and secessionist elements. The point that needs emphasis is that whatever evidence the Government has about such elements and their activities could not have been discovered suddenly on the eve of the elections necessitating quick pre-emptive action in the interest of national security and integrity. If any action was called for against such elements, it should have been taken much earlier. To arrest and extern people on the very eve of a general election lays the ruling party open to the charge not only of negligence in dealing with anti-national elements, but also of using a convenient ruse to put its opponents out of the way so as to ensure its victory at the polls. A great deal of praise has been showered in recent months on the central leadership particularly on the Prime Minister, for their political maturity and finesse. But I am constrained to say, with due respect, that the leadership has neither shown political maturity nor finesse in its present handling of the Kashmir situation.

(Indian Nation, 13 February 1972)

Background to Bangladesh and Election in J&K: Puri

I had endorsed JP's criticism of externment of Sheikh Abdullah, Mirza Abdul Beg and Ghulam Mohammad Shah from the State and arrest of the Plebiscite Front workers on the eve of the election to the state assembly in March 1972, through press statements. I also shared JP's disappointment about Sheikh Abdullah's stand on upsurge in the then East Pakistan. But parallel efforts that I made during the war in East Pakistan and before the election may be of interest to the readers.

I suggested to the Sheikh that if he offered support to the Government of India on Bangladesh on the condition that it applied the same principles to Kashmir for which it was fighting there, he was likely to get maximum concessions. For the Government was in desperate need of Muslim support and he was the tallest Muslim leader of the subcontinent. I had further warned him that it was his last opportunity to get any concession from the Government of India. For Bangladesh was bound to come into existence and Pakistan cut to size. Thereafter Kashmir would lose its bargaining capacity. If somehow, Bangladesh movement was crushed, it would only prove that might was right and it would apply to Kashmir also. The Sheikh agreed and asked me to draft a statement on the subject. But the draft was not approved by his other colleagues and instead a statement critical of Indian position was issued to which JP had taken an exception.

After Bangladesh came into existence, Sheikh Abdullah was prepared to accept finality of accession and take part in election provided the status of the State at the time of its accession to the Indian Union in 1947 was restored. I told him that he had no bargaining capacity left to demand any change in the status for the State. But if he accepted finality of accession, I presumed, he would be allowed to contest election and as chief minister he was entitled to demand any status for the State within India as many other chief ministers of the country were doing. Without such a commitment, I warned him , he would not be allowed to contest election and all I could then do was to make a protest. I assured him that JP would also do so.

On 10 March 1972, when results of election to the state assembly were declared, Sheikh Abdullah showed me a statement in which he declared: "my difference with the Government of India is not on the issue of accession but on the quantum of autonomy." I told him that no Government in New Delhi would dismiss a government it got elected in the State — through whatever means — soon after the election and instal him in power. He would have to wait for a few years. However, I arranged his meeting with the Prime Minister Indira Gandhi and the ice was thus broken.

(Ed.)

Abdullah's Letter to JP on Eradication of Communalism

10, Maulana Azad Road,
Srinagar Kashmir.
3rd November,1973

My dear J.P.,

I hope you are enjoying good health. It was so sweet of you to have issued a statement from Bombay, perhaps, in which you have said so many good thing about me. Unfortunately, the statement was brought to my notice very late and so I could not write to you earlier. Well, I am doing my humble bit and , I believe, it is having its effect. Both Jana Sangh and the Muslims league friends have expressed their displeasure and annoyance with my statements which has convinced me that I am on the right path. With God's blessings and the support of friends like you, I hope I shall be able to contribute something towards the eradication of the menace of communalism which is eating into the very vitals of the country.

I hope to visit Patna in the middle of November to participate in the deliberations of Muslim Educational Conference which is being held there between 16 & 18th. It will give me great pleasure to call upon you during that time and enquire about your health. Meanwhile please accept my best wishes and kindest regards.

Yours sincerely,

Sd/-

(Sheikh Mohammad Abdullah)

Shri J.P Narayan,
Kadam Kuan,
Patna

(NMM&L File No. 93)

17
Emergency and After

JP's Letter to Abdullah on Emergency

September 22, 1975

My dear Sheikh Saheb,

In this morning's *Tribune* (September 22), a PTI report from Srinagar is headlined 'Sheikh Favours Conciliation at all-India level'. I was naturally interested, and carefully read that report twice. The agency report says, inter-alia, the following (words within single quotes are the correspondent's and those within double quotes are reported to be yours):-

'He declined direct comment on reports of his mediatory efforts appearing in the Western press, saying he wishes such differences to be resolved in a spirit of conciliation.'

'When correspondents persisted in their attempts to drew him out.... The Sheikh said his services were always at the disposal of the Prime Minister. "It all depends on the situation ..... One must wait for the appropriate time," he said.'

Further on, 'He said it was a "delicate task" and a "delicate subject" for one to dwell on and emphasized that "everyone would like normalcy to be restored". He added that as far as he claimed to know the wishes of the Prime Minister, "she is more than keen to end the Emergency. It all depends on the overall situation."

Coming from a friend like you, with so much of goodwill in both camps, and occupying such an important position as you do your words are of extraordinary significance and interest for me.

I whole- heartedly reciprocate your view that differences, such as we had with the government, should be resolved in a

JP Calls NC to Merge with Janata

I had an occasion to disagree with JP on his call to National Conference to merge with the Janata Party that he had sponsored which included most of the opposition parties. Asoka Mehta, who was president of the Janata Party and visited the state to form the party unit, conveyed JP's message asking me to persuade Sheikh Abdullah, president of the NC to merge it with the Janata. My differences with JP on this proposal were two fold. Firstly without common ideological basis unity of heterogenous parties like the Jana Sangh and the Socialists, the party system in the country, so essential for democracy, would be damaged. Secondly, knowing Sheikh Abdullah, as I did, it was impossible for him to accept any proposal that undermines distinct identity of Kashmir. I, however, offered to discuss with Abdullah any proposal for adjustment of seats with the Janata Party in the elections that were due. Somehow this offer was not accepted. (Ed.)

On Jammu Agitation

Over three years after Sheikh Abdullah's return to power in the State, following his accord with Indira Gandhi, his alienation in Jammu region re-emerged (The reasons of which cannot be gone into here) till an incident of police firing on student demonstration against complaints of irregularities in recruitment of teachers in the border town of Poonch on 2 December 1978 provided the flash points of mass regional upsurge.

I pleaded with Sheikh Abdullah that instead of dealing with the symptoms, he should deal with the root cause of the malaise. As long as the people of Jammu were deprived of their legitimate share in political power, I said, their grievances, in the field of development, recruitment and admissions (to technical institutions) would not be effectively redressed; nor could their redressal be a substitute for political power. I reminded the chief minister of our joint commitment of regional autonomy. I did not get any response.

I convened an all party meeting and formed a 21 member committee. The Committee unanimously adopted my draft proposal as permanent solution for the Jammu problem which was as follows:

"There should be a statutory, political, democratic set up at regional, district, block and panchayat levels with a view to giving a sense of participation to all section of people and areas within each region." This was exactly what J&K state People's Convention convened by Sheikh Abdullah in 1968 had unanimously approved and reiterated by him on assumption of power.

I sought intervention of Prime Minister Morarji Desai, Janata Party President Chander Shekhar and Jayaprakash Narayan. JP wrote the following letter to Sheikh Abdullah and sent two of his emissaries — A.C. Sen and S.H. Kazi — to Jammu who met the chief minister and me in the jail where I was lodged after arrest as a Satyagrahi.

(Ed.)

JP's Letter to Abdullah

Patna

19th February, 1979

My dear Sheikh Sahib,

Newspaper reports of the recent happenings in Jammu have deeply concerned me. It appears that an atmosphere of deep distrust has been created which needs to be removed for a dispassionate consideration of the issues involved.

As I have telegraphically informed you, I am deputing two or three friends to visit Jammu to make an objective study of the situation and also of the issues that have cropped up.

What is most urgently needed is creation of an atmosphere of peace and goodwill. I hope you are taking suitable steps towards that end.

With affectionate regards,

Yours sincerely

Sd/-

(Jayaprakash Narayan)

Mr. Sheikh Abdullah

Chief Minister of Jammu & Kashmir,

Srinagar

EXPRESS TELEGRAM

Shri Sheikh Abdullah
Chief Minister
SRINAGAR

DEEPLY CONCERNED OVER SITUATION IN JAMMU AS REPORTED IN NEWSPAPERS (.) DEPUTING TWO OR THREE FRIENDS TO STUDY SITUATION OBJECTIVELY (.) SHALL SEND YOU THEIR NAMES WHEN THEIR CONSENT AVAILABLE (.) HOPE YOU ARE TAKING STEPS TO PREVENT FURTHER ESCALATION (.) LETTER FOLLOWS.

Jayaprakash

(NMM&L File No. 96) 18.2.79

Index

K

L

M

Q

R

S